INTRODUCTION TO
SEQUENCING AND SCHEDULING

Board of Advisors, Engineering

INTRODUCTION TO
SEQUENCING AND SCHEDULING

Kenneth R. Baker
Duke University

John Wiley & Sons, Inc.
New York London Sydney Toronto

Library of Congress Cataloging in Publication Data:

Baker, Kenneth R   1943–
  Introduction to sequencing and scheduling.

  Includes bibliographies.
  1. Scheduling (Management) I. Title.

TS157.5.B34   658.5'1   74-8010
ISBN 0-471-04555-1

Printed in the United States of America

10 9 8 7 6 5 4 3 2 1

76-1980

PREFACE

This book is intended for graduate students and advanced undergraduates in operations research, industrial engineering, and management science curricula. It is primarily a textbook on sequencing and scheduling, although it also can be used for reference, as a survey of the models and methodologies of the scheduling field. Since the material requires only little specific background, it can be accommodated rather easily, even in highly structured programs. The most desirable prerequisites are an exposure to probability and statistics and some experience with computer programming, which students can be expected to have upon or shortly after entry into a program where course work in scheduling is offered.

The text material is designed to be an integral part of the learning process. Thus, it proceeds from specialized models and specific results to more complex models and broader concepts. In the development of new material, detailed examples are given as a means of illustrating general principles and techniques. The exercises are intended to develop three types of skills: computational, conceptual, and algorithmic. The computational exercises require specific calculations so that the student is provided feedback on his understanding of the basic material. The conceptual exercises involve constructing proofs, creating counterexamples, building models, and discovering extensions, thereby providing feedback to the student on his understanding of the general concepts. The algorithmic exercises, which appear at the end of certain chapters, require the design and implementation of computerized solution methods. These computer exercises should clarify issues of computational practicality in scheduling problems. Moreover, they provide the student with an opportunity to learn to exploit the computer as a vehicle for testing his own new ideas. These exercises will complement the computing activities elsewhere in the curriculum.

Recent developments in the field have shown that many general techniques of combinatorial optimization, in addition to the specialized techniques of sequencing and scheduling, are particularly relevant to scheduling problems. The book reflects this trend by its comprehensive discussion of branch and bound methods, integer programming, and dynamic programming. General methodologies such as random sampling and discrete search, which have become more and more important especially in large-scale scheduling problems, are also discussed. Nevertheless, this is not a technique-oriented book. It is primarily concerned with scheduling problems and models, and it draws, where appropriate, on a variety of problem-solving approaches from several methodological disciplines.

Acknowledgements

The planning and preparation of this manuscript was a lengthy process, and several people influenced the finished product. I thank particularly Professor William L. Maxwell, whose own teaching and research first stimulated my interest in scheduling; Professor Salah E. Elmaghraby, who generously provided special materials and helpful discussions along the way; and Professor Ralph L. Disney, whose philosophy restored my faith in the published word. For their special help and encouragement I also thank Gerald E. Bennington, Stephen R. Kimbleton, J. C. Mathes, and Michael J. Magazine, who still believes a better title would have been *Everything You Always Wanted to Know About Scheduling but Were Afraid to Ask*. I am grateful to several students who helped me in preparing the manuscript, particularly Russell Deats, Charles Khuen, Leon McGinnis, and John Van Deman. Finally, I express my appreciation to Ms. Geraldine Cox, Ms. Mary Goodwin, Ms. Lillian Hamilton, and Ms. Liz Carpenter for their typing efforts.

Kenneth R. Baker

CONTENTS

5. PARALLEL-MACHINE MODELS

6. FLOW SHOP SCHEDULING

7. JOB SHOP SCHEDULING

8. SIMULATION STUDIES OF THE DYNAMIC JOB SHOP

9. NETWORK METHODS FOR PROJECT SCHEDULING

INTRODUCTION TO
SEQUENCING AND SCHEDULING

CHAPTER 1
INTRODUCTION

Scheduling is the allocation of resources over time to perform a collection of tasks. This rather general definition of the term does convey two different meanings that are important in understanding the purpose of this book. First, scheduling is a decision-making function: it is the process of determining a schedule. In this sense, much of what we learn about scheduling can apply to other kinds of decision making and therefore has general practical value. Second, scheduling is a body of theory: it is a collection of principles, models, techniques, and logical conclusions that provide insight into the scheduling function. In this sense, much of what we learn about scheduling can apply to other theories and therefore has general conceptual value. Thus there are two purposes to this book as a scheduling text: it is meant to provide both a practical and a conceptual learning experience. Let us now look more closely at the scheduling function and at scheduling theory.

1. THE SCHEDULING FUNCTION

The practical problem of allocating resources over time to perform a collection of tasks arises in a variety of situations. In most cases, however, scheduling does not become a concern until some fundamental planning problems are resolved, and it must be recognized that scheduling decisions are of secondary importance to a broader set of managerial decisions. For example, in manufacturing applications the fundamental managerial questions involve selecting a product to be manufactured and determining the scale of production. After market studies and economic analyses are used to resolve such issues, technological planning focuses on the question of how the product should be manufactured. Only after these planning questions have been answered, and the availability of resources is known, does it become appropriate to consider problems of scheduling. As another example, the fundamental managerial questions in the delivery of health care require the designation of services to be provided and the level at which each service will be offered. Then technological planning deals with questions of facility design, equipment utilization, and personnel deployment. Once these decisions have provided a profile of the resources available, it is then possible to deal with scheduling problems.

These examples indicate how the fundamental managerial decisions address themselves to three kinds of questions: (1) What product or service is to be provided? (2) On what scale will it be provided? and (3) What resources will be made available? Determining answers to these questions is the *planning* function; in contrast, the *scheduling* function presumes that answers to these questions already exist. Therefore, the function of scheduling *per se* becomes relevant in a situation where the nature of the tasks to be scheduled has been described and the configuration of the resources available has been determined.

In practice, of course, the scheduling and planning functions may not be completely independent. To illustrate these two functions, here is a typical scenario. The planner first identifies the tasks to be carried out and sets limits on the amount of resources available. The scheduler then takes this information as given and determines how to allocate the available resources to perform the specified tasks. When a tentative schedule is constructed, the scheduler can evaluate it and convey his evaluation to the planner. The planner may not be satisfied with the performance achieved by the tentative schedule and may alter the planned resource capacities (or even the tasks themselves), thereby providing revised input for the scheduler. The interplay between these two roles might be repeated in this manner over several exchanges before a final planning decision is reached. Ultimately, however, planning decisions represent the longer-range commitments, such as design or expansion of facilities, purchase and installation of equipment, and the determination of the labor force. While these decisions may be made originally by considering how scheduling would be accomplished, once they are resolved they determine the limits within which the scheduling function must be performed over a long period of time. Therefore, the scheduling process most often arises in a situation where resource availabilities are essentially fixed by the long-term commitments of a prior planning decision.

With this background in mind, we can describe the steps by which scheduling decisions are reached as the *systems approach*. Used informally, this term may mean only a rational method of arriving at decisions; but the systems approach does exhibit a formal structure, one that has found more and more support in contemporary managerial practice. The four primary stages of the systems approach are formulation, analysis, synthesis, and evaluation. In the first stage, basically, a problem is identified and the criteria that should guide decision making are determined. This is often a subtle and complicated activity, but good decisions can seldom be expected without a clear definition of the problem at hand and an explicit recognition of objectives. Analysis is the detailed process of examining the elements of a problem and their inter-relationships. This stage is aimed at identifying the decision variables and also at specifying the relationships among them and the constraints they must obey. Synthesis is the process of building alternative solutions to the problem. Its role is to characterize the feasible options that are available. Finally, evaluation is the process of comparing these feasible alternatives and selecting a desirable course of action. This selection is, of course, based on the criteria that were developed at the outset.

The study of scheduling models and methods will help develop these skills. Formulating a decision-making criterion is perhaps the most difficult of the four stages, but the scheduling problems given in subsequent chapters illustrate the types of goals commonly found in practice. The processes of analysis and synthesis are aided by a familiarity with suitable models. The models to be studied contain the important elements and relationships that frequently arise in scheduling problems, and they also suggest how feasible solutions can systematically be constructed. Finally, the process of evaluating alternatives may be a complicated task in large scheduling problems, and sophisticated solution techniques are often a vital part of the scheduling function. For this reason, the presentation in the following chapters uses a variety of techniques for determining solutions to scheduling problems.

Formal models are available to aid decision making in a variety of scheduling problems. For example, one of the simplest and most widely used models is the Gantt chart, which is a graphical representation of scheduling relationships. In its basic form the Gantt chart is a graph of resource allocation over time. Generally, specific resources are shown along the vertical axis and a time scale is shown along the horizontal axis, as in Figure 1.1. Since the graph breaks down resource allocation by time, it conveys basic information about system status for scheduling purposes. In this concise format, analysis of the graphical relationships can yield inferences about the behavior of a given schedule, while manipulation of the graphical elements can yield comparative information about alternative scheduling decisions. In this way, the Gantt chart serves as a focus for implementing the systems approach in scheduling. The following chapters will examine algebraic, logical, and simulation models, as well as graphical models, all of which can play the same valuable role in the scheduling function.

A final caveat needs to be added regarding the role of models in scheduling. We noted that models are inherent in the systems approach and provide a direct basis for making decisions when the systems approach is utilized. Indeed, when a model is actually a faithful representation of reality, it can

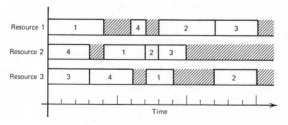

Figure 1.1
A Gantt chart.

become an integral part of the scheduling function. On the other hand, coarse and somewhat oversimplified models can also be of value, for on this level their role is to represent the general structure and essential properties of scheduling problems. It is the theory of scheduling that has developed this type of model, providing a useful framework for performing the scheduling function effectively.

2. SCHEDULING THEORY

Scheduling theory is concerned primarily with mathematical models that relate to the scheduling function, and the development of useful models and techniques has been the continuing interface between theory and practice. The theoretical perspective is predominantly a quantitative approach, one that attempts to capture problem structure in concise mathematical form. In particular, this quantitative approach begins with a translation of decision-making goals into an explicit objective function and decision-making restrictions into explicit constraints.

Ideally, the objective function should consist of all costs in the system that depend on scheduling decisions. In practice, however, such costs are often difficult to measure, or even to identify completely. In fact, the major operating costs—and the most readily identifiable—are determined by the planning function, while the short-term costs are difficult to isolate and often tend to appear fixed. Nevertheless, three types of decision-making goals seem to be prevalent in scheduling: efficient utilization of resources, rapid response to demands, and close conformance to prescribed deadlines. Frequently an important cost-related measure of system performance (such as machine idle time, job waiting time, or job lateness) can be used as a substitute for total system cost, and quantitative approaches to problems with these criteria appear throughout the literature on scheduling.

Two kinds of feasibility constraints are commonly found in scheduling problems. First, there are limits on the capacity of available resources and, second, there are technological restrictions on the order in which tasks can be performed. A solution to a scheduling problem is any feasible resolution of these two types of constraints, so that "solving" a scheduling problem amounts to answering two kinds of questions:

1. Which resources will be allocated to perform each task?
2. When will each task be performed?

In other words, the essence of scheduling problems gives rise to (1) allocation decisions and (2) sequencing decisions. The scheduling literature is replete with mathematical models for these two kinds of decision problems.

Traditionally, scheduling problems have been viewed as problems in optimization subject to constraints—specifically, problems in allocation and sequencing. Sometimes, scheduling is purely allocation, and in these cases mathematical programming models can usually be employed to determine optimal decisions. These general techniques are described in many available textbooks and will not be treated in the following chapters except in situations where sequencing, as well as allocation, is at issue and mathematical programming formulations are pertinent. On the other hand, problems that are purely sequencing are germane to the scheduling field and are the focus of much of this book.

The vital elements in scheduling models are resources and tasks. In the scheduling literature resources are typically characterized in terms of their qualitative and quantitative capabilities, so that a model describes the type and the amount of each resource. An individual task is described in terms of such information as its resource requirement, its duration, the time at which it may be started, and the time at which it is due. In addition, a collection of tasks may sometimes be described in terms of the technological constraints (precedence restrictions) that exist among its elements.

The theory of scheduling also includes a variety of techniques that are useful in solving scheduling problems. Indeed, the scheduling field has become a focal point for the development, application, and evaluation of combinatorial procedures, simulation techniques, network methods, and heuristic solution approaches. The selection of an appropriate technique depends on the complexity of the problem, the nature of the model, and the choice of a criterion as well as other factors; in many cases it might be appropriate to consider several alternative techniques. For this reason, scheduling theory is perhaps as much the study of methodologies as it is the study of models.

To classify the major scheduling models it is necessary to characterize the configuration of resources and the behavior of tasks. For instance, a model may contain one resource type or several resource types. If it contains one resource type, tasks are likely to be single stage, while multiple-resource models usually involve multistage tasks, and in either case resources may be available in unit amounts or in parallel. In addition, if the set of tasks available for scheduling does not change over time, the system is called *static*, in contrast to cases in which new tasks arise over time, where the system is called *dynamic*. Traditionally, static models have proven more tractable than dynamic models and have been subjected to more extensive study. Nevertheless, static models have often captured the essence of more complex, dynamic systems, and the analysis of static problems has frequently uncovered valuable insights and sound heuristic principles that are useful in more general situations.

Many of the early developments in the field of scheduling were motivated by problems arising in manufacturing. Therefore it was natural to employ the vocabulary of manufacturing when describing scheduling problems. Now even though scheduling work is of considerable significance in many non-manufacturing areas, the terminology of manufacturing is still frequently used. Thus, resources are usually called "machines" and basic task modules are called "jobs." Sometimes, jobs may consist of several elementary tasks that are interrelated by precedence restrictions; such elementary tasks are referred to as "operations." Therefore, it is possible to encounter, for example, a problem in the scheduling of outpatient visits to specialists in a diagnostic clinic and to find the system described generically as the processing of "jobs" by "machines."

3. OUTLINE OF THE BOOK

This book is made up of three major sections. The first section (Chapters 2 to 4) is a treatment of single-machine problems. Chapter 2 introduces the basic single-machine model to study static sequencing problems under the most simplifying set of assumptions and to examine a variety of scheduling criteria. By the end of Chapter 2, some reasonably challenging sequencing problems will have been encountered, thus motivating the study of solution methodologies in Chapter 3. In Chapter 4 the discussion returns to the basic model in order to relax several of the elementary assumptions and analyze the problem structures that result.

The second section of the book (Chapters 5 to 8) deals with multiple-resource models. Chapter 5 examines the scheduling of single-stage jobs with parallel machines, and Chapter 6 examines the flow shop model, which involves multistage jobs and machines in series. A hybrid model with both parallel and serial traits is the classical job shop model, which is examined in its static and dynamic forms in Chapters 7 and 8, respectively.

The final section of the book deals with network models and project scheduling. Chapter 9 introduces the techniques of project scheduling with CPM and PERT, and Chapter 10 integrates sequencing and network models in its treatment of resource-constrained project scheduling.

CHAPTER 2

SINGLE-MACHINE SEQUENCING
WITH INDEPENDENT JOBS

1. INTRODUCTION

The pure sequencing problem is a specialized scheduling problem in which an ordering of the jobs completely determines a schedule. Moreover, the simplest pure sequencing problem is one in which there is a single resource, or machine. As simple as it is, however, the single machine case is still very important for several reasons. First, in the learning process, the single machine problem is significant in that it can illustrate a variety of scheduling topics in a tractable model. It provides a context in which to investigate many different performance measures and several solution techniques. It is therefore a building block in the development of a comprehensive understanding of scheduling concepts, an understanding that should ultimately facilitate the modeling of complicated systems. In order to understand completely the behavior of a complex system, it is vital to understand the workings of its components, and quite often the single-machine problem appears as an elementary component in a larger scheduling problem. Sometimes it may even be possible to solve the imbedded single-machine problem independently and then to incorporate the result into the larger problem. For example, in multiple-operation processes there is often a bottleneck stage, and the treatment of the bottleneck itself with single-machine analysis may determine the properties of the entire schedule. At other times, the level at which decisions must be made may dictate that the processing facility should be treated in the aggregate, as a single resource.

The basic single-machine problem is characterized by these conditions.

C1. A set of n independent, single-operation jobs is available for processing at time zero.

C2. Setup times for the jobs are independent of job sequence and can be included in processing times.

C3. Job descriptors are known in advance.

C4. One machine is continuously available and is never kept idle while work is waiting.

C5. Once processing begins on a job, it is processed to completion without interruption.

Under these conditions there is a one-to-one correspondence between a sequence of the n jobs and a permutation of the job indices $1, 2, \ldots, n$. The total number of distinct solutions to the basic single-machine problem is therefore $n!$, which is the number of different permutations of n elements. Whenever a schedule can be completely characterized by a permutation of integers, it is called a *permutation schedule*, which is a classification that extends beyond single-machine cases. In describing permutation schedules, it is helpful to use brackets to indicate position in sequence. Thus $[5] = 2$ means that the fifth job in sequence is job 2. Similarly, $d_{[1]}$ refers to the due date of the first job in sequence.

After covering some preliminaries in Section 2 of this chapter, we review in Section 3 the elementary single-machine sequencing results for problems containing no due dates, and in Section 4 the elementary results for problems involving due dates. This chapter is organized to show how differences in the choice of a criterion will often lead to differences in methods of solution. In the next chapter we shall examine several general purpose methodologies that can be applied to single-machine problems.

2. PRELIMINARIES

In dealing with job attributes for the single-machine model, it is useful to distinguish between information that is known in advance and information that is generated as the result of scheduling decisions. Information that is known in advance serves as input to the scheduling function, and it is usually convenient to use lower case letters to denote this type of data. Three basic pieces of information that help to describe jobs in the deterministic single-machine case are:

Processing time (t_j).   The amount of processing required by job j.
Ready time (r_j).   The point in time at which job j is available for processing.
Due date (d_j).   The point in time at which the processing of job j is due to be completed.

We reiterate that under condition C2 the processing time t_j will generally include both direct processing time and facility setup time. The ready time can be thought of as an arrival time—the time when job j appears at the processing facility—and in the basic model the assumption in condition C1 is that $r_j = 0$ for all jobs. Due dates may not be pertinent in certain problems, but meeting deadlines is a common scheduling concern, and the basic model can shed some light on deadline-oriented objectives.

Information that is generated as a result of scheduling decisions represents output from the scheduling function, and it is usually convenient to use capital letters to denote this type of data. In deterministic cases, scheduling decisions will determine the most fundamental piece of data to be used in evaluating schedules:

Completion time (C_j).   The time at which the processing of job j is finished.

Quantitative measures for evaluating schedules are usually functions of job completion times. Two important quantities are:

Flowtime (F_j).   The amount of time job j spends in the system: $F_j = C_j - r_j$.

Lateness (L_j).   The amount of time by which the completion time of job j exceeds its due date: $L_j = C_j - d_j$.

These two quantities reflect two kinds of service. Flowtime measures the response of the system to individual demands for service and represents the interval a job waits between its arrival and its departure. (This interval is sometimes called the *turnaround* time.) Lateness measures the conformity of the schedule to a given due date, and it is important to note that the lateness quantity takes on negative values whenever a job is completed early. Negative lateness represents better service than requested, while positive lateness represents poorer service than requested. In many situations, distinct penalties and other costs will be associated with positive lateness, but no benefits will be associated with negative latenesses. Therefore it is often helpful to work with a quantity that measures only positive lateness:

Tardiness (T_j).   The lateness of job j if it fails to meet its due date, or zero otherwise: $T_j = \max \{0, L_j\}$.

Schedules are generally evaluated by aggregate quantities that involve information about all jobs, resulting in one-dimensional *performance measures*. Measures of schedule performance are usually functions of the set of completion times in a schedule. For example, suppose that n jobs are to be scheduled. Aggregate performance measures that might be defined include the following.

Mean flowtime:
$$\bar{F} = \frac{1}{n} \sum_{j=1}^{n} F_j$$

Mean tardiness:
$$\overline{T} = \frac{1}{n} \sum_{j=1}^{n} T_j$$

Maximum flowtime:
$$F_{\max} = \max_{1 \le j \le n} \{F_j\}$$

Maximum tardiness:
$$T_{\max} = \max_{1 \le j \le n} \{T_j\}$$

Number of tardy jobs:
$$N_T = \sum_{j=1}^{n} \delta(T_j)$$

$$\text{where} \quad \delta(x) = 1 \quad \text{if} \quad x > 0$$

$$\text{and} \quad \delta(x) = 0 \quad \text{otherwise}$$

Each of these measures is a function of the set of job completion times, so that their general form is always

$$Z = f(C_1, C_2, \ldots, C_n)$$

Furthermore, these quantities belong to an important class of performance measures that are called *regular* measures of performance. A performance measure Z is regular if

(a)　the scheduling objective is to minimize Z, and
(b)　Z can increase only if at least one of the completion times in the schedule increases.

More formally, suppose that $Z = f(C_1, C_2, \ldots, C_n)$ is the value of the measure that characterizes schedule S and that $Z' = f(C_1', C_2', \ldots, C_n')$ represents the value of the same measure under some different schedule S'. Then Z is regular as long as the following condition holds:

$$Z' > Z \text{ implies that } C_j' > C_j \text{ for some job } j$$

The aggregate measures introduced above are all regular measures, as are nearly all important scheduling criteria, and the following chapters will deal only with regular measures. The definition is significant because it is usually desirable to restrict attention to a limited set of schedules called a *dominant* set. In order to verify that a set D is a dominant set of schedules for regular measures of performance the following reasoning is used.

1.　Consider an arbitrary schedule S (containing completion times C_j) that is excluded from D.
2.　Show that there exists a schedule $S' \in D$ in which $C_j' \leq C_j$ for all j.
3.　Therefore $Z' \leq Z$ for any regular measure, and so S' is at least as good as S.
4.　Hence in searching for an optimum schedule it is sufficient to consider only schedules in D.

For example, it is possible to show that in the basic single-machine problem the set of permutation schedules is a dominant set for any regular measure of performance. In other words, assumption C5 could be relaxed, allowing jobs to be preempted, but preemption would never lead to a schedule that is better than the best permutation schedule. Similarly, assumption C4 could also be relaxed to allow idle time, but inserted idle time would never lead to a schedule that is better than the best permutation schedule. We prove the latter property below in order to illustrate the general reasoning in Steps 1 to 4.

Theorem 2.1

In the basic single-machine problem, schedules without inserted idle time constitute a dominant set.

Proof

1. Let S represent a schedule containing inserted idle time. In particular, suppose that under S the machine is idle for some interval (a, b).

2. Let S' represent a schedule that is identical to S through time a, and in which all the processing that occurs in S after time b is moved forward in time by an amount $b - a$. Then any job j for which $C_j \leq a$ under schedule S will have $C'_j = C_j$ under S'. Also, any job j for which $C_j > a$ under S will have $C'_j = C_j - (b - a)$ under S'. Hence $C'_j \leq C_j$ for all j.

3. It follows that $Z' \leq Z$ for any regular measure of performance Z; therefore removing inserted idle time can never lead to poorer performance.

4. Therefore schedules without idle time constitute a dominant set.

By using the same reasoning it can be shown that schedules without preemption form a dominant set.

Theorem 2.2

In the basic single-machine problem, schedules without preemption constitute a dominant set. The proof is given as Exercise 2.1.

As a consequence of these two theorems, it follows that conditions C4 and C5 need not be stated as explicit assumptions in the single-machine problem, since they characterize dominant sets of schedules under assumptions C1 to C3.

2.2 EXERCISES

2.1 Prove that in the basic single-machine problem, schedules without preemption constitute a dominant set (Theorem 2.2).

2.2 Give an example of a measure of performance that is not regular. Construct a single-machine problem in which this measure of performance is optimized by a schedule that is not a permutation schedule.

3. PROBLEMS WITHOUT DUE DATES: ELEMENTARY RESULTS

3.1 Flowtime and Inventory

Sometimes the costs associated with scheduling decisions involve service to customers, as reflected by their time spent in the system, and the scheduling objective is rapid turnaround. In other situations the costs involve investment in system resources, as reflected by the behavior of in-process inventories, and the scheduling objective is to maintain low inventory levels. The intimate relation between these two objectives can be illustrated in the basic single-machine model.

The time spent by a job in the system has been defined as its flowtime, and the "rapid turnaround" objective can be interpreted as minimizing mean flowtime. At the same time the "low inventory level" objective can be interpreted as minimizing the mean number of jobs in the system. Let $J(t)$ denote the number of jobs in the system at time t, and for a given time interval $[a, b]$ define the average number in the system to be $\bar{J}$ where

$$\bar{J} = \frac{1}{b-a} \int_a^b J(t)\, dt$$

In other words, $\bar{J}$ is the time average of the $J(t)$ function. For the basic single-machine model the behavior of $J(t)$ is easy to visualize. At time zero there are n jobs available in the system, and $J(0) = n$. There is no change in $J(t)$ until the completion of the first job, which occurs at time $F_{[1]} = t_{[1]}$. Then $J(t)$ drops to $n-1$ and remains there until the completion of the second job, which occurs at time $F_{[2]} = t_{[1]} + t_{[2]}$. If we continue in this manner, it is easy to see that $J(t)$ is a decreasing step function over the interval $[0, t_1 + t_2 + \cdots + t_n]$ as shown in Figure 2.1. Also note that $F_{\max} = t_1 + t_2 + \cdots + t_n$ and is independent of the sequence in which the jobs are

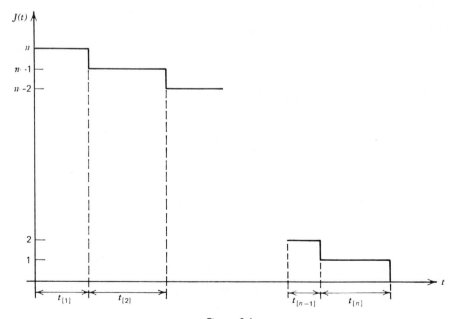

Figure 2.1
The $J(t)$ function.

processed. For the interval $[0, F_{\max}]$ then,

$$J = \frac{1}{F_{\max}} \{nt_{[1]} + (n-1)t_{[2]} + \cdots + 2t_{[n-1]} + t_{[n]}\}$$

The sum in the brackets is just the area A under the $J(t)$ function, expressed as the sum of the vertical strips in Figure 2.1. Thus $J = A/F_{\max}$.

Now recall that

$$\bar{F} = \frac{1}{n}(F_{[1]} + F_{[2]} + \cdots + F_{[n]})$$

and note that the sum in parentheses is also equal to A, expressed as the sum of the horizontal strips shown in Figure 2.2. Thus $\bar{F} = A/n$. Combining and rearranging these two relations, the algebraic result is

$$A = \bar{F}n = JF_{\max}$$

In other words, since n and $F_{\max}$ are both given constants, J is directly proportional to $\bar{F}$. This means, in particular, that the job sequence that minimizes $\bar{F}$ (average turnaround) will also minimize J (average in-process inventory). Whether the vantage point is one of optimizing customer service or one of minimizing in-process inventory levels, the problem is the same: find the sequence that minimizes $\bar{F}$.

This relation between flowtime and inventory extends well beyond the

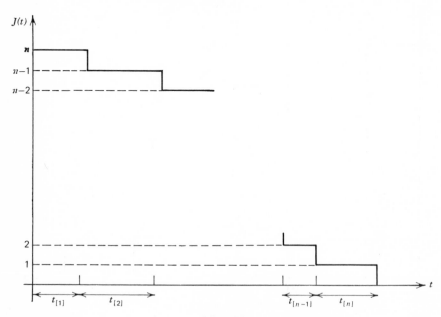

Figure 2.2
An alternative view of the $J(t)$ function.

single-machine sequencing problem. It arises in the dynamic environment (where jobs arrive over time), in infinite-horizon models, in probabilistic systems, and in situations where the inventory costs may vary among jobs (2).[1] Much of the theoretical work in scheduling has been directed to mean flowtime problems and their generalizations. What might at first seem to be undue emphasis on the turnaround criterion is not really so restrictive, in the light of this relation between flowtime and inventory, because mean flowtime actually encompasses a broader range of scheduling-related costs.

3.2 Minimizing Mean Flowtime

Consider the $J(t)$ graph and the problem of minimizing $\bar{F}$. An equivalent problem is that of minimizing the area under the $J(t)$ function. The selection of a sequence can be interpreted as the construction of a path on the $J(t)$ graph from the point $(0, n)$ to the point $(F_{max}, 0)$. The path consists of n vectors with given slopes, $-1/t_j$. Figure 2.3 shows the $J(t)$ graph for one such

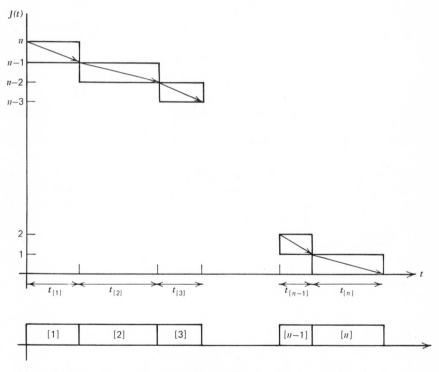

Figure 2.3
The $J(t)$ function, along with a corresponding Gantt chart.

[1] An italicized number indicates a specific reference listed at the end of the chapter.

sequence, along with the corresponding Gantt chart. Clearly the area can be minimized by placing the steepest slope to the left, then the next steepest slope, and so on. This configuration amounts to sequencing the processing times in nondecreasing order.

Sequencing the jobs in nondecreasing order of processing times is known as shortest processing time (SPT) sequencing, for obvious reasons, but it is also known by a variety of other names, such as shortest operation time and shortest imminent operation. Theorem 2.3 formalizes the optimality of SPT, and the proof of optimality illustrates a useful technique, called the method of *adjacent pairwise interchange*.

Theorem 2.3

Mean flowtime $(\bar{F})$ is minimized by SPT sequencing $(t_{[1]} \leq t_{[2]} \leq \cdots \leq t_{[n]})$.

Proof

Consider a sequence S that is not the SPT sequence. That is, somewhere in S there must exist a pair of adjacent jobs, i and j, with j following i, such that $t_i > t_j$. Now construct a new sequence, S', in which jobs i and j are interchanged in sequence and all other jobs are completed at the same time as in S. The situation is depicted in Figure 2.4, where t_B denotes the point in time at which job i begins in S and at which job j begins in S'. Also, B denotes the set of jobs that precede jobs i and j in both schedules, and A denotes the set of jobs that follow i and j in both schedules. We temporarily adopt the notation $F_k(S)$ to represent the flowtime of job k under schedule S.

It will suffice to deal with $\sum_{k=1}^{n} F_k$ as a criterion, since this differs from $\bar{F}$

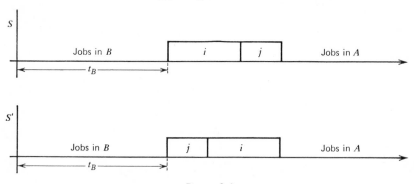

Figure 2.4

A pairwise interchange of adjacent jobs.

only in division by a constant. We first show that $\sum_{k=1}^{n} F_k$ is smaller under S' than under S.

$$\sum_{k=1}^{n} F_k(S) = \sum_{k \in B} F_k(S) + F_i(S) + F_j(S) + \sum_{k \in A} F_k(S)$$

$$= \sum_{k \in B} F_k(S) + (t_B + t_i) + (t_B + t_i + t_j) + \sum_{k \in A} F_k(S)$$

$$\sum_{k=1}^{n} F_k(S') = \sum_{k \in B} F_k(S') + (t_B + t_j) + (t_B + t_j + t_i) + \sum_{k \in A} F_k(S')$$

Therefore

$$\sum_{k=1}^{n} F_k(S) - \sum_{k=1}^{n} F_k(S') = t_i - t_j > 0$$

In other words, the interchange of jobs i and j reduces the value of $\bar{F}$. Therefore any sequence that is not the SPT sequence can be improved with respect to $\bar{F}$ by such an interchange of an adjacent pair of jobs. It follows that the SPT sequence itself must be optimal.

The overall thrust of the proof is essentially a proof by contradiction. (In other words, assume that some non-SPT sequence is "optimal." Then show via a pairwise interchange of an adjacent pair of jobs that a strict improvement can be made in this "optimal" sequence. Therefore conclude that it is impossible for a non-SPT sequence to be optimal.) However, it is also instructive to interpret the logic of the proof as that of a proof by construction.

1. Begin with any non-SPT sequence.
2. Locate a pair of adjacent jobs i and j, with j following i, such that $t_i > t_j$.
3. Interchange jobs i and j in sequence.
4. Return to Step 2 iteratively, improving the performance measure each time, until eventually the SPT sequence is constructed.

The method of adjacent pairwise interchange will be useful in other situations, as we shall see later on.

Another perspective on this derivation is sometimes useful. Note that the sum of the flowtimes is

$$\sum_{j=1}^{n} F_j = \sum_{j=1}^{n} \sum_{i=1}^{j} t_{[i]} = \sum_{j=1}^{n} (n - j + 1) t_{[j]} \tag{1}$$

This last sum of products can be viewed as the scalar product of two vectors with given elements—one containing the integers $1, 2, \ldots, n$ in descending order and the other containing the processing times in order of sequence. It is well known that in order to minimize such a scalar product, one sequence should be nonincreasing and the other should be nondecreasing. Since the terms $(n - j + 1)$ are already nonincreasing, the minimum is achieved by taking the t_j in nondecreasing order.

Associated with Theorem 2.3 are several related properties. First, by virtue of the relationship between flowtime and inventory, SPT sequencing minimizes J as well as $\bar{F}$. Second, if the waiting time of job j is defined to be its time spent in the system prior to the start of its processing, then it can be shown that SPT minimizes mean waiting time. Third, SPT minimizes the maximum waiting time. Finally, we shall find that even though SPT utilizes no information whatsoever about job due dates, it does have some optimizing properties in certain cases where the scheduling objective involves meeting due dates.

3.3 Minimizing Weighted Mean Flowtime

In a common variation of the $\bar{F}$ problem, the jobs do not have equal importance. One way to accommodate this characteristic is to assign a value or weighting factor, w_j, to each job and to incorporate the weighting factors into the performance measure. The weighted version of mean flowtime is called *weighted mean flowtime*, defined by

$$\bar{F}_w = \frac{\sum_{j=1}^{n} w_j F_j}{\sum_{j=1}^{n} w_j}$$

where the denominator is just a normalizing constant. There are direct weighted generalizations of the results described previously, and we shall specifically examine the extensions of the flowtime–inventory relation and the optimality of SPT.

In the presence of weighting factors, it is natural to define holding costs to be proportional to the value of in-process inventory. Job j contributes w_j to the value of total in-process inventory while it awaits completion, and we can define a function $V(t)$ to be the total value of inventory in the system at time t. The $V(t)$ function is a step function, but unlike $J(t)$, this step function decreases in steps of w_j rather than steps of 1. Figure 2.5 depicts $V(t)$. If $\bar{V}$ denotes the time average of $V(t)$ over the processing interval, we can again derive two expressions for the area under the $V(t)$ graph. Summing vertical strips, as shown in Figure 2.5, we obtain

$$A = \sum_{j=1}^{n} t_{[j]} \sum_{i=j}^{n} w_{[i]} = \bar{V} F_{\max}$$

Summing horizontal strips in a manner similar to that of Figure 2.2, we obtain

$$A = \sum_{j=1}^{n} w_j F_j = \bar{F}_w \sum_{j=1}^{n} w_j$$

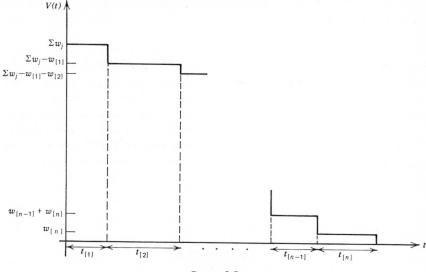

Figure 2.5
The $V(t)$ function.

If we now set these two expressions for A equal, we find that the generalized flowtime–inventory relation is given by

$$\bar{F}_w \sum_{j=1}^{n} w_j = \bar{V} F_{\max}$$

Now we observe that $\sum w_j$ and $F_{\max}$ are both constants that are independent of sequence; thus we conclude that $\bar{V}$ is directly proportional to $\bar{F}_w$, and that the sequence which minimizes one will minimize the other.

Having seen that the optimal sequencing rule for minimizing mean flow-time is shortest-first sequencing, it should be expected that the optimal rule for a weighted mean flowtime criterion should be a weighted version of SPT. As before, the nature of the optimal rule can be deduced from the graphical model. In this case, we seek a path on the $V(t)$ graph that connects the point $(0, \sum w_j)$ with the point $(F_{\max}, 0)$. This time the vectors that make up the path have slopes of $-w_j/t_j$, and we still place the steepest slope first in order to minimize the area under $V(t)$. In effect, the optimal rule is weighted shortest processing time (WSPT) sequencing. We state the result formally in the following way.

Theorem 2.4

Weighted mean flowtime $(\bar{F}_w)$ is minimized by WSPT sequencing

$$(t_{[1]}/w_{[1]} \leq t_{[2]}/w_{[2]} \leq \cdots \leq t_{[n]}/w_{[n]}).$$

A proof by the method of adjacent pairwise interchange is analogous to the proof of Theorem 2.3.

The optimality of WSPT when $\bar{F}_w$ is the objective may seem at first to be a specialized scheduling result. However, an examination of the vast literature on industrial engineering, operations research, information systems, and related fields will reveal that the sequencing model with a $\bar{F}_w$ objective is a rich model indeed. A specialized bibliography on the model can be found in (5), and some of the following exercises suggest its range of applicability. Note that when the job set contains unequal weights, WSPT will minimize $\bar{F}_w$ and $\bar{V}$, but not necessarily the mean number of jobs in the system.

2.3   EXERCISES

3.1　Prove that SPT sequencing minimizes mean waiting time.

3.2　An obvious definition of longest processing time (LPT) sequencing is

$$t_{[1]} \geq t_{[2]} \geq \cdots \geq t_{[n]}$$

It can be expected that, in general, LPT will exhibit properties that are antithetical to those of SPT. In particular, prove
(a) LPT maximizes $\bar{F}$.
(b) LPT maximizes $\bar{J}$.
(c) LPT maximizes mean waiting time.

3.3　Construct an example single-machine problem to show that SPT does not minimize mean tardiness.

3.4　Use the method of adjacent pairwise interchange to prove that WSPT minimizes $\bar{F}_w$.

3.5　A single-machine facility operates around the clock and faces the problem of sequencing the production work for the six customer orders described in the table below.

Order	1	2	3	4	5	6
Processing time (hours)	20	27	16	6	15	24

(a) What production sequence will minimize the mean flowtime of these orders, assuming all six arrived at the same time? What is the mean flowtime in this schedule?
(b) Suppose that customer orders 2 and 6 are considered three times as important as the rest. What production sequence would you propose?

3.6　(The least-cost testing sequence problem.) An item is subjected to a series of n tests (e.g., hardness, weight, and length.) Associated with the ith test are two known constants: K_i, the cost per item of carrying out the ith test, and

R_i, the probability of rejecting the item on the ith test. The tests are independent in the sense that they may be run in any order, and the constants K_i and R_i are independent of test order. For a given sequence of tests, an item is subjected to each test in the sequence in turn as long as the tests accept the item; if an item is rejected by any test, no further tests are performed. Determine the test sequence that minimizes the total expected cost of testing an item.

3.7   A magnetic tape contains n items. Requests for these items occur and are satisfied one at a time, and the tape is rewound after each request is satisfied. Item i has a known size, s_i, and is requested with a known probability, p_i. How should the items be sequenced on the file to minimize the expected time required to locate and transfer an item?

3.8   In the basic single-machine model suppose that job j has a known loss rate, c_j, which is the rate at which delay costs are incurred by job j until its completion. (If job j is completed at time T, then the associated delay cost is $c_j T$.)

   (a) What sequence will minimize total delay cost for the set of n jobs?

   (b) Suppose instead that costs are discounted continuously over time, and let r denote the discount rate. (In other words, at time zero the present value of the cost of keeping job j in the system until time T is $\int_0^T c_j e^{-rt}\, dt$.) Formulate the problem of minimizing total discounted delay costs, and determine the optimal sequence.

   (c) Are the optimal sequences in (a) and (b) identical?

3.9   The following sequence might be called the VIP sequence:

$$w_{[1]} \geq w_{[2]} \geq \cdots \geq w_{[n]}$$

Suppose that a scheduling objective is to minimize $\bar{F}_w$ and that weighting factors are assigned according to processing times. Show that

   (a) If $w_j = \alpha t_j$ (weighting factors are directly proportional to processing times), then all sequences are equivalent.

   (b) If $w_j = \alpha t_j^{\beta}$ then VIP is optimal when $\beta > 1$, but is the worst sequence when $\beta < 1$.

   (c) If $t_j = t$ (all processing times are equal), then VIP is optimal.

4.   PROBLEMS WITH DUE DATES: ELEMENTARY RESULTS

4.1   Lateness Criteria

   Recall that job lateness is defined as $L_j = C_j - d_j$, or the discrepancy between the due date of a job and its completion time. A simple and somewhat remarkable result is that minimum mean lateness is achieved by SPT.

Theorem 2.5

Mean lateness ($\bar{L}$) is minimized by SPT sequencing.

Proof

By definition

$$L = \frac{1}{n}\sum_{j=1}^{n}L_j = \frac{1}{n}\sum_{j=1}^{n}(C_j - d_j) = \frac{1}{n}\sum_{j=1}^{n}(F_j - d_j)$$

$$= \frac{1}{n}\sum_{j=1}^{n}F_j - \frac{1}{n}\sum_{j=1}^{n}d_j = \bar{F} - \bar{d}$$

where $\bar{d}$ is the average of the given set of due dates and is therefore a constant. Since $\bar{L}$ differs from $\bar{F}$ by a constant that is independent of sequence, the sequence that minimizes $\bar{L}$ will be the sequence that minimizes $\bar{F}$; this sequence is given by SPT.

This result is somewhat remarkable because a sequencing rule that ignores due-date information is optimal for a due-date oriented criterion. An intuitive approach to meeting due dates might well have been to sequence the jobs according to some measure of due-date urgency. One obvious measure of urgency for a given job is the time until its due date. Sequencing the jobs by earliest due date (EDD) cannot guarantee, however, that $\bar{L}$ will be minimized, because only SPT guarantees that. What can be shown is that EDD sequencing minimizes the maximum lateness in the schedule.

Theorem 2.6

The maximum job lateness ($L_{\max}$) and the maximum job tardiness ($T_{\max}$) are minimized by EDD sequencing ($d_{[1]} \leq d_{[2]} \leq \cdots \leq d_{[n]}$).

Proof

We again employ the method of adjacent pairwise interchange (see Figure 2.4). Consider a sequence S that is not the EDD sequence. That is, somewhere in S there must exist a pair of adjacent jobs, i and j, with j following i, such that $d_i > d_j$. Now construct a new sequence, S', in which jobs i and j are interchanged and all other jobs complete at the same time as in S. Then

$$L_i(S) = t_B + t_i - d_i \qquad\qquad L_j(S') = t_B + t_j - d_j$$

$$L_j(S) = t_B + t_i + t_j - d_j \qquad L_i(S') = t_B + t_j + t_i - d_i$$

from which it follows that $L_j(S) > L_i(S')$ and $L_j(S) > L_j(S')$. Hence

$$L_j(S) > \max\{L_i(S'), L_j(S')\}$$

Let $L = \max \{L_k \mid k \in A \text{ or } k \in B\}$ and notice that L is the same under both S and S'. Then

$$L_{\max}(S) = \max \{L, L_i(S), L_j(S)\} \geq \max \{L, L_i(S'), L_j(S')\} = L_{\max}(S')$$

In other words the interchange of jobs i and j does not increase the value of $L_{\max}$, and may actually reduce (improve) it. Therefore an optimal sequence can be constructed as follows.

1. Begin with an arbitrary non-EDD sequence.

2. Locate a pair of adjacent jobs i and j, with j following i, such that $d_i > d_j$.

3. Interchange jobs i and j.

4. Return to Step 2 iteratively until the EDD sequence is constructed. At each iteration $L_{\max}$ either remains the same or is reduced. Since the EDD sequence can be reached from any other sequence in this manner, there can be no other sequence with a value of $L_{\max}$ lower than that corresponding to EDD sequencing.

A similar argument will establish that EDD minimizes $T_{\max}$, beginning with the inequality

$$T_{\max}(S) = \max \{0, L_{\max}(S)\} \geq \max \{0, L_{\max}(S')\} = T_{\max}(S')$$

A second measure of urgency for a given job is the time until its due date minus the time required to process it. (In particular, among jobs with identical due dates, the longest is most urgent.) This urgency measure is called *slack time* and may appear to be a more sophisticated quantification of urgency than the due date alone. Nevertheless, there is little to be said for optimality of minimum slack time (MST) sequencing in the single-machine problem. Its only general property involves a mirror image of Theorem 2.6, and is of questionable usefulness in this situation. The practical value of slack time information does appear, however, in more complicated problems, especially when used in combination with SPT sequencing.

Theorem 2.7

The minimum job lateness $(L_{\min})$ is maximized, among permutation schedules, by MST sequencing $(d_{[1]} - p_{[1]} \leq d_{[2]} - p_{[2]} \leq \cdots \leq d_{[n]} - p_{[n]})$.

Proof

The proof is also a mirror image of the proof of Theorem 2.6, and utilizes an adjacent pairwise interchange argument. Observe that $L_{\min}$ is not a regular measure of performance; hence the need, in Theorem 2.7, to restrict consideration to permutation schedules.

An important variation of the single-criterion problem involves the designation of both a primary and a secondary measure of performance. The primary measure is the dominant criterion, but if there are alternate optima with respect to the primary measure it is then desired to identify the best sequence among these alternatives with respect to a secondary measure.

For example, suppose that some tardiness-based measure (such as $\bar{T}$) is the primary measure and that there are several sequences that are considered "perfect" because they contain no tardy jobs. Furthermore, suppose that $\bar{F}$ is the secondary measure. Then to construct a perfect sequence that minimizes $\bar{F}$, we can employ Smith's rule (7):

Job i may be assigned the last position in sequence only if

(1) $d_i \geq \sum_{j=1}^{n} t_j$, and

(2) $t_i \geq t_k$ among all jobs k such that $d_k \geq \sum_{j=1}^{n} t_j$

This rule should seem quite logical, for if some other job were to come last in some sequence, then an obvious improvement in $\bar{F}$ could be achieved simply by shifting job i to the end of the sequence. Once Smith's rule has identified the last job among n, there remain $(n - 1)$ jobs to which the rule can again be applied. If we continue in this fashion, the rule will eventually construct an optimal sequence, working backwards.

For example, consider the following problem.

Job j	t_j	d_j
1	4	16
2	7	16
3	1	8
4	6	21
5	3	9

It is not hard to verify (see Exercise 4.2) that a perfect sequence exists. Then the application of Smith's rule generates a perfect sequence with $\bar{F} = 9.8$, by following the steps shown in the worksheet of Table 2.1. At each stage, the jobs that are candidates for the last available position are those that satisfy condition 1. The candidate job with the largest processing time is selected at each stage, yielding an optimal sequence of 3–5–1–2–4.

4.2 Minimizing the Number of Tardy Jobs

If the EDD sequence should yield zero tardy jobs, or should it yield exactly one tardy job, then it is an optimal sequence for N_T (see Exercise 4.5). If it

Table 2.1

STAGE 1

$\sum t_j = 21$ Candidates for job [5] must have $d_j \geq 21$: job 4
Hence [5] = 4

STAGE 2

$\sum t_j = 15$ Candidates for job [4]: jobs 1, 2
Hence [4] = 2, since $t_2 > t_1$

STAGE 3

$\sum t_j = 8$ Candidates for job [3]: jobs 1, 3, 5
Hence [3] = 1, since $t_1 > t_5 > t_3$

STAGE 4

$\sum t_j = 4$ Candidates for job [2]: jobs 3, 5
Hence [2] = 5, since $t_5 > t_3$

STAGE 5

[1] = 3

Optimal Sequence: 3–5–1–2–4   ($\bar{T} = 0, \bar{F} = 9.8$)

yields more than one tardy job, however, the EDD sequence may not be optimal. An efficient algorithm for the general case is given below. The solution method assumes that the form of an optimal sequence is as follows (Figure 2.6);

(a) First, a set (E^*) of early jobs, in EDD order.

(b) Then, a set (L^*) of late jobs, in any order.

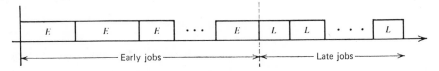

Figure 2.6
The form of a sequence that minimizes N_T.

The early jobs are assumed to be in EDD order without loss of generality because if any sequence (or subsequence) of jobs has no tardiness, then we are assured that the EDD sequence for those jobs must have no tardiness (see Exercise 4.2).

ALGORITHM 2.1   HODGSON'S ALGORITHM (4)
(To Minimize N_T)

Step 1.   Place all the jobs in set E using EDD order. Let set L be empty.

Step 2.   If no jobs in E are late, stop: E must be optimal. Otherwise, identify the first late job in E. Suppose this turns out to be job [k].

Step 3. Identify the longest job among the first k jobs in sequence. Remove this job from E and place it in L. Revise the completion times of the jobs remaining in E and return to Step 2.

For example, consider the job set in the table below.

Job j	t_j	d_j
1	1	2
2	5	7
3	3	8
4	9	13
5	7	11

A worksheet for minimizing N_T using Algorithm 2.1 is shown in Table 2.2.

Table 2.2

STAGE 1		
Step 1. Initialize.	$E = \{1\text{--}2\text{--}3\text{--}5\text{--}4\}$	$L = \phi$
Step 2. Job 3 is the first late job.		
Step 3. Job 2 is removed from E.	$E = \{1\text{--}3\text{--}5\text{--}4\}$	$L = \{2\}$
STAGE 2		
Step 2. Job 4 is the first late job.		
Step 3. Job 4 is removed from E.	$E = \{1\text{--}3\text{--}5\}$	$L = \{2, 4\}$
STAGE 3		
Step 2. No jobs in E are late. An optimal sequence is		
$\qquad$ 1–3–5–2–4 $\qquad$ ($N_T = 2$)		

In Stage 1, the jobs are ordered by EDD and job 3 is found to be the first late job. The longest job in the sequence up to and including job 3 is job 2; thus job 2 is removed from E and placed in L. At Stage 2, job 4 is removed from E and placed in L, and at Stage 3 no tardy jobs remain in E. The algorithm therefore yields two optimal sequences: 1–3–5–2–4 and 1–3–5–4–2, since the late jobs can appear in any order.

Several papers have discussed proofs of Algorithm 2.1 or its closely related original form, including references *3, 4, 6,* and *8.*

4.3   Minimizing Mean Tardiness

The performance objective of meeting job due dates is one of the scheduling criteria most frequently encountered in practical problems. While meeting due dates is only a qualitative goal, it usually implies that time-dependent penalties are assessed on late jobs but that no benefits derive from completing jobs early. A natural quantification of the objective of meeting due dates thus involves the tardiness measure, and a fundamental sequencing problem is the minimization of mean job tardiness. The difficulty of dealing with mean tardiness, and also with most other tardiness-based performance measures, arises from the fact that tardiness is not a linear function of completion time. This means that to find optimal solutions to such problems it is usually necessary to rely on the concepts of combinatorial optimization. Furthermore, because of the complexities of combinatorial methods, there is apt to be more attention paid to efficient but suboptimal solution techniques. In this section we examine in detail a suboptimal procedure, originated by Wilkerson and Irwin (9), for minimizing mean tardiness. In Chapter 3 we shall deal with general purpose combinatorial optimization techniques that might also be applied to the mean tardiness criterion.

The logical first approach to the $\bar{T}$ problem is to use adjacent pairwise interchange properties, and this is the basic idea of the Wilkerson-Irwin procedure. Consider a schedule S in which jobs i and j are adjacent in sequence, and the schedule S' that is identical to S except that jobs i and j are interchanged (see Figure 2.4). We assume that $t_i \geq t_j$, and we seek conditions under which the job with the earlier due date (between jobs i and j) should appear earlier in the sequence. Rather than comparing $\bar{T}$ for both sequences, it will suffice to compare the contributions to total tardiness that come from jobs i and j, since the total contributions of the other jobs will be the same in both sequences. Thus let

$$T_{ij} = T_i(S) + T_j(S) = \max \{t_B + t_i - d_i, 0\} + \max \{t_B + t_i + t_j - d_j, 0\}$$
$$T_{ji} = T_j(S') + T_i(S') = \max \{t_B + t_j - d_j, 0\} + \max \{t_B + t_j + t_i - d_i, 0\}$$

where, as before, t_B denotes the time at which job i or job j can be started. There are several distinct cases to consider.

Case 1. $d_i \geq d_j$

Case 1.1 $t_B + t_i \leq d_i$

$$T_{ij} = \max \{t_B + t_i + t_j - d_j, 0\}$$
$$T_{ji} = \max \{t_B + t_j - d_j, 0\} + \max \{t_B + t_j + t_i - d_i, 0\}$$

Notice that T_{ij} is at least as large as the first maximum in T_{ji} (since $t_i > 0$) and at least as large as the second (since $d_i \geq d_j$). Therefore if one or both of the maxima in T_{ji} are zero, we will have $T_{ij} \geq T_{ji}$.
Now suppose that neither term in T_{ji} is zero. Then

$$T_{ij} - T_{ji} = (t_B + t_i + t_j - d_j) - (t_B + t_j - d_j) - (t_B + t_j + t_i - d_i)$$
$$= -t_B - t_j + d_i \geq -t_B - t_i + d_i \geq 0 \quad \text{(in this case)}$$

Therefore case 1.1 yields $T_{ij} \geq T_{ji}$; thus it is preferable to have job j (the job with the earlier due date) precede job i.

Case 1.2 $d_i < t_B + t_i$

$$T_{ij} = t_B + t_i - d_i + t_B + t_i + t_j - d_j$$
$$T_{ji} = \max \{t_B + t_j - d_j, 0\} + t_B + t_j + t_i - d_i$$
$$T_{ij} - T_{ji} = t_B + t_i - d_j - \max \{t_B + t_j - d_j, 0\}$$

If $(t_B + t_j - d_j)$ is negative, then

$$T_{ij} - T_{ji} = t_B + t_i - d_j \geq t_B + t_i - d_i \geq 0 \quad \text{(in this case)}$$

Otherwise

$$T_{ij} - T_{ji} = t_B + t_i - d_j - (t_B + t_j - d_j) = t_i - t_j \geq 0$$

Therefore case 1.2 yields $T_{ij} \geq T_{ji}$; thus it is preferable to have job j (the job with the earlier due date) precede job i.

Case 2. $d_i < d_j$

Case 2.1 $t_B + t_i \leq d_i$

$$T_{ij} = \max \{t_B + t_i + t_j - d_j, 0\}$$
$$T_{ji} = \max \{t_B + t_j + t_i - d_i, 0\} \geq T_{ij}$$

Therefore, case 2.1 yields $T_{ji} \geq T_{ij}$, and so it is preferable to have job i (the job with the earlier due date) precede job j.

Case 2.2 $d_i < t_B + t_i$

(Case 2.2.1) $t_B + t_i + t_j \leq d_j$

$$T_{ij} = t_B + t_i - d_i$$
$$T_{ji} = t_B + t_j + t_i - d_i \geq T_{ij}$$

Therefore case 2.2.1 yields $T_{ji} \geq T_{ij}$, and so it is preferable to have job i (the job with the earlier due date) precede job j.

(Case 2.2.2) $t_B + t_j \leq d_j < t_B + t_i + t_j$

$$T_{ij} = t_B + t_i - d_i + t_B + t_i + t_j - d_j$$
$$T_{ji} = t_B + t_j + t_i - d_i$$
$$T_{ij} - T_{ji} = t_B + t_i - d_j$$

Notice in this case that the desirability of S or S' depends on t_B and that a choice could not be made without knowing where in the sequence jobs i and j are located. The conclusion is that it is preferable to have job i (the job with the earlier due date) precede job j unless $t_B + t_i > d_j$, in which case job j (the shorter job) should precede job i.

(Case 2.2.3) $d_j < t_B + t_j$

$$T_{ij} = t_B + t_i - d_i + t_B + t_i + t_j - d_j$$

$$T_{ji} = t_B + t_j - d_j + t_B + t_j + t_i - d_i$$

$$T_{ij} - T_{ji} = t_i - t_j \geq 0$$

Therefore case 2.2.3 yields $T_{ij} \geq T_{ji}$; thus it is preferable to have job j (the shorter job) precede job i.

We have now exhausted all the cases and subcases. We conclude that it is preferable to have the job with the earlier due date come first (between i and j) except when

$$d_i < d_j, d_i < t_B + t_i \quad \text{and} \quad d_j < t_B + t_i$$

or when

$$d_i < d_j, d_i < t_B + t_i \quad \text{and} \quad d_j < t_B + t_j$$

in which case the shorter job should come first. We can easily remove the redundant conditions and restate this result: *It is preferable to have the job with the earlier due date come first except when*

$$t_B + \max \{t_i, t_j\} > \max \{d_i, d_j\}$$

in which case the shorter job should come first. (This form follows from the fact that $t_i \geq t_j$ was assumed at the outset and that $d_i < d_j$ characterized both exceptional subcases.)

The Wilkerson-Irwin algorithm uses this decision rule in a heuristic procedure that employs pairwise job comparisons in the construction of a sequence. The algorithm involves two ordered lists: a list of unscheduled jobs and a list of scheduled jobs. The scheduled list is a partially completed job sequence that is subject to possible revisions, and the unscheduled list contains the remaining jobs in EDD order. At each stage, the first job on the unscheduled list is removed in order to implement the decision rule. We call this the *pivot* job. Let

$\alpha = $ the index of the last job on the scheduled list

$\beta = $ the index of the pivot job

$\gamma = $ the index of the first job on the unscheduled list

so that for the evaluation of the decision rule, we will use $t_B = F_\alpha$. Figure 2.7a depicts the locations of jobs α, β, and γ.

At each stage, the algorithm applies the pairwise decision rule to jobs β and γ, where $d_\beta \leq d_\gamma$. If $F_\alpha + \max \{t_\beta, t_\gamma\} \leq d_\gamma$, or if $t_\beta \leq t_\gamma$, then it is desirable

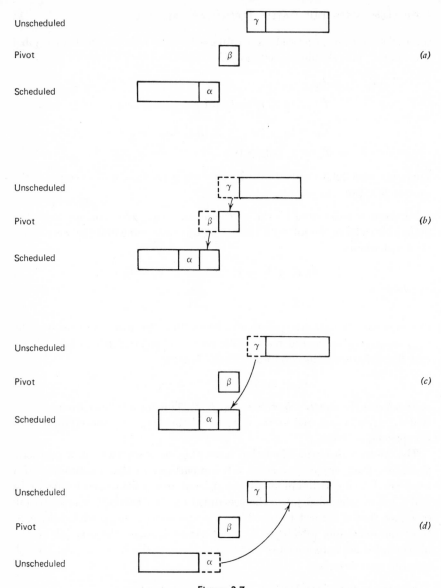

Figure 2.7
Job manipulations under the Wilkerson-Irwin algorithm.

to have β precede γ at this stage in the sequence; thus β is added to the scheduled list (Figure 2.7b). If these conditions fail, the decision rule is applied to jobs α and γ. If $(F_\alpha - t_\alpha) + \max \{t_\alpha, t_\gamma\} \leq \max \{d_\alpha, d_\gamma\}$ or if $t_\alpha \leq t_\gamma$, then it is desirable to have γ follow α and so γ is added to the scheduled list (Figure 2.7c). However, if this decision rule also fails, a *jump condition* results. Under the jump condition, job α is removed from the scheduled list and placed on the unscheduled list in EDD order. The decision rule is then applied to job γ and the job that preceded job α on the scheduled list (Figure 2.7d). The jump condition occurs infrequently, but it may be employed several times in succession in order to schedule job γ. The algorithm is initialized by applying the decision rule (with $t_B = 0$) to the jobs with the two earliest due dates.

In order to illustrate the method in detail, consider the four-job example shown below and the accompanying worksheet (Table 2.3). Initially, jobs 1

Job j	t_j	d_j
1	5	6
2	7	8
3	6	9
4	4	10

and 2 are compared, and the decision rule selects job 1 to be scheduled first, since

$$\max \{t_1, t_2\} \leq d_2$$

At the second stage (see Table 2.3) job 1 is the last job scheduled, and job 2 is the pivot job. The decision rule fails when comparing jobs 2 and 3, since

$$F_1 + \max \{t_2, t_3\} > d_3 \quad \text{and} \quad t_2 > t_3$$

Table 2.3

Stage	Scheduled List	F_α	α	β	γ	Unscheduled List	Decision Rule Result
1	Empty	0	—	1	2	2–3–4	$\alpha = 1$
2	1	5	1	2	3	3–4	$\alpha = 3$
3	1–3	11	3	2	4	4	Jump condition
3'	1	5	1	—	4	2–3	$\alpha = 4$
4	1–4	9	4	2	3	3	$\alpha = 3$

Final sequence is 1–4–3–2 ($\bar{T} = 5$)

Therefore the decision rule is applied to jobs 1 and 3. This time the decision rule holds, so that job 3 is added to the scheduled list.

At the third stage, the decision rule fails in attempting to schedule both jobs 2 and 4, and a jump condition results. Thereafter (Stage 3′) the decision rule holds, since

$$(F_1 - t_1) + \max \{t_1, t_4\} \leq \max \{d_1, d_4\}$$

and so job 4 is assigned to follow job 1 in sequence. Finally, at the fourth stage, the decision rule fails when attempting to schedule job 2 but succeeds in scheduling job 3. Thus the algorithm constructs the complete sequence 1–4–3–2, for which $\bar{T} = 5$.

A formal statement of the algorithm, organized in a manner suitable for adaptation as a computer code, is given below.

ALGORITHM 2.2　THE WILKERSON-IRWIN ALGORITHM (9)
(A Heuristic Procedure for Minimizing $\bar{T}$)

Step 1.　(Initialization) Place all the jobs on the unscheduled list in EDD order. Let a and b denote the first two jobs on this list. If $\max \{t_a, t_b\} \leq \max \{d_a, d_b\}$, then assign the first position in sequence to the job with the earlier due date; otherwise assign the first position in sequence to the shorter job. The assigned job becomes α and the other job becomes β, the pivot job.

Step 2.　If $F_\alpha + \max \{t_\beta, t_\gamma\} \leq \max \{d_\beta, d_\gamma\}$ or if $t_\beta \leq t_\gamma$, then add job β to the scheduled list. Job β now becomes job α; job γ is removed from the unscheduled list and now becomes job β; and the next job on the unscheduled list now becomes job γ. Repeat Step 2 unless the unscheduled list is empty, in which case add job β to the scheduled list and stop. If, on the other hand, $F_\alpha + \max \{t_\beta, t_\alpha\} > \max \{d_\beta, d_\alpha\}$ and $t_\beta > t_\alpha$, then return job β to the unscheduled list and let job γ now become job β. Proceed to Step 3.

Step 3.　If $F_\alpha - t_\alpha + \max \{t_\alpha, t_\beta\} \leq \max \{d_\alpha, d_\beta\}$ or if $t_\alpha \leq t_\beta$, then add job β to the scheduled list. Job β now becomes job α; the first unscheduled job now becomes the pivot job; and the next job on the unscheduled list now becomes job γ. Go to Step 2. If, on the other hand, $F_\alpha - t_\alpha + \max \{t_\alpha, t_\beta\} > \max \{d_\alpha, d_\beta\}$ and $t_\alpha > t_\beta$, then a jump condition results. Go to Step 4.

Step 4.　(Jump condition) Remove job α from the scheduled list and return it to the unscheduled list in EDD order. If jobs remain on the scheduled list, the last remaining job now becomes job α Return to Step 3. If there are no jobs on the scheduled list, job β is assigned first position on the scheduled list and becomes job α; the first unscheduled job now becomes the pivot job; and the next job on the unscheduled list now becomes job γ. Go to Step 2.

Algorithm 2.2 will sometimes, but not always, produce an optimal sequence. The outcome of the decision rule, when applied to a given pair of jobs, may depend on whether the jobs are considered early or late in the sequence. If the adjacent pairs in a given sequence happen to satisfy the decision rule, then the sequence is at least a local optimum, but there is no guarantee that a better sequence cannot be found. (This subject is examined more generally in Chapter 3.) It is sometimes possible to determine whether the sequence generated by Algorithm 2.2 is a global optimum as well as a local optimum. For each tardy job in the final sequence we define its tardiness interval to be the time interval between its due date and its completion. More formally, we define the tardiness interval for job j as follows:

$$I_j \quad \text{is empty} \quad \text{if} \quad C_j \le d_j$$

$$I_j = [d_j, C_j] \quad \text{if} \quad C_j > d_j$$

If Algorithm 2.2 produces a schedule in which the tardiness intervals are nonoverlapping, then the solution is optimal. This relation is stated explicitly in the following theorem.

Theorem 2.8

The sequence produced by Algorithm 2.2 minimizes $\overline{T}$ if there is no point in time t for which

$$t \in I_j \quad \text{and} \quad t \in I_i$$

for the tardiness intervals of any pair of jobs i and j.

The proof of Theorem 2.8 is lengthy and tedious. It relies on two properties (see Exercise 4.10) that require detailed examination of subcases in a manner reminiscent of the pairwise interchange analysis performed above. Note, however, that Theorem 2.8 provides only a sufficient condition for optimality. Even when tardiness intervals overlap, the final sequence may still be optimal, but there is no simple way to know.

The evaluation of a heuristic procedure, such as Algorithm 2.2, is based on two considerations. First, its primary advantage lies in the fact that it can generate good solutions to the $\overline{T}$ problem rapidly. Compared to optimizing methods and general purpose heuristic procedures, as we shall see in the next chapter, this specialized algorithm requires relatively few calculations. On the other hand, its primary disadvantage is that it cannot guarantee finding an optimal sequence. Empirical investigations have provided some perspective on this trade-off.

In their original study, Wilkerson and Irwin found that the solution was quite likely to satisfy the hypothesis of Theorem 2.8 when the due dates were distributed over nearly all of the total processing interval $[0, F_{\max}]$, but

Table 2.4

Problem Size	Number of Problems	Optimum Found	Optimality Condition (Theorem 2.8) Held
8	16	14	2
10	16	9	1
12	16	10	3
15	16	9	3

relatively less likely when the due dates were distributed over less than 85 % of the total processing interval. A later study (1) in a series of test problems found that the algorithm tended to locate an optimum much more frequently than Theorem 2.8 might indicate (see Table 2.4). Also, in 64 test problems[2] with between 8 and 15 jobs, the algorithm found a solution that on the average was about 2 % above optimum and only once was greater than 10 % above optimum.

We conclude our treatment of the $\bar{T}$ problem with some specialized results concerning optimal sequences.

Theorem 2.9

If the EDD sequence produces no more than one tardy job, it yields the minimum value of $\bar{T}$.

Theorem 2.10

If all jobs have the same due date, then $\bar{T}$ is minimized by SPT sequencing.

Theorem 2.11

If it is impossible for any job to be on time in any sequence, then $\bar{T}$ is minimized by SPT sequencing.

Theorem 2.12

If SPT sequencing yields no jobs on time, then it minimizes $\bar{T}$.

2.4 EXERCISES

4.1 Prove that MST sequencing maximizes $L_{\min}$.

4.2 Prove this corollary to Theorem 2.6:
    In the basic single-machine problem, a sequence containing no late jobs exists if and only if the EDD sequence contains no late jobs.

[2] The 16 test problems in which $n = 8$ are reproduced in Appendix A.

4.3 Generalize the procedure for optimizing secondary measures in the following sequencing problems:

(a) Minimize $\bar{F}_w$ among sequences with no tardiness.

(b) Minimize $\bar{F}$ among sequences that minimize T_{max}.

4.4 The following general algorithm can be employed to minimize the maximum cost of a job sequence. Let $g_j(t)$ be a nondecreasing cost function, representing the cost associated with the completion of job j at time t. To minimize $\max_j \{g_j(C_j)\}$

Step 1. Compute $T = \sum_{j=1}^{n} t_j$.

Step 2. Determine j such that $g_j(T)$ is minimal among the n jobs.

Step 3. Sequence job j (identified at Step 2) last in sequence among the n jobs. This leaves a smaller single-machine problem with $(n-1)$ jobs. Hence replace n by $(n-1)$ and return to Step 1 until all jobs are sequenced.

(a) Prove the optimality of the algorithm. (*Hint.* Suppose that the algorithm made an incorrect job assignment to the last position at some stage. Show that a contradiction results.)

(b) Discuss how the algorithm behaves when $g_j(t) = \max \{0, t - d_j\}$.

4.5 Suppose that an EDD sequence contains one late job. Prove that this is then an optimal sequence with respect to minimizing N_T.

4.6 Discuss the difficulties involved in extending Smith's rule to this situation: Minimize $\bar{F}$ among sequences that minimize N_T. Compare Exercise 4.3b.

4.7 A computer systems consulting company is under contract to carry out seven projects, all with deadlines, measured in days from now. The consultants are a small group and must work together on each project, so that the projects will be started and completed sequentially. Under the terms of the contract, the consultants will receive $800 for each project completed on time, but they will incur $500 in penalties for each project completed late. Each project has an associated duration, which is the anticipated number of days required to carry the project out, as shown below. How should the projects be sequenced in order to maximize net revenues?

Project ID	1	2	3	4	5	6	7
Duration	2	4	6	8	10	12	14
Deadline	6	12	30	19	12	18	24

4.8 (a) Prove Theorem 2.9 and determine whether Algorithm 2.2 generates an optimal sequence when the hypothesis of the theorem is satisfied.

(b) Repeat (a) for Theorem 2.10.

(c) Repeat (a) for Theorem 2.11.

(d) Repeat (a) for Theorem 2.12.

4.9 Apply Theorem 2.8 to the four-job example in Section 4.3. What conclusion can be drawn regarding optimality of the sequence 1-4-3-2?

4.10   Prove the following elements of the justification of Theorem 2.8.

(a) Suppose that Algorithm 2.2 generates nonoverlapping tardiness intervals. If any job is removed from the final sequence, then the remaining tardiness intervals are still nonoverlapping.

(b) Consider a sequence generated by Algorithm 2.2 in which there are nonoverlapping tardiness intervals. If any job is shifted to a later position in sequence, while the order of the remaining jobs is preserved, then the net change in $\overline{T}$ cannot be a reduction.

(c) Show that any sequence can be constructed from the sequence produced by Algorithm 2.2 by a series of adjustments in which each adjustment is of the form described in (b): that is, shifting one job to a later position in sequence.

(d) Justify the claim in Theorem 2.8.

5. SUMMARY

The basic single-machine model is fundamental in the study of sequencing and scheduling. It is considered a rather simple *scheduling* problem because it does not have distinct sequencing and resource allocation dimensions. Nevertheless, as the $\overline{T}$ problem begins to illustrate, the sequencing problem itself may sometimes be fairly complicated. Even in this fundamental type of problem the set of feasible solutions can be quite large, and the determination of an optimum can be a formidable combinatorial problem. In some special cases optima can be found readily, most notably in the minimization of $\overline{F}_w$ and T_{max}, but in general it may be necessary to resort to general purpose methodologies, such as those described in the next chapter.

Several important scheduling objectives can be illustrated in the single-machine model, and these often give rise to a variety of solution strategies. Geometric and algebraic methods were used to prove the optimality of WSPT for $\overline{F}_w$ and the optimality of EDD for T_{max}, respectively. In these cases, knowledge of an optimum pairwise job ordering allows the optimal sequence to be constructed with a simple sorting mechanism. A more intricate construction is required to minimize the number of tardy jobs. For more complicated criteria, including $\overline{T}$, the general purpose methodologies treated in Chapter 3 can be utilized in the problem.

All of these comments serve to describe the role of the basic single-machine model in the learning process. It is also worth repeating, as noted at the beginning of this chapter, that the solution of practical scheduling problems can make direct use of these results in certain situations and can usually build on the understanding of their fundamental components.

REFERENCES

1. Baker, K. R., and Martin, J. B. "An Experimental Comparison of Solution Algorithms for the Single-Machine Tardiness Problem," *Naval Research Logistics Quarterly*, Vol. 21, No. 1 (March, 1974).
2. Maxwell, W. L. "On the Generality of the Equation $L = \lambda W$," *Operations Research*, Vol. 18, No. 1 (January–February, 1970).
3. Maxwell, W. L. "On Sequencing n jobs on One Machine to Minimize the Number of Late Jobs," *Management Science*, Vol. 16, No. 5 (January, 1970).
4. Moore, J. M. "Sequencing n Jobs on One Machine to Minimize the Number of Tardy Jobs," *Management Science*, Vol. 17, No. 1 (September, 1968).
5. Rau, J. G. "Selected Comments Concerning Optimization Theory for Functions of Permutations," *Symposium on the Theory of Scheduling and its Applications*, S. E. Elmaghraby, Ed., Springer-Verlag, New York, 1973.
6. Sidney, J. B. "A Comment on a Paper of Maxwell," *Management Science*, Vol. 18, No. 11 (July, 1972).
7. Smith, W. E. "Various Optimizers for Single Stage Production," *Naval Research Logistics Quarterly*, Vol. 3, No. 1 (March, 1956).
8. Sturm, L. J. M. "A Simple Optimality Proof of Moore's Sequencing Algorithm," *Management Science*, Vol. 17, No. 1 (September, 1970).
9. Wilkerson, L. J., and Irwin, J. D. "An Improved Algorithm for Scheduling Independent Tasks," *AIIE Transactions*, Vol. 3, No. 3 (September, 1971).

CHAPTER 3

GENERAL PURPOSE METHODOLOGIES FOR THE SINGLE-MACHINE PROBLEM

1. INTRODUCTION

In the previous chapter we explored the fundamental performance measures for the single-machine problem and observed that different scheduling procedures were appropriate for different measures. With the question of minimizing $\bar{T}$ we encountered a relatively simple problem where the determination of an optimal sequence was not a simple matter. Now to generalize this discussion we can examine a slightly more complex criterion.

Suppose that a penalty is assessed on the tardiness of each job and that the size of the penalty is proportional to the amount of tardiness. Thus the total penalty associated with a given sequence is $\sum_{j=1}^{n} w_j T_j$. Quite often, this problem has been described as the minimization of total cost where costs arise from linear tardiness penalties. In effect, this objective is equivalent to minimizing weighted mean tardiness ($\bar{T}_w$), and for this reason weighting factors are used to represent unit penalty costs.

There has been relatively little progress in exploiting the special structure of the $\bar{T}_w$ problem in order to develop a solution algorithm. Instead, solutions have usually been obtained through the use of general purpose techniques. The major purpose of this chapter is to discuss several of the general purpose methodologies that can be employed in sequencing and scheduling problems and to illustrate their application to tardiness criteria in the single-machine case.

In the implementation of combinatorial optimization techniques for sequencing problems, it is usually desirable to take advantage of dominance properties whenever possible. A simple dominance property is illustrated in the following statement.

Property 3.1

Suppose that $\bar{T}_w$ is the measure of performance and that there exists a job k that satisfies

$$d_k \geq \sum_{j=1}^{n} t_j$$

Then there exists an optimal sequence in which job k is assigned the last position in sequence.

The value of Property 3.1 is that it defines a dominant set of sequences, characterized by $[n] = k$. In effect, the problem is reduced in size, for it remains only to determine how to assign the first $(n - 1)$ positions to the remaining $(n - 1)$ jobs. In describing general purpose techniques in the following sections, we assume that at the outset Property 3.1 is applied as many times as possible, ultimately leaving a problem in which no a priori reasoning can directly assign the last job in sequence.

2.   ADJACENT PAIRWISE INTERCHANGE METHODS

It has been shown that an adjacent pairwise interchange argument can be used in proving the optimality of certain sequencing rules (e.g., WSPT minimizes $\bar{F}_w$ and EDD minimizes $T_{\max}$). The thrust of the adjacent pairwise interchange argument may be stated as follows: a sequence is sought for which all adjacent pairwise interchanges lead to a deterioration in the criterion; this will be an optimal sequence. It is important to recognize, however, that there are definite limitations to this approach.

Suppose that the single-machine problem is concerned with minimizing Z and that a sequence S is found for which all adjacent pairwise interchanges lead to an increase in Z. Does this condition imply that S is the optimal sequence? The answer, as we have seen, is certainly yes when, for example, Z is $\bar{F}$ and S corresponds to SPT sequencing, but the answer is not always yes. Suppose that Z is $\bar{T}$ for the following three-job set:

Job j	t_j	d_j
1	1	4
2	2	2
3	3	3

The optimal sequence is 2–1–3, with $\bar{T} = 1$. However, if all six sequences are examined, the complete set of solutions can be depicted as in Figure 3.1. Notice that for sequence 3–1–2 all (two) adjacent pairwise interchanges lead to an increase in $\bar{T}$, yet 3–1–2 is not an optimal sequence. This example shows that the adjacent pairwise interchange property will not be sufficient for identifying optimal sequences in the $\bar{T}$ problem, but might lead only to identification of a local optimum. In Section 4.3 of Chapter 2 we observed a clue as to why this local optimality might arise: in general the result of an adjacent pairwise interchange between a given pair of jobs may depend on where in the sequence the interchange occurs. In particular, the decision rule that emerged involved information (t_B) about jobs not involved in the interchange. By contrast, the decision rule that emerged in the $\bar{F}$ problem involved only a comparison of the processing times of the jobs being interchanged.

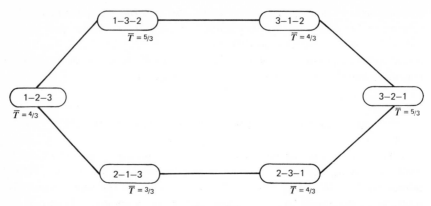

Figure 3.1

The complete set of permutation schedules for the example problem, organized so that each sequence is linked to the schedules attainable via an adjacent pairwise interchange.

The adjacent pairwise interchange method is sufficient to prove optimality for only a limited class of sequencing rules. For sequencing rules that employ only information about individual jobs in constructing a sequence, a crucial property involves the transitivity of the optimal job ordering. For such rules as WSPT, EDD, and MST, the optimal sequence is characterized by a transitive pairwise ordering of the jobs. (An ordering relation R between two jobs is transitive whenever iRj and jRk implies iRk.) In the case of the measure $\bar{T}$, however, we can conclude only that the optimal sequencing rule (whatever it might be) is not transitive in general.

These observations point to a simple way of using adjacent pairwise interchange methods in solving new sequencing problems. Under the hypothesis that transitivity will result, an interchange can be analyzed and a condition that specifies how two jobs should be ordered can be derived. If this condition turns out to be transitive, the ordering will indeed be optimal. Otherwise, only a more complicated approach will be able to locate an optimum.

For a more comprehensive discussion of adjacent pairwise interchange methods (also referred to as "contiguous binary switching") see references *3* and *10*.

3.2 EXERCISES

2.1 Prove that Dominance Property 3.1 holds when the criterion is $\bar{T}_w$ or when the criterion is weighted number of tardy jobs.

2.2   Verify that the optimal sequencing rule in Exercise 3.8*b* of Chapter 2 is transitive.

2.3   The sequencing rule R' is called the antithetical rule of sequencing rule R if the job that is assigned position j in sequence under R is assigned position $(n - j + 1)$ under R'. Suppose that a measure of performance Z is minimized by a particular transitive rule R_0. Show that Z is maximized (among permutation sequences) by R_0'.

3.   A DYNAMIC PROGRAMMING APPROACH

A regular measure of performance is a function of job completion times, and in general we may interpret a regular measure Z as a cost function.

$$Z = f(C_1, C_2, \ldots, C_n)$$

In many problems, the function f that defines Z is of a special additive structure and we can write

$$Z = \sum_{j=1}^{n} g_j(C_j)$$

For example, if Z is total tardiness penalty then

$$g_j(C_j) = w_j(C_j - d_j) \qquad \text{if} \qquad C_j > d_j$$
$$= 0 \qquad \text{if} \qquad C_j \leq d_j$$

When Z has this additive form (and even in more general cases) an optimum sequence can be found by employing dynamic programming.

Let J denote some subset of the n jobs and let J' denote the complement of set J (i.e., all jobs not contained in J). Also, let q_J denote the total time required to process the jobs in set J':

$$q_J = \sum_{j \in J'} t_j$$

Suppose that a sequence has been constructed in which all the jobs in set J' precede every job in set J, as shown in Figure 3.2. If such a sequence is optimal then the principle of optimality of dynamic programming requires

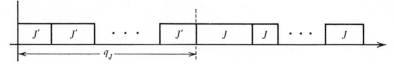

Figure 3.2
The structure of a job sequence for the purposes of dynamic programming.

that *no matter how the jobs in J' are sequenced, the jobs in J must be sequenced optimally, subject to the constraint that none may begin prior to q_J.* Now let

$G(J) = $ the minimum cost realizable for the jobs in set J,
    subject to the constraint that none begin prior to q_J

Finally, let K denote the set of all jobs. Observing that the cost function G is defined on subsets of jobs, we can see that the minimum cost will be $G(K)$, where

$$G(K) = \min_{j \in K} [g_j(t_j) + G(K - \{j\})] \tag{1}$$

and in general

$$G(J) = \min_{j \in J} [g_j(q_J + t_j) + G(J - \{j\})] \tag{2}$$

where

$$G(\phi) = 0 \tag{3}$$

At each stage the function $G(J)$ measures the total tardiness contributed by the jobs in set J, when set J occurs at the end of the schedule and is sequenced optimally. The recursion relations 1 and 2 indicate that in order to calculate the value of G for any particular subset of size k, we first have to know the value of G for k subsets of size $k - 1$. Therefore the procedure begins with knowledge of the value of G for a subset of size zero, from (3). Then, by using (2), we can calculate the value of G for all subsets of size 1, then the value of G for all subsets of size 2, and so on.[1] In this manner the procedure works backward, considering ever larger sets J, until at the final stage the procedure determines which job should be scheduled first and calculates from (1) the optimal value of Z as $G(K)$. If we keep track of where minima in (2) occurred at each stage, then after finding $G(K)$ we will be able to reconstruct the optimal sequence.

To illustrate the method, suppose that $\overline{T}$ (or, equivalently, total tardiness) is the performance measure and that the following job set is to be sequenced:

Job j	t_j	d_j	w_j
1	1	2	1
2	2	7	1
3	3	5	1
4	4	6	1

The essential dynamic programming calculations are displayed in Table 3.1.

---

[1] It is not absolutely necessary to perform the calculations in exactly this order; in fact, a slightly different order may be more appropriate for implementation on a computer.

Table 3.1

	STAGE 1			
J	{1}	{2}	{3}	{4}
q_J	9	8	7	6
$j \in J$	1	2	3	4
g_j	8	3	5	4
$G(J - \{j\})$	0	0	0	0
$G(J)$	$\overline{8}$	$\overline{3}$	$\overline{5}$	$\overline{4}$

	STAGE 2					
J	{1, 2}	{1, 3}	{1, 4}	{2, 3}	{2, 4}	{3, 4}
q_J	7	6	5	5	4	3
$j \in J$	1* 2	1* 3	1* 4	2* 3	2* 4	3* 4
g_j	6 2	5 4	4 3	0 3	0 2	1 1
$G(J - \{j\})$	3 8	5 8	4 8	5 3	4 3	4 5
$G(J)$	$\overline{9}$	$\overline{10}$	$\overline{8}$	$\overline{5}$	$\overline{4}$	$\overline{5}$

	STAGE 3			
J	{1, 2, 3}	{1, 2, 4}	{1, 3, 4}	{2, 3, 4}
q_J	4	3	2	1
$j \in J$	1* 2 3	1* 2 4	1* 3 4	2 3* 4
g_j	3 0 2	2 0 1	1 0 0	0 0 0
$G(J - \{j\})$	5 10 9	4 8 9	5 8 10	5 4 5
$G(J)$	$\overline{8}$	$\overline{6}$	$\overline{6}$	$\overline{4}$

	STAGE 4	
J	{1, 2, 3, 4}	
q_J	0	Optimal Sequence
$j \in J$	1* 2 3 4	1–3–2–4
g_j	0 0 0 0	$\sum T_j = 4$
$G(J - \{j\})$	4 6 6 8	
$G(J)$	$\overline{4}$	

To illustrate these calculations, consider the set $J = \{1, 2, 4\}$ that is encountered at Stage 3. For this set $q_J = 3$, since only job 3 is contained in J'. If job 1 comes first in the set J, then $g_1(C_1) = 2$ and for the remaining jobs $G(\{2, 4\}) = 4$, so that the total contribution from this set, when job 1 comes first, is 6. An adjacent column indicates that if job 2 comes first, $g_2(C_2) = 0$ and $G(\{1, 4\}) = 8$, totaling 8; and if job 4 comes first, $g_4(C_4) = 1$ and $G(\{1, 2\}) = 9$, totaling 10. The minimum of these three totals is 6, which is designated as $G(J)$ in the table; this is achieved when job 1 comes first, as denoted by the asterisk.

To reconstruct the optimal sequence in the example, note that at Stage 4 the asterisk indicates that job 1 should come first in sequence. Since this leaves jobs 2, 3, and 4 to be sequenced, we examine the set {2, 3, 4} that was evaluated at Stage 3. Here the previous calculations show that job 3 should come first in this set, thus job 3 should occupy the second position in the optimal sequence. Continuing in this fashion, we construct the optimal sequence, 1–3–2–4, for which the total tardiness is $G(K) = 4$.

It is important to recognize the computational properties of the dynamic programming procedure. One characteristic is immediately clear: the number of subsets considered by the procedure is 2^n, since that is the total number of subsets of n elements. (A more specific measure of computational effort is suggested in Exercise 3.1.) In this respect, dynamic programming is typical of many general purpose procedures for combinatorial optimization, in that the effort required to solve the problem grows at an exponential rate with increasing problem size. This trait makes dynamic programming an inefficient procedure for finding optimal sequences in some of the simple problems we have examined. For example, when $\bar{F}_w$ is the criterion, we could employ dynamic programming with

$$g_j(C_j) = w_j C_j$$

Also, when N_T is the criterion, we could employ dynamic programming with

$$g_j(C_j) = 1 \quad \text{if} \quad C_j > d_j$$
$$= 0 \quad \text{if} \quad C_j \le d_j$$

But in both instances it is computationally more efficient to use the specialized results developed in Chapter 2. On the other hand, for problems in which efficient optimizing procedures have not been developed (such as weighted mean tardiness or weighted number of tardy jobs), dynamic programming may be a reasonable approach.

Even though the computational demands of dynamic programming grow at an exponential rate with increasing problem size, the approach is more efficient than complete enumeration of all feasible sequences, for the computational demands of complete enumeration grow at a rate that increases as the factorial of the problem size. Because dynamic programming considers certain sequences only indirectly, without actually evaluating them explicitly, the technique is often described as an *implicit enumeration* technique. Even though it is a more efficient technique than complete enumeration, the fact that its computational requirement exhibits an exponential growth trait places a premium on the ability to curtail the dynamic programming calculations whenever possible. Such a strategy is described in the next section.

Appendix B describes a strategy for implementing the dynamic programming algorithm on a computer and includes a sample computer code for doing so.

3.3   EXERCISES

3.1   Derive formulas for (a) the number of additions and (b) the number of comparisons required by a dynamic programming solution to an n-job problem. Compare these with comparable expressions for a procedure consisting of complete enumeration of all feasible sequences. In particular, what numbers are obtained from the formulas for $n = 5$, 10, and 20?

3.2   Verify the optimal sequences (for minimal N_T) in the example of Section 4.2 of Chapter 2 by using dynamic programming.

3.3   Consider the four-job problem used to illustrate Algorithm 2.2 in Section 4.3 of Chapter 2. Use dynamic programming to determine whether the solution obtained by Algorithm 2.2 is optimal.

3.4   Formulate the problem of minimizing $T_{\max}$ as a dynamic programming problem (i.e., write the appropriate recursion relations.)

3.5   Indicate how to identify alternate optima (assuming they exist) with dynamic programming.

4.   A HYBRID ALGORITHM FOR THE MEAN TARDINESS PROBLEM

The hybrid algorithm devised by Srinivasan (12) improves on dynamic programming by exploiting specialized dominance properties that can be developed for the $\bar{T}$ problem. In particular, the hybrid algorithm was originally developed with two dominance properties that had been discovered by Emmons (4). Let

A_i = the set of jobs that have been shown to follow job i in an optimal sequence

A_i' = the complement of set A_i

B_i = the set of jobs that have been shown to precede job i in an optimal sequence

Furthermore, it is convenient to employ the notation $i\rho j$ to denote the following relation between two jobs i and j:

$$i\rho j \quad \text{if} \quad (1)\ t_i < t_j \quad \text{or} \quad (2)\ t_i = t_j \quad \text{and} \quad d_i \leq d_j$$

Emmons proved the following properties.

Property 3.2

In the $\bar{T}$ problem, if $i\rho j$ and

$$d_i \leq \max \left\{ d_j, t_j + \sum_{k \in B_j} t_k \right\}$$

then there exists an optimal schedule in which $i \in B_j$ and $j \in A_i$.

Property 3.3

In the $\bar{T}$ problem if $i\rho j$ and

(1) $d_i > \max \left\{ d_j, t_j + \sum_{k \in B_j} t_k \right\}$ and

(2) $d_i + t_i \geq \sum_{k \in A_j'} t_k$

then there exists an optimal sequence in which $j \in B_i$ and $i \in A_j$.

Phase 1 of the hybrid algorithm collects the dominance information systematically in a dominance matrix P. The (i, j)-th element of P is $p_{ij} = 1$ if $j \in A_i$ (or $i \in B_j$) and $p_{ij} = 0$ otherwise. To implement Phase 1, renumber the jobs so that they are in SPT order with ties broken by EDD. This means that if job i appears before job j in the renumbered sequence then $i\rho j$. Two quantities that appear in Properties 3.2 and 3.3 are denoted as follows:

$$Q_i = \sum_{k \in A_i'} t_k \quad \text{and} \quad R_j = t_j + \sum_{k \in B_j} t_k$$

Also let $|A_j|$ and $|B_j|$ denote the sizes of the sets A_j and B_j, respectively. Then a computational display for Phase 1 is shown in Table 3.2. The matrix is filled in with the following algorithm.

Table 3.2

			Job j			
	p_{11}	p_{12}	$\cdots$	p_{1n}	Q_1	$|A_1|$
	p_{21}	p_{22}	$\cdots$	p_{2n}	Q_2	$|A_2|$
	$\cdot$	$\cdot$		$\cdot$	$\cdot$	$\cdot$
Job i	$\cdot$	$\cdot$		$\cdot$	$\cdot$	$\cdot$
	$\cdot$	$\cdot$		$\cdot$	$\cdot$	$\cdot$
	p_{n1}	p_{n2}	$\cdots$	p_{nn}	Q_n	$|A_n|$
	R_1	R_2	$\cdots$	R_n		
	$|B_1|$	$|B_2|$	$\cdots$	$|B_n|$		

ALGORITHM 3.1
(Phase 1 of the Hybrid Algorithm)

Step 1. (Initialization) All $p_{ij} = 0$ initially. Set $Q_i = \sum_{k=1}^{n} t_k$, set $R_i = t_i$, and set $|A_i| = |B_i| = 0$ for $1 \leq i \leq n$. Then begin with $i = 1$ and $j = n$.

Step 2. Test Dominance Property 3.2 for the pair of jobs (i, j). If it holds go to Step 3, otherwise go to Step 4.

Step 3. Set $p_{ij} = 1$. Increment $|A_i|$ and $|B_j|$ by 1. Add t_i to R_j and subtract t_j from Q_i. Increment i by 1. If this leaves $i = j$, then reset i to 1, and in any case return to Step 2.

Step 4. Test Dominance Property 3.3 for the pair of jobs (i, j). If it holds go to Step 5; otherwise go to Step 6.

Step 5. Set $p_{ji} = 1$. Increment $|A_j|$ and $|B_i|$ by 1. Add t_j to R_i and subtract t_i from Q_j. Increment i by 1. If this leaves $i = j$, then reset i to 1 and in any case return to Step 2.

Step 6. (a) If for the current value of j no change in the matrix has occurred in the last $(j - 2)$ applications of Step 2, decrease j by 1, set $i = 1$, and return to Step 2 unless this leaves $j = 1$; in such a case stop.
(b) Otherwise, increment i by 1. If this leaves $i = j$, then reset i to 1, and in any case return to Step 2.

The algorithm works from right to left in the matrix. Step 3 enters 1's in the matrix above the diagonal, while Step 5 enters 1's below the diagonal. When a 1 is entered in a column, it may then be possible to satisfy Property 3.2 more easily elsewhere in the column (since B_j has been augmented); thus the signal that no more entries can be made is that a full pass down the column has failed to provide an additional entry, as specified in Step 6*a*.

Once the matrix is filled in, it may be possible to reduce the size of the problem even further. If $|B_j| = n - 1$, then job j may be assigned the last position in sequence, and n can in effect be reduced by 1. If $|A_j| = n - 1$, then job j may be assigned the first position in sequence, and n can in effect be reduced by 1. (In this case, the problem that remains is reformulated by subtracting t_j from each due date.) When no more of these reductions are possible, the optimization algorithm proceeds to Phase 2.

In Phase 2, the reduced problem is solved by dynamic programming. The information in the P matrix may also help to shrink the computational task, and in his original exposition, Srinivasan recommended four mechanisms that reduce the computational effort. We state these mechanisms below, with reference to the dynamic programming notation introduced in the previous section. In particular, consider the recursion relation (2) for some subset J containing k elements.

Lemma 3.1

For any $j \in J$, if $|A_j| \geq k$, then J need not be considered at all.

Lemma 3.2

For any $j \in J$, if $|A_j| = k - 1$, then (2) simplifies to

$$G(J) = \max \{0, q_J + t_j - d_j\} + G(A_j)$$

if we assume there is only one element of J with $|A_j| = k - 1$.

Lemma 3.3

In general suppose that $p_{ij} = 1$ for $j = i_1, i_2, \ldots, i_m$ (where $m < k - 1$). Then of the sets J in which job i appears, it is necessary to consider only those in which jobs $i_1, i_2, \ldots,$ and i_m also appear.

Lemma 3.4

For any $j \in J$, if $|B_j| > n - k$, then j need not be considered as the lead job in J. Hence (2) becomes

$$G(J) = \min_{\substack{j \in J \\ |B_j| \leq n-k}} \{\max [0, q_J + t_j - d_j] + G(J - \{j\})\}$$

The frequency with which these conditions will hold in a given problem will depend on the data in the job set. Nevertheless, it appears that a substantial reduction in computational effort can often be achieved with the use of Lemmas 3.1 to 3.4.

For example, consider the job set shown in Table 3.3. The application of Algorithm 3.1 yields a P matrix that is shown in Table 3.4. (While these calculations are somewhat tedious when done by hand, they are fairly rapid when programmed for a computer.) From Table 3.4, it is clear that $B_{10} = 9$; therefore, job 10 may be placed last in sequence. Also $A_2 = 9$; thus job 2 may be placed first. In fact, the first six positions in the job sequence can be filled immediately, yielding the partial solution

$$2-5-1-4-6-7-?-?-?-10$$

Table 3.3

Job j	1	2	3	4	5	6	7	8	9	10
t_j	32	75	80	86	93	107	109	115	136	144
d_j	216	53	681	288	66	33	445	716	424	424

Table 3.4

	1	2	3	4	5	6	7	8	9	10	$|A|$
1	0	0	1	1	0	1	1	1	1	1	7
2	1	0	1	1	1	1	1	1	1	1	9
3	0	0	0	0	0	0	0	1	0	1	2
4	0	0	1	0	0	1	1	1	1	1	6
5	1	0	1	1	0	1	1	1	1	1	8
6	0	0	1	0	0	0	1	1	1	1	5
7	0	0	1	0	0	0	0	1	1	1	4
8	0	0	0	0	0	0	0	0	0	1	1
9	0	0	0	0	0	0	0	0	0	1	1
10	0	0	0	0	0	0	0	0	0	0	0
$|B|$	2	0	6	3	1	4	5	7	6	9	

This leaves only a three-job problem to be solved. For this smaller problem, subtraction of the processing times of jobs already scheduled from each d_j yields:

Job j	t_j	d_j
3	80	179
8	115	214
9	136	−78

The accompanying P matrix is made up of the pertinent rows and columns from Table 3.4.

	3	8	9
3	0	1	0
8	0	0	0
9	0	0	0

Even though the matrix has but one nonzero entry, several of the calculations in dynamic programming are affected, as demonstrated in the worksheet shown in Table 3.5, where x's indicate calculations avoided under the conditions of one of the lemmas. The solution to the three-job problem completes the sequence as 2–5–1–4–6–7–9–3–8–10, for which $\bar{T} = 146.2$.

Table 3.5

	STAGE 1		
J	$\{3\}$	$\{8\}$	$\{9\}$
q_J	x	216	195
$j \in J$	x	8	9
g_j	x	117	409
$G(J - \{j\})$	x	0	0
$G(J)$	x	117	409

	STAGE 2					
J	$\{3, 8\}$		$\{3, 9\}$		$\{8, 9\}$	
q_J	136		x		80	
$j \in J$	3*	8	3	9	8*	9
g_j	37	x	x	x	0	294
$G(J - \{j\})$	117	x	x	x	409	117
$G(J)$	154	x	x	x	409	

	STAGE 3		
J	$\{3, 8, 9\}$		
q_J	0		
$j \in J$	3	8	9*
g_j	0	x	214
$G(J - \{j\})$	409	x	158
$G(J)$		x	368

Optimal subsequence
9–3–8

Thus the hybrid algorithm is based on dynamic programming and is actually a sophisticated mechanism for what is called *curtailed enumeration*, meaning that the enumeration of all solutions is curtailed by means of characteristics found in the data. The approach is significant in that it suggests a general method for solving sequencing problems. Basically, the approach uses Properties 3.2 and 3.3 to describe a dominant set of sequences for the $\overline{T}$ problem. Sometimes this dominant set might contain only one sequence, in which case enumeration is avoided entirely, but in most instances the dominant set at least represents a substantial reduction in the size of the original problem. Then, the pairwise relations among unsequenced jobs can be used to limit the effort involved in dynamic programming. To adapt this approach to other performance measures, it would be necessary to develop specialized theoretical relations between pairs of jobs in order to describe a dominant set. Lemmas 3.1 to 3.4 could then be employed in a reduced dynamic programming algorithm for the final phase.

3.4 EXERCISES

4.1 Suppose that in Phase 1 of the hybrid algorithm it is found that $|A_j| = n - 1$ for job j. The procedure calls for setting $[1] = j$ and proceeding to the reduced problem obtained by subtracting t_j from all remaining due dates. What new relationships can be obtained by applying Property 3.2 to the reduced problem?

4.2 Prove Properties 3.2 and 3.3. (*Hint.* In each instance, attempt a proof by contradiction. That is, suppose that some sequence not in the dominant set is actually "optimal." Show that the sequence described in the dominance property can never have a larger value of $\bar{T}$ than that of the "optimum.")

4.3 Use the hybrid algorithm to determine the minimum value of $\bar{T}$ in the following job sets:

(a)

j	1	2	3	4	5	6	7	8
t_j	121	147	102	79	130	83	96	88
d_j	260	269	400	266	337	336	683	719

(b)

j	1	2	3	4	5	6	7	8
t_j	138	132	153	89	141	131	107	103
d_j	466	459	402	422	478	392	368	385

5. A BRANCH AND BOUND APPROACH

A useful method for solving many combinatorial problems is a general purpose strategy for curtailed enumeration known as *branch and bound*. As its name implies, the approach consists of two fundamental procedures. *Branching* is the process of partitioning a large problem into two or more subproblems, and *bounding* is the process of calculating a lower bound on the optimal solution of a given subproblem.

The branching procedure replaces an original problem by a set of new problems that are

(a) mutually exclusive and exhaustive subproblems of the original,
(b) partially solved versions of the original, and
(c) smaller problems than the original.

Furthermore, the subproblems can themselves be partitioned in a similar fashion. As an example of a branching procedure, let P^0 denote a single-machine sequencing problems containing n jobs. The problem P^0 can be partioned into n subproblems, P_1^1, P_2^1, ..., P_n^1 by assigning the last position in sequence. Thus P_1^1 is the same problem, but with job 1 fixed in the last position; P_2^1 is similar, but with job 2 fixed in the last position; and so on. Clearly, these subproblems are smaller than P^0 because only $(n-1)$ positions remain to be assigned, and obviously each P_i^1 is a partially solved version of P^0. In addition, the set of subproblems P_i^1 is a mutually exclusive and exhaustive partition of P^0 in the sense that if each P_i^1 is solved, the best of these n solutions will represent an optimal solution to P^0. Therefore the P_i^1 satisfy conditions (a), (b), and (c) above.

Next, each of the subproblems can be partitioned (see Figure 3.3). For instance, P_2^1 can be partitioned into P_{12}^2, P_{32}^2, P_{42}^2, ..., P_{n2}^2. In P_{12}^2, jobs

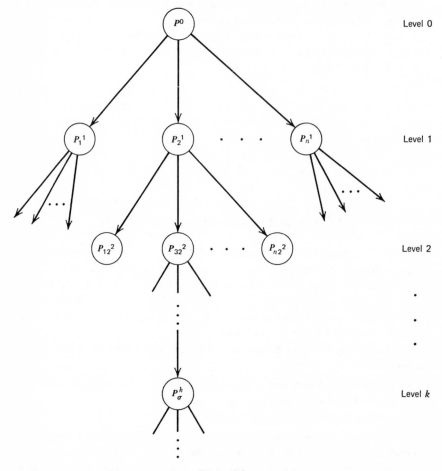

Figure 3.3
A branching scheme for single-machine problems.

1 and 2 occupy the last two positions in sequence in that order; and in $P_{32}{}^2$, jobs 3 and 2 occupy the last two positions. Therefore the second-level partition $P_{i2}{}^2$ bears the same relation to $P_2{}^1$ as the first level partition $P_i{}^1$ bears to P^0. That is, the partitions at each level satisfy conditions (a), (b), and (c). At level k, then, each subproblem contains k fixed positions and can be further partitioned into $(n - k)$ subproblems, which form part of level $(k + 1)$. If this branching procedure were to be carried out completely there would be $n!$ subproblems at level n, each corresponding to a distinct feasible solution to the original problem. In other words, exhaustive pursuit of the branching tree would be equivalent to complete enumeration of all sequences. The function of the bounding process is to provide a means for curtailing this enumeration.

The bounding procedure calculates a lower bound on the solution to each subproblem generated in the branching process. Suppose that at some intermediate stage a complete solution has been obtained that has an associated performance measure Z. Suppose also that a subproblem encountered in the branching process has an associated lower bound $b > Z$. Then the subproblem need not be considered any further in the search for an optimum. That is, no matter how the remainder of the subproblem is solved, the resulting solution can never have a value better than Z. When such a subproblem is found, its branch is said to be *fathomed*. By not branching any further from fathomed branches, the enumeration process is curtailed, and the entire set of feasible solutions is enumerated implicitly in the search for an optimum.

The complete solution used in comparisons that allow branches to be fathomed is called a *trial solution*. It may be obtained at the very outset by applying a heuristic procedure; or it can be obtained in the course of the tree search, perhaps by pursuing the tree directly to the bottom as rapidly as possible.

We can now illustrate how these concepts are applied in the problem of minimizing total tardiness penalty, once we introduce some convenient notation. Let σ denote a partial sequence of jobs from among the n jobs originally in the problem. Also let $i\sigma$ denote the partial sequence in which σ is immediately preceded by job i. We can treat σ as an ordered set of jobs, so that as before

$$\sigma' = \text{the complement of } \sigma$$

$$q_\sigma = \sum_{j \in \sigma'} t_j$$

Let $P_\sigma{}^k$ represent a subproblem at level k in the branching tree. This subproblem will be the original problem P^0 with the last k positions in sequence assigned, where σ specifies the assigned partial sequence. Associated with $P_\sigma{}^k$ is a *value*, v_σ, which is the contribution of assigned jobs to total tardiness penalty. That is,

$$v_\sigma = \sum_{j \in \sigma} w_j T_j$$

The T_j values in this sum can be calculated because the completion time of each $j \in \sigma$ is known even though the complete sequence has not yet been determined.

Normally the branching process will partition $P_\sigma{}^k$ into $(n - k)$ subproblems. Each subproblem, $P_{i\sigma}^{k+1}$, is constructed by selecting some job $i \in \sigma'$ to be last in the remaining sequence, where i can be chosen $(n - k)$ distinct ways. Notice that the completion time of job i in the partial sequence $i\sigma$ is q_σ. Therefore the value associated with $P_{i\sigma}^{k+1}$ is

$$v_{i\sigma} = w_i \max \{0, q_\sigma - d_i\} + v_\sigma$$

It is important to realize that $P_\sigma{}^k$ may be treated as a single-machine sequencing problem containing $(n - k)$ jobs. This means, in particular, that Dominance Property 3.1 may be invoked. In other words, if there exists a job $i \in \sigma'$ such that $d_i \geq q_\sigma$, then it is sufficient in solving $P_\sigma{}^k$ to let $[n - k] = i$. The implication of this property is that it is unnecessary to partition $P_\sigma{}^k$ into $(n - k)$ subproblems in search of an optimum. Instead $P_\sigma{}^k$ can be partitioned into just one subproblem, $P_{i\sigma}^{k+1}$. Thus it may be possible to exploit dominance properties within the branching tree so that some branches are implicitly enumerated. Curtailing the branching process with dominance properties is sometimes called *elimination*.

In the bounding process, we seek a means of calculating a lower bound b_σ on the total tardiness penalty associated with any completion of the partial sequence σ. One way of calculating a bound is obvious:

$$b_\sigma = v_\sigma \tag{4}$$

A slightly stronger bound can be obtained by pursuing the fact that some job $i \in \sigma'$ must be completed at q_σ. We may use

$$b_\sigma = v_\sigma + \min_{j \in \sigma'} (w_j \max \{0, q_\sigma - d_j\}) \tag{5}$$

Other more complicated procedures may be employed for calculating an even stronger lower bound (*11*).

Once b_σ is calculated, it may be possible to determine whether a completion of the subproblem $P_\sigma{}^k$ might lead to an optimum. If a complete solution is available with a total penalty of Z, Z and b_σ can then be compared. If $b_\sigma < Z$, then a completion of σ could be an optimum; therefore the subproblems $P_{i\sigma}^{k+1}$ must be constructed and examined. On the other hand, if $b_\sigma \geq Z$, then no completion of the partial sequence σ could ever achieve a total tardiness penalty less than Z. Therefore the completions of σ need not be enumerated in the search for an optimum, and in this case the enumeration is curtailed.

The branch and bound algorithm maintains a list of unsolved subproblems. This list contains all subproblems that have been encountered in the branching process but that have not been eliminated by dominance properties and whose own subproblems have not yet been generated. These are called *active* subproblems, and it is sufficient to solve all active subproblems to determine an optimal solution to P^0. In the following version of the algorithm, the active list is ranked by lower bound, smallest first. At each stage, the first subproblem on the active list is replaced by its own subproblems. This strategy is equivalent to continuing the branching process from the subproblem with the lowest bound, wherever that may be in the branching tree. The algorithm terminates when a trial solution appears at the head of the active list, because then no other subproblem could lead to a better solution. Also in this form of the algorithm, no trial solution is obtained until the branching process itself reaches the bottom of the branching tree at some stage.

ALGORITHM 3.2
(Branch and Bound)

Step 1. (Initialization) Place $P_0^{\,0}$ on the active list; its associated value is $v_0 = 0$ and $q_0 = \sum_{j=1}^n t_j$.

Step 2. Remove the first subproblem, $P_\sigma^{\,k}$ from the active list. If $k = n$, stop: the complete sequence σ is optimal. Otherwise test Dominance Property 3.1 for $P_\sigma^{\,k}$. If the property holds, go to Step 3; otherwise go to Step 4.

Step 3. Let job j be the job with the latest due date in σ'. Create the subproblem $P_{j\sigma}^{k+1}$ with

$$q_{j\sigma} = q_\sigma - t_j$$

$$v_{j\sigma} = v_\sigma$$

$$b_{j\sigma} = v_\sigma$$

Place $P_{j\sigma}^{k+1}$ on the active list, ranked by its lower bound. Return to Step 2.

Step 4. Create $(n - k)$ subproblems $P_{i\sigma}^{k+1}$, one for each $i \in \sigma'$. For $P_{i\sigma}^{k+1}$, let

$$q_{i\sigma} = q_\sigma - t_i$$

$$v_{i\sigma} = v_\sigma + q_\sigma - d_i$$

$$b_{i\sigma} = v_{i\sigma}$$

Now place each $P_{i\sigma}^{k+1}$ on the active list, ranked by its lower bound. Return to Step 2.

The particular version of the branch and bound algorithm given above has invoked three important options, all of which are open to some scrutiny. First, the algorithm employs the lower bounds given in equation 4. An obvious alternative is to use equation 5.

A second option involves the use of a trial solution. At any stage the best trial solution yet found can be used in reducing the list of active subproblems. First, no subproblem need ever be placed below the trial solution on the active list, for such a subproblem can never lead to an optimum. Second, whenever a complete sequence is placed on the active list, all active subproblems with greater bounds can be discarded. Notice, however, that no trial solution can be encountered until the branching process has reached level n. An obvious alternative is to obtain a trial solution in Step 1. In fact, if the branch and bound approach is used in the $\bar{T}$ problem, then a desirable initialization phase might be the use of Algorithm 2.2 in order to obtain a trial solution.

A third option involves the branching tactic itself; that is, the selection of the subproblem with the smallest bound as the candidate for further branching. This tactic is known as *jumptracking*, because the branching process tends to jump from one part of the branching tree to another at successive stages in the algorithm. An alternative is a tactic known as *backtracking*, in which the branching process first proceeds directly to level n along some path to obtain a trial solution. Then the algorithm retraces that path upward until it reaches a level on which unsolved subproblems remain. It selects one of these and again proceeds toward level n along a single path. The process may actually reach another trial solution or it may fathom the branch it pursues by utilizing the value of the on-hand trial solution. In either case the algorithm once again backtracks up to the first level at which an unfathomed branch remains and then proceeds again toward level n (see Appendix C).

The characteristics of jumptracking and backtracking are considerably different. Backtracking maintains relatively few subproblems on the active list at any one time, while jumptracking tends to construct a fairly large active list. This is a disadvantage for jumptracking, mainly because each time it places a subproblem on the ranked list, it must search the list to determine exactly where on the list the subproblem must be placed. This searching may become quite time consuming in problems of moderate size. This disadvantage may be remedied somewhat by clearing the list below any trial solution that gets placed on it. In addition, the list size requirement may restrict computerized versions of the algorithm when storage capacity does not readily accommodate a large list. On the other hand an advantage in jumptracking is that the trial solutions it encounters tend to be very close to optimal, while the early trial solutions obtained by backtracking might be relatively poor. Thus jumptracking will usually do less branching in total, and this may compensate for its larger time per branch. Jumptracking will branch from every subproblem that has a bound less than the value of an optimal sequence, and it may also generate some nonoptimal trial solutions. Backtracking may in addition branch from several subproblems that have bounds greater than the optimal value and may also generate very many nonoptimal trial solutions. Other kinds of related considerations are examined in surveys on branch and bound methods in references 1, 6, and 7.

In addition to the trade-offs discussed above in connection with the choice of branching tactics, there are other choices to be considered in implementation. For example, the lower bound in (5) is stronger than the bound in (4) and would be more effective in curtailing the branching process, yet there are more calculations involved in computing the better bounds. Also, starting the algorithm initially with a good trial solution can curtail the branching process considerably, yet more effort must be invested to obtain a better initial trial solution. In many respects, Algorithm 3.2 is a general prototype for a whole spectrum of branch and bound methods, and the specific choice of tactics might be described as somewhat of an art.

In order to illustrate Algorithm 3.2 in its present form, consider this example.

Job j	t_j	d_j
1	4	5
2	3	6
3	7	8
4	2	8
5	2	17

The branching tree for this example problem is displayed in Figure 3.4. The lower bound v_σ for each subproblem is entered just below the corresponding node in the figure. The order of branching is indicated by the number that appears just above the corresponding node. Initially, the tree consists of P_0^0, with $v_0 = 0$ and $q_0 = 18$. At step 2, the initial problem is removed from the active list and subsequently replaced by P_1^1, P_2^1, P_3^1, P_4^1, and P_5^1. As shown in the figure, $v_1 = 13$, $v_2 = 12$, $v_3 = 10$, $v_4 = 10$, and $v_5 = 1$. The jump-tracking strategy calls for branching next from P_5^1, since it is first on the active list. At the next stage, P_{35}^2 and P_{45}^2 both have the lowest bound on the active list, and the tie between them is broken arbitrarily in favor of the latter, so that the subproblems of P_{45}^2 are created. At this point, P_{35}^2 is alone at the head of the active list and so its subproblems are generated next. Thereafter the active list contains three subproblems with lower bounds of 10. (These are P_3^1, P_4^1, and P_{435}^3). In this type of situation it is a good idea to

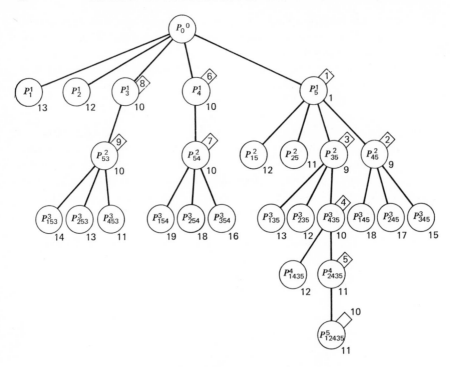

Figure 3.4
The branching tree for the example problem.

break ties by branching from the problem that is closest to being completely solved (P^3_{435} here). In other words, priority is given to the subproblem with the largest $|\sigma|$. Eventually, at the 10th branching iteration, the tree reaches the trial solution P^5_{12435} for which $v_{12435} = 11$. At this point, the trial solution is first on the active list, since $|\sigma|$ is being used as a tie breaker; therefore the algorithm terminates in Step 2. In effect, all branches have been fathomed at this stage, for the active list contains the 17 subproblems shown in Table 3.6. The optimal sequence 1–2–4–3–5 has a total tardiness equal to 11.

In general it is sometimes possible to curtail the enumeration even further by using the v_σ values in an additional dominance check.

Property 3.4

Let $P_{\sigma_1}{}^r$ and $P_{\sigma_2}{}^s$ denote two subproblems that appear on the active list at some stage. If $v_{\sigma_1} \geq v_{\sigma_2}$ and $\sigma_1 \subseteq \sigma_2$ then $P_{\sigma_1}{}^r$ need no longer be considered in the search for an optimum.

Table 3.6

Subproblem	Bound	
P^5_{12435}	11	Trial solution
P^3_{453}	11	
P^4_{1435}	12	
P^3_{235}	12	
$P_{15}{}^2$	12	
$P_2{}^1$	12	
P^3_{135}	13	
P^3_{253}	13	
$P_1{}^1$	13	
P^3_{153}	14	
P^3_{345}	15	
P^3_{354}	16	
P^3_{245}	17	
P^3_{254}	18	
P^3_{145}	18	
P^3_{154}	19	

One way to prove Property 3.4 is to assume that it is necessary to solve $P_{\sigma_1}{}^r$, to find an optimum. It will then be possible to show that a contradiction results (see Exercise 5.1). Assuming that an efficient device can be found for carrying out the dominance check of Property 3.4, it may then be utilized for further elimination.

In order to illustrate the use of Property 3.4, consider the branching tree in Figure 3.4 once again. Among the first set of subproblems created at level 2 is $P_{35}{}^2$. Comparing this subproblem with $P_3{}^1$, we can see that the hypotheses of Property 3.4 are satisfied, with $\sigma_1 = 3$ and $\sigma_2 = 35$. Therefore $P_3{}^1$ may be removed from the active list. Further application of Property 3.4 in the example problem curtails the branching process by more than 25 %.

Unfortunately, it is not always easy to implement this dominance condition because the condition $\sigma_1 \subseteq \sigma_2$ is difficult to detect without a detailed examination of the active list. A device to assist this dominance checking involves a branching process patterned after the dynamic programming logic (Table 3.1). Each node in the dynamic programming "tree" corresponds to an unordered set rather than a partial sequence. Thus subproblems $P_{54}{}^2$ and $P_{45}{}^2$ would be associated with the same node in the dynamic programming tree. Notice that in the dynamic programming tree a subproblem might be created from one of several subproblems at the previous level, whereas in Figure 3.4 there was a unique subproblem associated with the

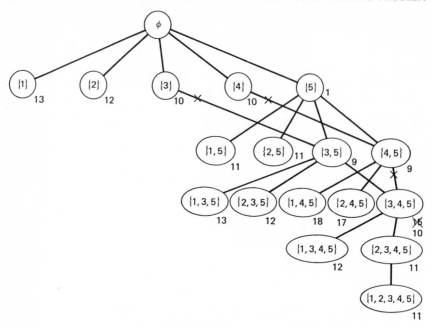

Figure 3.5
The dynamic programming tree for the example problem.

previous level. Now consider how the example problem is handled on the dynamic programming tree (Figure 3.5). The node corresponding to the set $\{3, 4, 5\}$ is generated when P^3_{345} is created, and the corresponding value is $v_{345} = 15$. At the next stage, the set $\{3, 4, 5\}$ is encountered again when P^3_{435} is generated. The new value, $v_{435} = 10$, is better than the old value. In effect, this means that the new path for reaching $\{3, 4, 5\}$ is preferable to the earlier path. On Figure 3.5, the new value is recorded and the poorer branch leading to $\{3, 4, 5\}$ is deleted. (Deleting branches this way keeps track of the specific sequence that attained the best value yet found for the set, so that the optimal sequence can be reconstructed once the branching process terminates.) Later, branches are deleted when subproblems P^2_{53} and P^2_{54} are generated, as shown in the illustration.

It is important to recognize that Dominance Property 3.4 can be implemented, in whole or in part, either on the partial sequence tree or on the dynamic programming tree. In either case, full implementation of the dominance check may be difficult to accomplish efficiently in a computerized adaptation of Algorithm 3.2. The advantage of the dynamic programming tree is that it represents a convenient device for carrying out some of the dominance checks efficiently. A further discussion of the dynamic programming tree can be found in the original exposition, given by Elmaghraby (2).

3.5 EXERCISES

5.1   Prove Property 3.4. Hint. First prove that $v_{\sigma_1} \leq v_{\sigma_2}$ whenever σ_2 contains σ_1.

5.2   Discuss the effect of obtaining a trial solution initially in branch and bound, when jumptracking is used and when backtracking is used. What trade-offs are involved in deciding whether to generate an initial trial solution?

5.3   Show how backtracking can be implemented by ranking the subproblems on the active list.

5.4   Write a version of a branch and bound algorithm that incorporates Dominance Property 3.4.

5.5   Solve the example problem in this section by branch and bound
   (a) Using equation 5 to compute bounds.
   (b) Using equation 4 to compute bounds and also using Dominance Property 3.4. Compare the number of nodes generated in each case to those in the example problem.

6. NEIGHBORHOOD SEARCH TECHNIQUES

As mentioned earlier, the computational effort required to solve combinatorial problems grows remarkably fast as problem size increases. Suppose, for instance, that a computer code for the dynamic programming algorithm allows 1000 subsets to be evaluated per second. Then the solution of a 25-job problem would consume several hours of computer time. This much computer time may not be accessible; and even if it is, the cost of using so much computer time may well outweigh the benefits to be derived from using dynamic programming in the first place. The same might often be said of other implicit enumeration techniques, where the solution effort required depends on the data in the problem and can certainly be substantial when $n = 25$.

Although it would be difficult to claim that a particular problem size is typical of practical problems, it is still important to consider the computational demands of an optimizing technique whenever its use is contemplated. Five or 10-job problems can usually be solved quite rapidly, but 20-job problems might not be practical to solve where computing capability is scarce or expensive, or where scheduling decisions need to be resolved in minutes. In such cases it is quite reasonable to consider suboptimal methods, or *heuristic* procedures, which are capable of obtaining good solutions very quickly but which do not necessarily yield optimal solutions.

We turn now to a general purpose heuristic procedure that is applicable to a wide variety of combinatorial problems. In contrast to the methodologies of dynamic programming and branch and bound, the neighborhood search technique is not generally an optimizing procedure; still it is a simple and flexible method of obtaining good solutions quickly.

The basic elements in the neighborhood search approach are the concept of a neighborhood of a sequence and a mechanism for generating neighborhoods. The generating mechanism is a method of taking one sequence as a seed and systematically creating a collection of related sequences. For example the adjacent pairwise interchange operation might serve as a generating mechanism. If the seed sequence were $1, 2, 3, \ldots, n$, then any of the following sequences could be formed by a single adjacent pairwise interchange:

$$2, 1, 3, 4, \ldots, n - 2, n - 1, n$$
$$1, 3, 2, 4, \ldots, n - 2, n - 1, n$$
$$\cdot$$
$$\cdot$$
$$\cdot$$
$$1, 2, 3, 4, \ldots, n - 1, n - 2, n$$
$$1, 2, 3, 4, \ldots, n - 2, n, n - 1$$

This is a list of $(n - 1)$ distinct sequences, which is called the *neighborhood* of the seed sequence, for this particular generating mechanism. It is not difficult to envision other methods for generating neighborhoods. Another mechanism is to insert the last job of the seed sequence into other positions. Thus the neighborhood of the sequence $1, 2, \ldots, n$ would be

$$n, 1, 2, \ldots, n - 1$$
$$1, n, 2, \ldots, n - 1$$
$$\cdot$$
$$\cdot$$
$$\cdot$$
$$1, 2, 3, \ldots, n, n - 1$$

which is again a list of $(n - 1)$ sequences in the neighborhood. The choice of a generating mechanism can affect the size of the neighborhood. For example, a neighborhood could be generated by all pairwise interchanges (not necessarily just the adjacent ones), and this would lead to a list of $n(n - 1)/2$ sequences in each neighborhood. In general, given a seed and a generating mechanism, any sequence that can be formed from the seed by a single application of the generating mechanism is defined to be in the neighborhood of the seed. In this context, a search algorithm requires the specification of a generating mechanism. A general description of a neighborhood search algorithm is given below.

ALGORITHM 3.3
(Neighborhood Search Procedure)

Step 1. Obtain a sequence to be an initial seed and evaluate it with respect to the given measure of performance.

Step 2. Generate and evaluate all the sequences in the neighborhood of the seed. If none of the sequences are better than the seed with respect to the given measure of performance, stop. Otherwise proceed.

Step 3. Select one of the sequences in the neighborhood that improved the measure of performance. Let this sequence be the new seed. Return to step 2.

Within this general framework, these options must still be specified.

1. A method of obtaining the initial seed.
2. A particular generating mechanism.
3. A method of selecting a particular sequence to be the new seed.

To illustrate the search algorithm, suppose that the objective is to minimize N_T and consider the five-job example introduced in Section 4.2 of Chapter 2.

Job j	t_j	d_j
1	1	2
2	5	7
3	3	8
4	9	13
5	7	11

Suppose that the following rules resolve the three options shown above.

1. The initial seed is obtained from SPT sequencing.
2. The generating mechanism is adjacent pairwise interchanges.
3. The first improvement in the neighborhood identifies the new seed.

Table 3.7 provides a worksheet for the implementation of Algorithm 3.3, in which it is shown that an optimal sequence is obtained by the search procedure. (It can also be verified that if the initial seed is obtained by EDD sequencing, then the search procedure will terminate without finding an optimum.)

The search procedure of Algorithm 3.3 terminates with a sequence that is a local optimum (with respect to the given neighborhood structure.) Unfortunately there is in general no way to know whether the terminal sequence is also a global optimum. As in other kinds of search procedures, it is possible

Table 3.7

	STAGE 1	
Seed:	1–3–2–5–4	$N_T = 3$
Neighborhood:	3–1–2–5–4	$N_T = 4$
	1–2–3–5–4	$N_T = 3$
	1–3–5–2–4	$N_T = 2^*$ selection
	1–3–2–4–5	$N_T = 3$
	STAGE 2	
New seed:	1–3–5–2–4	$N_T = 2$
Neighborhood:	3–1–5–2–4	$N_T = 3$
	1–5–3–2–4	$N_T = 3$
	1–3–2–5–4	$N_T = 3$
	1–3–5–4–2	$N_T = 2$
	Terminates with $N_T = 2$	

to augment the basic algorithm and improve its chances of converging to a global optimum in the following ways.

1. Generate *several* sequences to serve as initial seed. Employ the full search procedure for each initial seed, and take the best terminal sequence that is found.
2. In each neighborhood, keep track of *all* sequences that improve on the seed. Use each of these as a seed to a new neighborhood.
3. Choose a generating mechanism that creates large neighborhoods.

While these and other augmentation methods are eminently logical, they still cannot offer a guarantee that a global optimum will be found. Nevertheless, a few experimental studies have indicated that even the fundamental version of Algorithm 3.3 is fairly reliable as a general purpose heuristic procedure. As an example, Algorithm 3.3 was tested on the $\bar{T}$ problems in Appendix A, with (a) adjacent pairwise interchange neighborhoods, and then with (b) all pairwise interchange neighborhoods. The results are compared in Table 3.8

Table 3.8

Algorithm	Optimizing Performance	Ratio of Solution to Optimum, Averaged over All 16 Problems
2.2	14 out of 16	1.004
3.3a (random)	4 out of 16	1.20
3.3b (random)	14 out of 16	1.0002
3.3a (EDD)	14 out of 16	1.0002

with the performance of Algorithm 2.2. (The initial seed is indicated in parentheses and, in each case, the first improvement in the neighborhood identified the new neighborhood.)

A knowledge of the principles of neighborhood search can provide added perspective on the Wilkerson–Irwin algorithm for the $\bar{T}$ problem. The algorithm produces a sequence that is a local optimum with respect to adjacent pairwise interchanges. This local optimality results from the fact that the decision rule criterion was equivalent to determining an ordering of two jobs that was no worse than its pairwise interchange alternative. The algorithm did not require that the full sequence of scheduled jobs be evaluated before and after each interchange because the decision rule was a simple method of determining the same information. An important lesson emerges for the application of Algorithm 3.3 to other problems: in Step 2, it is desirable to avoid, where possible, the explicit evaluation from scratch of all sequences in the neighborhood. It may instead be sufficient to impute the value of each sequence by exploiting special properties of the generating mechanism. Thus, if the neighborhood is generated by adjacent pairwise interchanges, the special property which applies is that the $(n-2)$ jobs not involved in the interchange will have the same completion times before and after the interchange. Hence the full impact of the interchange can be evaluated by considering the impact on the interchanged jobs only.

We can apply this lesson again in the $\bar{T}$ problem in the case of neighborhoods generated by all pairwise interchanges. Suppose that job i and a later job j are interchanged in sequence (Figure 3.6). The completion times of jobs in B_i and A_j are unaffected by the interchange, and it is necessary to consider only the remaining jobs, those in set $A_i \cap B_j$ in addition to jobs i and j. Let $t = t_j - t_i$, and let primes denote values after interchange. Then

$$C'_i = C_j$$

$$C'_j = C_i + t$$

$$C'_k = C_k + t \qquad k \in A_i \cap B_j$$

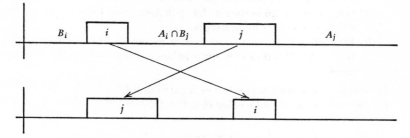

Figure 3.6
A pairwise interchange of nonadjacent jobs.

Now it is possible to evaluate the potential value of certain interchanges without actually computing the new tardiness values. Here is an example.

Property 3.5

If $t_j > t_i$ and $C_j \leq d_j$, then the interchange of i and j (as in Figure 3.6) will not lead to a reduction in $\overline{T}$.

In their original presentation, Wilkerson and Irwin actually examined pairwise interchange neighborhoods in cases where the sequence generated by their algorithm did not satisfy Theorem 2.8. In effect, their algorithm consisted of two phases. The first phase constructed a local optimum with respect to adjacent pairwise interchange neighborhoods, and the second phase constructed a local optimum with respect to pairwise interchange neighborhoods.

The neighborhood search technique generally appears to be a promising heuristic procedure for solving sequencing problems. Several research topics still remain to be investigated, however, including efficient methods of finding an initial seed, selecting a generating mechanism, and proceeding to a new seed. In the context of these unanswered questions, the implementation of a search procedure is still very much an art.

3.6 EXERCISES

6.1 Prove Property 3.5.

6.2 One crucial trade-off in implementing a neighborhood search involves the quality of the terminal solution versus the time required to reach termination. Discuss the implications of the following options for this trade-off:

(a) Generating neighborhoods by pairwise interchanges or by only adjacent pairwise interchanges.

(b) Proceeding to a new seed as soon as an improvement is discovered in the neighborhood or only after exhaustively searching the neighborhood.

6.3 Discuss the optimizing properties of Algorithm 3.3 in the case that $\overline{F}$ is the performance measure and neighborhoods are generated by adjacent pairwise interchanges.

6.4 Apply a neighborhood search procedure to find a solution (i.e., a local optimum) to each of the two $\overline{T}$ problems in Exercise 4.3. How good are your results?

7.   RANDOM SAMPLING

It is somewhat surprising at first to learn that statistical techniques can be useful in the solution of combinatorial problems that are strictly deterministic. Nevertheless, random sampling has been employed successfully in such complex problems and may be of value in problems arising in connection with the basic single-machine model. But even in problems with simple structure there are some important topics still to be explored. As we shall see, a fundamental question pertains to the choice of specific tactics by which sampling is carried out. Then there is the question of how much sampling should be done. And finally, when a sampling procedure is fully designed, there is the question of how effective a solution method it really is.

The essence of a sampling procedure is easy enough to describe: *using some random device, construct and evaluate N sequences and identify the best sequence in the sample.* Random sampling can be viewed as a solution method that lies on a continuum between a specialized heuristic procedure and an optimizing procedure. Most specialized heuristic procedures (such as Algorithm 2.2, for the $\bar{T}$ problem) construct one sequence, while an optimizing procedure (such as branch and bound) must enumerate all $n!$ sequences, at least implicitly. The strategy of random sampling is to construct some intermediate number of sequences and to select the best. The difficult aspect of designing a sampling scheme involves two tactical problems:

1.   Specifying a particular device for carrying out sampling.
2.   Drawing conclusions regarding the best sequence found in the sample.

Much of the literature on sampling techniques has attempted to provide some insight into these tactical problems, which we can now examine in some detail.

It is not easy to draw substantive conclusions about the best sequence found in the sample. The ideal information is knowledge of how likely a sample is to contain an optimum or how close to optimum the best sequence sampled is likely to be. Unfortunately, these relationships are generally known only qualitatively: a larger sample is more likely than a small sample to contain an optimum, and the best sequence in a larger sample will also tend to be closer to optimum. But without quantitative information about these relationships, there is virtually no logical way to select a sample size. In principle there is a certain probability p that on a particular trial a specified sampling procedure will construct an optimum for a given problem. Therefore, since sampling is essentially done with replacement, the probability that an optimum will be found in a sample of size N is $1 - (1 - p)^N$. The difficulty is to estimate p.

In the basic single-machine problem there is perhaps one situation in which some quantitative conclusions can be drawn. Suppose that a sequence is constructed by assigning the first position in sequence, then the second, and so on. In order to assign the first sequence position, suppose that a random device (such as a random number generator) is used and that each job is assigned to this position with probability $1/n$. After this assignment suppose that each remaining job is assigned to second position with probability $1/(n-1)$. If we continue in this manner, each position is assigned by an equally likely selection device. Then all of the $n!$ sequences are equally likely to be included in the sample. If the optimum is unique, then $p = 1/n!$; thus in this procedure we can conclude that the best sequence in a sample of size N is an optimum with probability $1 - (1 - 1/n!)^N$. On the subject of how close to optimum the best sequence in the sample may be, it is still not possible to provide quantitative conclusions. In order to suggest the kind of behavior that might be found, some eight-job test problems for $\bar{T}$ (Appendix A) were used in a set of sampling experiments that employed equally likely mechanisms. Three different sample sizes were tested and the results evaluated in two ways. First, the ratio of the solution found to the optimum was averaged over all 16 problems and, second, the maximum of these ratios was recorded. The results are shown in Table 3.9. While reasonably high solution efficiency

Table 3.9

Procedure	Average Ratio	Maximum Ratio	Optima Found
Sampling ($N = 25$)	1.47	4.68	0
Sampling ($N = 250$)	1.14	1.48	1
Sampling ($N = 2500$)	1.02	1.10	9
Algorithm 2.2	1.004	1.05	14

is obtained with a sample size of 2500, the sampling procedure is not nearly as effective as Algorithm 2.2.

At this point we should recognize that perhaps a different sampling mechanism might yield a value of p that is much larger than $1/n!$, and in general we should think in terms of selection devices that are not equally likely in nature.

The following is an example of a simple method for performing *biased random sampling*. Begin by ordering the jobs according to some sequencing rule (such as EDD). In assigning the first position in sequence, job $[j]$ on the ordered list is selected with probability $p_j^{(1)}$ ($j = 1, 2, \ldots, n$). The job assigned is then removed from the list, and the second position is assigned by selecting job $[j]$ on the ordered list with probability $p_j^{(2)}$ ($j = 1, 2, \ldots,$

$n - 1$). In this way a discrete distribution $p_j^{(k)}$ is employed at the kth stage. Moreover, a widely used method involves a set of $p_j^{(k)}$ values that have a truncated geometric distribution with parameter α. In this case the selection device corresponds to

$$p_j^{(k)} = Q_k \alpha^j \qquad j = 1, 2, \ldots, k$$

where Q_k is simply a normalizing constant. With this structure, the first job on the ordered list has the highest probability of being selected next, the second job has the second highest probability, and so on. In addition, the probabilities decrease in a geometric manner, but the nature of that decrease can be controlled by selecting the parameter α. For example when $n = 8$ and α is set to 0.6, then the first set of probabilities is

j	1	2	3	4	5	6	7	8
$p_j^{(1)}$	0.407	0.244	0.146	0.088	0.053	0.032	0.019	0.011

A larger value of α would make the jobs early on the list more likely to be selected, while a smaller α would distribute the selection probabilities in more of an equally likely fashion. (In particular, the equally likely case can be viewed as the limiting case corresponding to $\alpha = 0$.) With this facility to choose one member of a family of sampling distributions, the efficiency of the sampling approach is improved. Table 3.10 compares some biased sampling plans

Table 3.10

Procedure	Average Ratio	Maximum Ratio	Optima Found
Sampling ($\alpha = 0, N = 100$)	1.25	2.27	0
Sampling ($\alpha = 0.7, N = 100$; SPT)	1.28	3.81	2
Sampling ($\alpha = 0.8, N = 100$, SPT)	1.13	1.50	2
Sampling ($\alpha = 0.7, N = 100$; MRM)	1.04	1.18	4
Sampling ($\alpha = 0.8, N = 100$; MRM)	1.07	1.32	0
Sampling ($\alpha = 0.7, N = 100$; EDD)	1.03	1.13	5
Sampling ($\alpha = 0.8, N = 100$; EDD)	1.06	1.32	4

with the equally likely plan described above. Each plan is described by a value of α, a sample size, and an initial job ordering. The acronym MRM represents Montagne's ratio method (8), in which the n jobs in a $\bar{T}_w$ problem are ranked in nondecreasing order of the quantity θ_j where

$$\theta_j = \frac{t_j}{w_j} \cdot \frac{1}{1 - d_j/\sum_{i=1}^{n} t_i}$$

The results in Table 3.10 suggest that an effective combination of an initial job ordering and a choice of α can be worth more than a large amount of sampling.

In short, random sampling is a viable procedure for obtaining good solutions to combinatorial problems with limited computational effort. In more complicated problems, both in and out of the scheduling field, sampling techniques have provided effective heuristic procedures. Although it appears to be competitive with other general purpose heuristic procedures, sampling may have found only limited acceptance as a solution technique because so many options are left to the discretion of the scheduler. These options include initial ordering of the jobs for biased sampling; selection of a probability distribution—or perhaps a family of distributions—for the assignment of jobs to positions; and, most importantly, a rational determination of sample size. The task for research in scheduling is to determine how these options should be resolved to arrive at an effective sampling procedure.

The foregoing treatment has assumed throughout that the sample size should be fixed beforehand. However, we can borrow from the theory of sequential decision making and suggest a different approach, because it is possible, at least in theory, to allow the partial results of sampling to dictate the extent of sampling. In order to illustrate the decision-theoretic reasoning embodied in this approach, we shall make several assumptions. Let the scheduling measure of performance Z denote the total cost associated with a given job sequence. Also suppose that the $n!$ sequences give rise to a population of Z-values that can be approximated by the probability density function $h(z)$, where

$$h(z) = \Pr \{z \le Z \le z + dz\}$$

Let c_s denote the sampling cost of constructing and evaluating one schedule as part of the sampling procedure. Suppose that after some amount of sampling, the best sequence yet found attained a scheduling cost of Z^*. At this point, the expected reduction in total scheduling cost associated with taking one more sample is

$$\int_0^{Z^*} (Z^* - z)h(z)\, dz$$

On the other hand the incremental cost associated with taking one more sample is just c_s. Consequently it can be shown that the form of an optimal sampling rule is:

Take another sample if $c_s < \int_0^{Z^*} (Z^* - z)h(z)\, dz$

In order to devise a procedure containing a stopping rule of this sort, it is necessary to know or to estimate $h(z)$. While extensive experimental work, along the lines of that carried out by Heller (5), might provide this type of information, it appears that more sophisticated statistical techniques— which are beyond the scope of this text—are required to implement such a strategy. Efforts in this direction have begun with the work of Randolph (9).

3.7 EXERCISES

7.1 Suppose that an equally likely mechanism is used for generating a random sample of sequences when there are eight jobs. How many sequences must be evaluated in order to yield a probability of 1/2 that an optimum will be found in the sample (assuming that a unique optimum exists)? How many sequences must be evaluated in complete enumeration?

7.2 Calculate $p_j^{(k)}$ by using the geometric probability model and $\alpha = 0.5$ for $k = 1$ and $k = 2$, when $n = 8$.

8. SUMMARY

Challenging combinatorial optimization problems are encountered even in the simplest of scheduling problems. The previous chapter discussed the relatively few situations in which general optimal solutions are known. For other cases, and especially for most tardiness-based criteria, general purpose techniques must be brought to bear on the problem. Nevertheless, each of the general methodologies described in this chapter contains many optional features that can determine its effectiveness in a given implementation. Some of these options are reviewed below.

The dynamic programming approach (Section 3) is a highly flexible implicit enumeration strategy that can be applied directly to most single-machine sequencing problems. Although there are no important design options involved in applying the technique to a given class of problems, an intriguing question is how to develop an efficient computer code for the algorithm. (Appendix B is devoted to this particular question.) Because the computational demands of dynamic programming grow exponentially with problem size, it is particularly crucial to use an efficient code for moderate-sized problems. In situations where all alternate optima are desired, efficient coding may require different tactics than if only one optimum is desired.

In Srinivasan's hybrid algorithm (Section 4) the dynamic programming calculations are curtailed by invoking Lemmas 3.1 to 3.4. Each lemma requires that a certain condition be checked to exploit the possibility that some of the dynamic programming calculations could be avoided entirely. However, the very process of checking those conditions might introduce computational overhead that could offset the associated gains. Perhaps there are combinations of the lemmas that are beneficial in some circumstances but not in others. While this aspect of implementation has never been thoroughly explored, it serves to illustrate that within the broad limits of a solution strategy there may be considerable room for discretion.

The branch and bound approach (Section 5) might be the best illustration of how implementing a mathematical technique can require a good deal of individual judgment. The list of tactical options in which this judgment must be exercised includes the choice of a lower bound calculation, the potential utilization of an initial trial solution, the incorporation of complicated dominance checks, and the specification of a branching mechanism. In spite of the existence of these options, and the fact that they cannot be evaluated independently, branch and bound approaches have met with success in the solution of a wide variety of problems.

The neighborhood search heuristic procedure (Section 6) embodies a simple but valuable concept in sequencing problems. The primary tactical options that were examined in Section 6, include the specification of an initializing phase (to obtain the first seed), the choice of a mechanism for generating neighborhoods, and the specification of a rule for determining a new seed. Likewise, the random sampling heuristic procedure (Section 7) contained such options as the choice of an initial ordering and a sample size, and the specification of a random device for generating sequences. An intriguing question is how effective both of these general purpose heuristic procedures would be when used in tandem.

There are two important reasons for delineating these options. First, it should now be evident that there are important considerations in linking methodology to implementation, even in the basic single-machine problem. Second, the treatment of more complicated models in subsequent chapters often includes a suggestion that a particular optimization technique or a particular heuristic strategy is suitable for a given scheduling problem. It is important to be sensitive, on these occasions, to the fact that implementation itself may involve a host of significant questions, even once the general methodology is developed.

Now, armed with a variety of methodological capabilities, we can investigate more complex problems in sequencing and scheduling. But before proceeding to larger scheduling models, it is worth reexamining the assumptions of the basic single-machine model. By relaxing some of these assumptions, as discussed in the next chapter, a broader modeling capability can be developed and additional scheduling insights can be discovered.

3.8. COMPUTATIONAL EXERCISES

The following exercises involve writing computer programs to solve sequencing problems. Where investigation of a given algorithm or comparison of two algorithms is involved, it is suggested that several job sets be constructed as test data for such studies. The design of meaningful data sets for test purposes is not necessarily a simple task. In the following problems, questions such as those regarding size of job sets, generation of job data, and special characteristics of job set data are left open.

8.1   Write a computer program to solve the single-machine mean tardiness problem by dynamic programming. The program should read as input the number of jobs (n), their processing times (t_j), and their due dates (d_j).

8.2   Write a computer program for the hybrid algorithm.

(a) Construct some test data in order to investigate the general behavior of Phase 1 (e.g., how many jobs does it actually assign to positions in sequence? How much of the P matrix does it fill?)

(b) Construct some test data in order to compare the run-time performance of the hybrid algorithm and the dynamic programming algorithm (Exercise 8.1).

8.3   Write a computer program to solve the $\bar{T}$ problem by branch and bound. Compare the performance of the program under the following options.

(a) Lower bounds from equation 4 versus lower bounds from equation 5.

(b) Jumptracking versus backtracking.

(c) The addition of Algorithm 2.2 to provide a trial solution for backtracking.

8.4   Write a computer program to solve the $\bar{T}_w$ problem using neighborhood search. Compare the following options in terms of run time and solution value:

(a) Initial seed obtained by WSPT, EDD, and MRM.

(b) Adjacent pairwise interchange neighborhoods versus pairwise interchange neighborhoods.

(c) Single initial seeds versus multiple initial seeds.

8.5   Write a computer program to solve the $\bar{T}_w$ problem by using biased random sampling. Compare the following options in terms of run time and solution value:

(a) Initial ordering by WSPT, EDD, MRM.

(b) Sample size (two values of N).

(c) Random device (two values of α).

For the best combination of options (a) and (c), set N so that run times are comparable to one method studied in Exercise 8.4. Which procedure produces better schedules?

REFERENCES

1. Agin, N. "Optimum Seeking With Branch and Bound," *Management Science*, Vol. 13, No. 4 (December, 1966).
2. Elmaghraby, S. E. "The One-Machine Sequencing Problem with Delay Costs," *Journal of Industrial Engineering*, Vol. 19, No. 2 (February, 1968).
3. Elmaghraby, S. E. "A Graph-Theoretic Interpretation of the Sufficiency Conditions for the Contiguous-Binary-Switching (CBS) Rule," *Naval Research Logistics Quarterly*, Vol. 18, No. 3 (September, 1971).
4. Emmons, H. "One-Machine Sequencing to Minimize Certain Functions of Job Tardiness," *Operations Research*, Vol. 17, No. 4 (July–August, 1969).
5. Heller, J. "Some Numerical Experiments for an $M \times J$ Flow Shop and its Decision-Theoretical Aspects," *Operations Research*, Vol. 8, No. 2 (March–April, 1960).
6. Lawler, E. L., and Wood, D. E. "Branch and Bound Methods: A Survey," *Operations Research*, Vol. 14, No. 4 (July–August, 1966).
7. Mitten, L. G. "Branch and Bound Methods: General Formulation and Properties," *Operations Research*, Vol. 18, No. 1 (January–February, 1970).
8. Montagne, E. R., Jr. "Sequencing with Time Delay Costs," *Industrial Engineering Research Bulletin*, No. 5, Arizona State University (January, 1969).
9. Randolph, P. H., Swinson, G. H., and Ellingsen, C. "Stopping Rules for Sequencing Problems," *Operations Research*, Vol. 21, No. 6 (November–December, 1973).
10. Rau, J. G. "Minimizing a Function of Permutations of n Integers," *Operations Research*, Vol. 19, No. 2 (March–April, 1971).
11. Shwimer, J. "On the n-Job, One-Machine, Sequence-Independent Scheduling Problem with Tardiness Penalties: A Branch-Bound Solution," *Management Science*, Vol. 18, No. 6 (February, 1972).
12. Srinivasan, V. "A Hybrid Algorithm for the One-Machine Sequencing Problem to Minimize Total Tardiness," *Naval Research Logistics Quarterly*, Vol. 18, No. 3 (September, 1971).

CHAPTER 4

EXTENSIONS OF THE BASIC MODEL

1. INTRODUCTION

As some of the exercises in Chapter 2 indicated, single-machine sequencing models are relevant for problems in such areas as quality control and computer system design in addition to production scheduling. The development of more general models and methods extends the applicability of sequencing theory even further, and this chapter deals with structures in which some of the assumptions in the basic model are relaxed.

Recall that five assumptions for the basic model were stated in Chapter 2, and that assumptions C4 and C5 turned out to be derived conditions for the model. The three primary conditions were:

C1. A set of n independent, single-operation jobs is available for processing at time zero.

C2. Setup times for the jobs are independent of job sequence.

C3. Job descriptors are known in advance.

There are several ways of generalizing C1, such as allowing different ready times or dependent sets of jobs. These two situations are discussed in Sections 2 and 3. Condition C2 can be generalized by allowing sequence-dependent setup times. Such a model relies on a well-known problem known as the "traveling salesman problem," which is treated in detail in Section 4. The generalization of C3 clearly involves the use of probabilistic methods, and since some of these are beyond the scope of this book, Section 5 surveys the major sequencing results that have been obtained for probabilistic models.

2. NONSIMULTANEOUS ARRIVALS

The *static* version of a single-machine problem refers to the situation in which all jobs are simultaneously available for processing. Many sequencing problems, however, require that different ready times be accommodated. For example, when computer programs are to be scheduled for execution in a large business data processing facility, allowances typically must be made for such preliminary work as data collection, keypunch, and validation. Since this preprocessing activity will vary for different types of programs, the jobs will actually have different ready times.

In the case of different ready times, the set of tasks to be scheduled changes over time, giving rise to a *dynamic* version of the single-machine problem. An immediate consequence of allowing different ready times is the need to reexamine the questions of inserted idle time (condition C4) and job preemption (condition C5). To illustrate the role of these two factors, consider the two-job example shown below, in which total job tardiness is the criterion.

Job j	1	2
r_j	0	1
t_j	5	2
d_j	7	2

There is only one sequence that satisfies conditions C4 and C5 by avoiding all inserted idle time and preemption; this is the sequence 1–2 (see Figure 4.1a). This sequence has a total tardiness of 5. When inserted idle time is permitted, the sequence 2–1 (Figure 4.1b) gives rise to a total tardiness of 2. Furthermore, if a job can be preempted and later continued from the point in its processing at which the interruption occurred, then a total tardiness of 1 can be achieved, as shown in Figure 4.1c.

The type of preemption illustrated in Figure 4.1c is called the *preempt-resume* mode, because processing can be resumed from the point at which

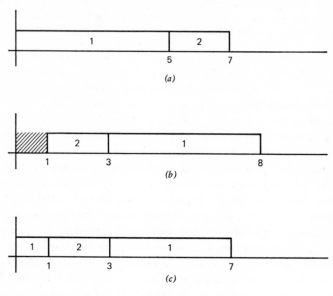

Figure 4.1
Three different schedules for the example problem.

preemption occurred. In other words, the total amount of processing required by job j is always t_j and is unaffected by the number of times the job is preempted. In cases where preempt-resume applies, inserted idle time can never be beneficial; therefore schedules without inserted idle time constitute a dominant set for all regular measures of performance.

The opposite extreme is the case in which a job must be started over again each time it is interrupted. This type of preemption is called the *preempt-repeat* mode, for obvious reasons. The difference between these two modes of processing is reflected in the way that scheduling decisions are made in each case. Under a preempt-repeat mode, there is no reason to begin processing on a job unless it is to be completed. In deterministic situations, then, jobs might as well be scheduled as if no preemption were permitted, and schedules without preemption constitute a dominant set.

When preempt-resume prevails, the properties associated with transitive rules are essentially unchanged. Consider, for example, the problem of minimizing $T_{\max}$ in a dynamic problem where preempt resume applies. The optimal rule is: *Always keep the machine assigned to the available job with the earliest due date*. The machine is assigned at completion times and at ready times as follows:

1. At each job completion, examine the set of available jobs and assign the machine to process the job with the earliest due date.

2. At each job arrival, compare the due date of the newly available job j with the due date of the job currently being processed. If d_j is lower, allow job j to preempt the job being processed; otherwise simply add job j to the available list.

In this case, the vital information (d_j) on which scheduling decisions are based does not change over time. By contrast, consider the minimization of $\bar{F}$. The optimal rule is: *Always keep the machine assigned to the available job with minimum remaining processing time*. The vital information in this case is a job's remaining processing time, which will certainly change over time while it is being processed. Thus a job may enter the system with a large t_j (and relatively low priority), but after some partial processing it will have a smaller remaining processing time (and higher priority). This dynamic sequencing rule is known as shortest remaining processing time (SRPT) sequencing. Notice that in the dynamic version of both EDD and SPT the implementation of an optimal scheduling rule requires no look-ahead features, even though jobs become ready intermittently. At each decision point (i.e., a completion time or a ready time) the necessary information is obtained only from the current set of available jobs. Consequently the actual scheduling decisions can be made at chronologically ordered points in time, and on the basis of current status each time. This decision-making structure is called *dispatching*, and its significance lies in the fact that dispatching is easier to implement than a decision-making scheme based on look-ahead information.

When preempt-repeat prevails, dispatching procedures are no longer sufficient, but it is helpful to recognize, as indicated earlier, that permutation schedules constitute a dominant set. This means that even though inserted idle time may be desirable, the choice of a permutation schedule will uniquely determine the allocation of idle time. Nevertheless, there has been virtually no progress up to now in exploiting special structures in this problem; therefore it appears necessary to use general purpose techniques to find the best permutation schedule. A promising strategy in many problems seems to be the branch and bound approach, because quite often it is possible to calculate very strong lower bounds for subproblems (partial sequences) in the branching tree. In particular, consider the $T_{\max}$ problem and suppose that a partial sequence at level k corresponds to a specific assignment of the *first* k jobs in sequence. (This branching structure complements the structure introduced in Chapter 3.) The associated subproblem involves the non-preemptive sequencing of the remaining $(n - k)$ jobs, but an excellent lower bound for this problem is represented by the value obtained by using preempt-resume scheduling (which can never do worse than preempt-repeat scheduling). As described above, the preempt-resume solution is constructed by using just a one-pass dispatching rule, and this calculation can be made quite efficiently. In general, whenever the preempt-resume version of the problem can be solved readily, then the branch and bound approach should be seriously considered for the preempt-repeat version.

An experimental study of the $T_{\max}$ problem, described in reference *1*, pursued this reasoning and tested the branch and bound approach on 90 example problems with $n = 10$, 20, or 30. It was necessary in the experimental procedure to terminate the jumptracking algorithm after 1000 nodes had been created in the branching process. Even though this termination rule is restrictive for moderate-sized problems (less than half a minute of computer time was involved) more than 93% of the test problems were completely solved prior to termination. Moreover, the number of nodes created in the branching tree for these solved problems was quite small on the average, as shown in Table 4.1. (Keep in mind that the number of nodes at

Table 4.1

Problem Size	10	20	30
Very tight due dates	14.8	40.4	84.9
Moderate due dates	11.1	35.4	91.9
Loose due dates	8.9	39.5	72.8
Maximum nodes	22	78	132

level n of the branching tree when $n = 30$ is greater than 2×10^{32}.) The conclusion of this study was that lower bounds obtained from the preempt-resume version of the problem were fairly tight, leading to a brief tree search in a very high percentage of problems. While there was still a small proportion of problems in which the algorithm did not locate an optimum quickly, this was not deemed to be a major disadvantage, since other combinatorial optimization schemes are not even practicable for 30-job problems. Whereas problems of this size are normally solved with heuristic procedures, the study demonstrated that only in relatively few cases is it actually necessary to resort to heuristic approaches.

In short, the crucial property in the dynamic single-machine problem is the nature of job preemption. If processing can be carried out in a preempt-resume mode, then many of the scheduling rules for optimal sequencing in the static problem can be extended. In particular, the extension of transitive job orderings can be implemented as a dispatching procedure, and there is no need to rely on inserted idle time. On the other hand, if processing requires a preempt-repeat mode, inserted idle time can be helpful, and it may be necessary to employ a general purpose technique to find an optimal job permutation.

4.2. EXERCISES

2.1   Describe how to adapt Algorithm 2.1 (for minimizing N_T) to the dynamic single-machine problem.

2.2   Construct an example to demonstrate that EDD sequencing will not guarantee minimum $T_{\max}$ in the dynamic single-machine problem with no preemption allowed.

2.3   Consider the following three-job example of a dynamic single-machine problem with preempt-repeat processing.

Job j	1	2	3
r_j	0	2	3
t_j	4	1	2

For any regular measure of performance it is sufficient in seeking an optimum to consider only the six permutation schedules. Show that regardless of the regular measure involved, there is in fact a dominant set in this problem containing fewer than six schedules.

3. DEPENDENT JOBS

Throughout the discussion of the basic single-machine model, the only active type of constraint was the resource capacity constraint represented by the single processor. As discussed in connection with the definition of scheduling in Chapter 1, the other type of constraint typical of scheduling problems is a technological constraint, represented by the existence of a precedence restriction. The presence of such restrictions, which may sometimes reflect externally imposed priorities, reduces the set of feasible solutions, but this does not mean that optimal solutions can be found more readily.

The existence of technological restrictions on job sequence is interpreted as the existence of a partial ordering among the jobs based on the *precedence* relation. The notation $i < j$ denotes the fact that job i precedes job j. In other words, job j may not begin until job i is complete. When $i < j$, job i is said to be a *predecessor* of job j, and job j is said to be a *successor* of job i. Job i is also called a *direct predecessor* of job j (denoted $i \ll j$) if there exists no job k such that $i < k < j$.

As an example, consider the computer programs submitted for processing by a payroll department. Program A reads daily employee time cards, sorts the information, and updates the monthly records that are maintained on tape. Program B reads the tape and punches out paychecks. On the last day of the month, both programs are submitted, but B cannot be run until A is complete. Therefore job A precedes job B.

To illustrate the effect of adding precedence constraints to a sequencing problem, consider minimizing mean flowtime in a single-machine problem with three jobs. Suppose the jobs are labeled a, b, and c, and suppose that $t_a < t_b < t_c$. Then without precedence constraints the optimal sequence is clearly a–b–c. Now suppose there exists one precedence constraint, $c < a$. Although job b "ought" to follow job a and precede job c, it is not immediately clear in such a situation whether sequence c–a–b or sequence b–c–a is most desirable. (We can, however, rule out the possibility that c–b–a is best with a simple adjacent pairwise interchange argument.) The specific properties of this problem can be examined more closely (see Exercise 3.1), but the main point is that the existence of precedence constraints can complicate even the simplest scheduling problems. With more than three jobs and more than one precedence constraint the problem is considerably more difficult to solve.

3.1 A Generalization of EDD Sequencing

One of the few results for independent jobs that can be extended to dependent job sets without major modifications is the minimization of L_{max} and T_{max}. For a set of independent jobs, it was shown in Section 4.1 of Chapter 2 that EDD sequencing is optimal. Now suppose a dependent job set is to be sequenced. Define

$$d'_j = \min (d_j, \min \{d_i \mid j < i\})$$

In words, d'_j is either the due date of job j itself or else the earliest due date among successors of job j, whichever is smaller. A feasible sequence that minimizes $L_{\max}$ and $T_{\max}$ can be constructed by satisfying the precedence constraints and sequencing the jobs in nondecreasing order of d'_j.

Theorem 4.1

In the single-machine problem with arbitrary precedence constraints, $L_{\max}$ and $T_{\max}$ are minimized by the sequence

$$d'_{[1]} \le d'_{[2]} \le \cdots \le d'_{[n]}$$

Proof (Adjacent Pairwise Interchange)

Let S be a feasible sequence that does not obey the d' ordering specified in the theorem. There must exist a pair of adjacent jobs i and j in sequence S, with j following i, such that $d'_i > d'_j$. Let S' be the sequence obtained by interchanging jobs i and j in sequence. (The interchange cannot violate precedence constraints since $i < j$ would imply $d'_i \le d'_j$.) There are two cases to consider.

Case 1. $d_i > d_j$
In this case the value of $L_{\max}(T_{\max})$ associated with schedule S' is at least as good as the value associated with schedule S, by exactly the same reasoning that was employed in the independent job problem (Theorem 2.6), that is, $L_{\max}(S') \le L_{\max}(S)$.

Case 2. $d_i \le d_j$
Since $d'_j < d'_i$ by hypothesis, there must exist a job k for which $j < k$ and $d_k < d_j$. Also $d_k = d'_j < d'_i \le d_i$, so that $d_k < d_i$. Because both schedules S and S' are feasible, it follows that $C_k > C_j$ and $C_k > C_i$ (under either schedule). Therefore

$$C_k - d_k > C_i - d_i$$
$$C_k - d_k > C_j - d_j$$

under both schedules, and $L_{\max}$ cannot occur for job i or for job j. Consequently $L_{\max}(S') = L_{\max}(S)$.

Combining both cases, we find that $L_{\max}(S') \le L_{\max}(S)$, which allows the adjacent pairwise argument to be invoked to prove optimality. (Notice that the optimal job ordering is transitive.)

3.2   An Extension of SPT to Sequences of Strings

When $\bar{F}$ is the measure of performance, it is sometimes possible to develop optimal sequencing rules when precedence constraints apply. One such result involves the sequencing of job strings. A string is a set of jobs that must be processed in a fixed order without interruption, and the sequencing problem for job strings is one of sequencing these special job sets. Suppose that there are s strings given to be sequenced and that

$$n_k = \text{the number of jobs in string } k \ (1 \leq k \leq s)$$

$$t_{kj} = \text{processing time of job } j \text{ in string } k \ (1 \leq j \leq n_k)$$

$$t_k = \sum_{j=1}^{n_k} t_{kj} = \text{total processing time in string } k$$

Also, let

$$F_{kj} = \text{flowtime of job } j \text{ in string } k$$

$$F_k = F_{k,n_k} = \text{completion time of string } k$$

First, if the objective is to minimize mean string flowtime, that is,

$$\frac{1}{s} \sum_{k=1}^{s} F_k$$

then the strings may each be treated as "jobs," yielding an optimal sequence characterized by

$$t_{[1]} \leq t_{[2]} \leq \cdots \leq t_{[s]}$$

On the other hand, if the objective is to minimize mean job flowtime, that is,

$$\bar{F} = \frac{1}{n} \sum_{k=1}^{s} \sum_{j=1}^{n_k} F_{kj}$$

then in general a different sequence is optimal, as stated in the following theorem.

Theorem 4.2

In the single-machine problem with job strings, $\bar{F}$ is minimized by sequencing the strings in the order

$$\frac{t_{[1]}}{n_{[1]}} \leq \frac{t_{[2]}}{n_{[2]}} \leq \cdots \leq \frac{t_{[s]}}{n_{[s]}}$$

Proof

It is helpful to define a quantity r_{kj} to represent the processing time in string k that follows job j. In other words, r_{kj} may be interpreted as a residual processing time.

$$r_{kj} = \sum_{i=j+1}^{n_k} t_{ki}$$

Then

$$\bar{F} = \frac{1}{n} \sum_{k=1}^{s} \sum_{j=1}^{n_k} F_{kj} = \frac{1}{n} \sum_{k=1}^{s} \sum_{j=1}^{n} \left(F_{kn_k} - \sum_{i=j+1}^{n_k} t_{ki} \right)$$

$$= \frac{1}{n} \sum_{k=1}^{s} \sum_{j=1}^{n_k} (F_{kn_k} - r_{kj}) = \frac{1}{n} \sum_{k=1}^{s} \sum_{j=1}^{n} F_{kn_k} - \frac{1}{n} \sum_{k=1}^{s} \sum_{j=1}^{n_k} r_{kj}$$

Notice that the second double sum is a constant, independent of sequence. Consequently, minimizing $\bar{F}$ is equivalent to minimizing the first double sum, which is

$$\frac{1}{n} \sum_{k=1}^{s} \sum_{j=1}^{n_k} F_{kn_k} = \frac{1}{n} \sum_{k=1}^{s} n_k F_k$$

But minimizing this sum corresponds to minimizing weighted mean flowtime for the strings, where the weighting factor associated with string k is just n_k. Hence, by Theorem 2.4, the optimal string sequence must be in nondecreasing order of t_k/n_k.

The job-string model may seem restrictive because it requires that a collection of jobs be processed in a specific sequence. However the model may actually be most valuable in situations where the string requirement is not technologically necessary. For example, the technological requirement may be a *contiguity constraint* (6), under which a collection of jobs must be performed together (e.g., all electrical tests together and all drilling operations together) but without specification of their sequence. In this situation the collection of jobs within a given contiguity set can be ordered optimally (by SPT) and then the ordered set can be treated as a string for the purpose of sequencing all the contiguity sets, at which point Theorem 4.2 can be invoked. In addition, a weighted version of Theorem 4.2 can easily be derived (see Exercise 3.3).

3.3   A Generalization of WSPT Sequencing

A slightly more general extension of the basic model can be developed for a precedence structure that forms a *tree*. To be specific, a set of jobs in which each job has at most one direct successor is called an *assembly tree*. A set of jobs in which each job has at most one direct predecessor is referred to as a *branching tree*, and is essentially an assembly tree with all precedence relations reversed. Figure 4.2 shows an assembly tree and a branching tree that exhibit this complementary relationship. (Jobs are represented by nodes in the figure.)

A useful aspect of network structure is the concept of a collection of jobs consisting of a lead job and a subset of its successors. When the entire set can be processed in some order once the lead job is complete, without requiring the completion of jobs outside the set, such a collection is called a

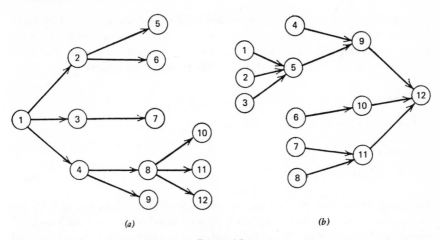

Figure 4.2

The two types of tree structures for precedence-related jobs. (*a*) Branching tree. (*b*) Assembly tree.

feasible subset and is identified with its lead job. Thus a feasible subset, S_j, of job j must satisfy

(a) $j \in S_j$,

(b) If $i \in S_j$ and $i \neq j$, then $j < i$,

(c) If $i \in S_j$ and $k < i$, then either $k \in S_j$ or else $k < j$.

Also let U_j denote the union of all feasible subsets of job j (so that U_j contains job j and all of its successors.)

Now suppose that $\bar{F}_w$ is the performance measure for a single-machine problem with precedence constraints. If the precedence relationships form a branching tree, the following procedure will construct an optimal sequence,

ALGORITHM 4.1

(To minimize $\bar{F}_w$ in a Branching Tree)

1. For each job j calculate the quantity z_j, where

$$z_j = \min_{S_j \subseteq U_j} \left\{ \frac{\sum\limits_{i \in S_j} t_i}{\sum\limits_{i \in S_j} w_i} \right\}$$

2. Sequence the jobs in nondecreasing order of z_j subject to the given precedence restrictions, as follows:

   (a) Consider jobs for which all predecessors have been scheduled.

   (b) Select the job with minimal z_j to be next in sequence.

   (c) Return to (a) until the sequence is complete.

The optimality of this job-by-job procedure was first demonstrated by Horn (8), but there are some special characteristics of the optimal sequence with more general significance. Let S_j^* denote the largest feasible subset of job j on which z_j is attained. Then it is possible to show the following.

Lemma 4.1

If $k \in S_j^*$, then $z_k \leq z_j$.

Lemma 4.2

If $k \in S_j^*$, then $S_k^* \subseteq S_j^*$.

By using these two properties, we can argue that when the job-by-job procedure sequences job j, it will then proceed to schedule all of the jobs in S_j^* immediately thereafter. Thus the scheduling mechanism can be interpreted as a set-by-set procedure, as follows. First calculate z_j for each job that has all predecessors scheduled, and identify each corresponding S_j^*. Select the job with minimum z_j and schedule its S_j^* next. Continue in this manner until all jobs are sequenced. (In carrying out the scheduling of some S_j^*, it may be necessary to reapply the procedure to S_j^* itself in order to generate a specific sequence.) This nesting of the procedure within itself is illustrated by the nine-job problem shown in Figure 4.3, where all w_j are equal so that the

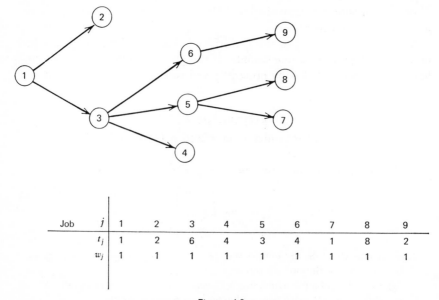

Job	j	1	2	3	4	5	6	7	8	9
	t_j	1	2	6	4	3	4	1	8	2
	w_j	1	1	1	1	1	1	1	1	1

Figure 4.3

A set of jobs related by a tree-structured set of precedence constraints.

measure of performance is simply $\bar{F}$. Determination of the z_j values identifies the nine S_j^* shown below.

Job j	1	2	3	4	5	6	7	8	9
S_j^*	1	2	3, 5, 6, 7, 9	4	5, 7	6, 9	7	8	9

The given branching tree structure provides the actual sequence within S_5^* and S_6^*. But in order to sequence all the jobs in S_3^*, the algorithm must be reapplied to the five jobs in the set. From the given precedence structure, job 3 must come first. Then to sequence S_5^* and S_6^*, which make up the rest of S_3^*, note that $z_5 = 2$ and $z_6 = 3$. Therefore S_5^* precedes S_6^* and the complete sequence is 1–2–3–5–7–6–9–4–8.

The problem of calculating z_j values and identifying the S_j^* efficiently is still a significant one, and the computational aspects of this part of the solution procedure have not been thoroughly investigated.

The problem of dealing with assembly trees is essentially a mirror image of the branching tree case. It is not difficult to show that any sequence is feasible in the assembly tree problem if and only if its antithetical sequence is feasible in the branching tree problem that results when the precedence constraints of the assembly tree are all reversed. By using this property and the result given as Exercise 2.3 in Chapter 3, we can easily construct an optimal procedure for the assembly tree problem (Exercise 3.5).

The ability to handle both kinds of tree structures actually makes it possible to construct optimal sequences for more general precedence structures that decompose into trees. Consider the 14-job set in Figure 4.4. The sequencing problem decomposes around jobs 4 and 9 in a manner that might be depicted as

$$\{1, 2, 3\}; 4; \{5, 6, 7, 8\}; 9; \{10, 11, 12, 13, 14\}$$

First, jobs 1, 2, and 3 can be sequenced as independent jobs. Then job 4 must

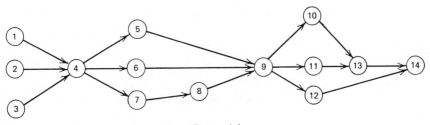

Figure 4.4

A set of jobs related by a complex set of precedence constraints, which may be decomposed.

follow in sequence. After job 4, the set containing jobs 5 to 8 can be sequenced using the branching tree procedure. Then job 9 must follow. Finally jobs 10 to 14 can be sequenced using the assembly tree procedure.

In general, the optimal procedures for tree-structured precedence constraints will break down in more complicated cases. Consider, for example, the five-job problem of Figure 4.5, where the criterion is $\bar{F}$. Suppose first that the set-by-set version of the procedure is employed. Here are the results.

Stage 1 $z_1 = 11.5$ $S_1^* = \{1, 4\}$; $z_2 = 13$, $z_3 = 12$

Stage 2 $z_3 = 12$ $S_3^* = \{3\}$; $z_2 = 13$

Stage 3 $z_2 = 7$ $S_2^* = \{2, 5\}$

The full sequence is 1–4–3–2–5, for which $\sum F_j = 169$. Now suppose that the job-by-job version is employed:

Stage 1 $z_1 = 11.5$ $S_1^* = \{1, 4\}$; $z_2 = 13$, $z_3 = 12$

Stage 2 $z_4 = 9$ $S_4^* = \{4\}$; $z_2 = 13$, $z_3 = 12$

Stage 3 $z_3 = 12$ $S_3^* = \{3\}$; $z_2 = 13$

Stage 4 $z_2 = 7$ $S_2^* = \{2, 5\}$

Stage 5 $z_5 = 1$ $S_5^* = \{5\}$

The full sequence, based on these z_j values is 2–1–4–3–5, for which $\sum F_j = 173$. The obvious problem relates to the fact that the revised value of z_2 became 7 only after other jobs were removed from consideration and it was impossible to place S_2^* early in the sequence. As it happens, the minimum value of $\sum F_j$ is less than 169.

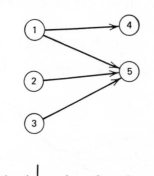

Figure 4.5
An example job set.

Job	j	1	2	3	4	5
	t_j	14	13	12	9	1

Nevertheless, the general approach can be adapted to arbitrary precedence structures as discussed by Sidney (13). Instead of working with feasible subsets, however, the generalized algorithm works with *initial sets*. A collection of jobs, S, is an initial set if the following condition holds:

If $i \in S$ and $k < i$, then $k \in S$.

This is one of the conditions that define a feasible subset. Indeed, a feasible subset is a special kind of initial set. The major distinction is that a feasible subset has a unique lead job associated with it, while an initial set may not. The general form of the solution procedure is given below.

ALGORITHM 4.2 SIDNEY'S ALGORITHM (14)
(To Decompose the $\bar{F}_w$ Problem with Precedence Constraints)

Step 1. Consider all initial sets among the unscheduled jobs and find the largest initial set, S^*, that minimizes the quantity

$$\frac{\sum_{i \in S} t_i}{\sum_{i \in S} w_i}$$

Step 2. Add the jobs in S^* to the sequence.

Step 3. Delete the jobs in S^* from consideration and return to Step 1 until all jobs are scheduled.

Effective implementation of Algorithm 4.2 requires that two crucial steps be carried out efficiently:

1. Identification of S^* (Step 1).
2. Sequencing of the individual jobs in S^* (Step 2).

These two facets of the algorithm are not difficult to implement for tree structures, but they are fairly difficult to perform efficiently in the general case. The general problem will not truly be solved until efficient mechanisms have been designed for these two steps. Notice also that the degree to which Algorithm 4.2 actually decomposes the problem is unpredictable, as might be suggested by Exercise 3.6.

4.3 EXERCISES

3.1 Solve the three-job $\bar{F}$ problem with a single precedence constraint, as formulated at the beginning of this section.

3.2   Consider the algorithm presented in Exercise 4.4 of Chapter 2. Show how the algorithm would be extended to sequencing problems with precedence constraints. Hence prove Theorem 4.1 as a special case.

3.3   Develop a sequencing rule that will minimize $\bar{F}_w$ for the single-machine problem with job strings (i.e., generalize Theorem 4.2.).

3.4   Prove Lemmas 4.1 and 4.2.

3.5   Describe an algorithm that will minimize $\bar{F}_w$ for the single-machine problem with assembly tree precedence structure.

3.6   Find an optimal sequence for the problem in Figure 4.5. What is the optimal initial set?

3.7   Consider the least cost testing sequence problem (Exercise 3.6 of Chapter 2). Discuss how realistic testing systems may actually involve precedence constraints among tests. What precedence structures would you expect to find?

3.8   Find the sequence that minimizes $\bar{F}$ in the following problem:

$$\begin{array}{ccccc} j & 1 & 2 & 3 & 4 \\ t_j & 8 & 6 & 3 & 1 \end{array}$$

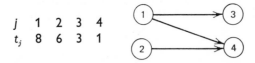

3.9   The following problem arises in the sorting of mail by destination. Mail must be sorted into a rather large number of categories (e.g., 90,000 zip codes), but devices available can separate their inputs into only a relatively small number of categories (e.g., 10). Therefore, full sorting of input requires several sorting passes, with progressively more refined classification each time, until sorting by specific destination is achieved. At each stage a sorting device takes as input an unsorted or partially sorted subset of objects and generates several subsubsets. (These may include both final sorts and items requiring even further sorting.)

Suppose that the distribution of mail among destination categories is known. Formulate the problem of minimizing the average time objects spend in the sorting process, assuming that only one sorting device is available.

4.   SEQUENCE-DEPENDENT SETUP TIMES

In many realistic problems setup times depend on the type of job just completed as well as on the job to be processed. In such situations it is not valid to absorb the setup time for job j in the processing time t_j, and explicit modifications must be made. The time interval in which job j occupies the single machine is expressed $s_{ij} + t_j$, where i is the job that precedes j in sequence, s_{ij} is the setup time required for job j after job i is completed, and t_j is the amount of direct processing time required to complete job j.

Sequence-dependent setups are commonly found where a single facility produces several different kinds of items, or where a multipurpose machine carries out an assortment of tasks. The use of a single system to produce different chemical compounds may require that some amount of cleansing be carried out between process runs on different compounds, to insure that tolerably low impurity levels are maintained. Furthermore, it should not be hard to envision situations in which the extent of the cleansing depends on both the chemical most recently processed and the chemical about to be processed. Similar setup properties can be found, for instance, in the production of different colors of paint, strengths of detergent, and blends of fuel. The same observations apply to certain assembly lines where retooling, inspection, or rearrangement of work stations represent the setup activity.

For example, suppose that a process line manufactures four types of gasoline: racing fuel, premium, regular, and leadfree. The matrix of setup times, s_{ij}, might resemble the one shown in Table 4.2. In a full production

Table 4.2

		(1)	(2)	(3)	(4)
Racing	(1)	—	30	50	90
Premium	(2)	40	—	20	80
Regular	(3)	30	30	—	60
Leadfree	(4)	20	15	10	—

cycle, the amount of nonproductive time (i.e., setup time) depends on the sequence in which these fuels are manufactured. In particular, the total amount of setup time in each of the six distinct sequences that include all four products is different.

$$s(1\text{–}2\text{–}3\text{–}4\text{–}1) \qquad 30 + 20 + 60 + 20 = 130$$
$$s(1\text{–}2\text{–}4\text{–}3\text{–}1) \qquad 30 + 80 + 10 + 30 = 150$$
$$s(1\text{–}3\text{–}2\text{–}4\text{–}1) \qquad 50 + 30 + 80 + 20 = 180$$
$$s(1\text{–}3\text{–}4\text{–}2\text{–}1) \qquad 50 + 60 + 15 + 40 = 165$$
$$s(1\text{–}4\text{–}2\text{–}3\text{–}1) \qquad 90 + 15 + 20 + 30 = 155$$
$$s(1\text{–}4\text{–}3\text{–}2\text{–}1) \qquad 90 + 10 + 30 + 40 = 170$$

The implicit assumption in these numbers is that production is continuous, and that a cyclic plan is always followed.

In the basic single-machine problem, the time to complete all jobs is a constant. The length of time required to complete all jobs is called the *makespan* and will be denoted M. With sequence-dependent setups, however, the makespan depends on which sequence is chosen:

$$F_{[1]} = s_{0,[1]} + t_{[1]}$$

$$F_{[2]} = s_{[1],[2]} + t_{[2]} + F_{[1]}$$

$$F_{[n-1]} = s_{[n-2],[n-1]} + t_{[n-1]} + F_{[n-2]}$$

$$F_{[n]} = s_{[n-1],[n]} + t_{[n]} + F_{[n-1]}$$

where state 0 corresponds to an initial idle state. Also, if state $n + 1$ is treated as a terminal idle state (perhaps identical to state 0), then the schedule makespan is

$$M = F_{[n]} + s_{[n],[n+1]} = \sum_{j=1}^{n+1} s_{[j-1],[j]} + \sum_{j=1}^{n} t_j$$

Since the second summation is a constant, the problem of minimizing makespan is equivalent to minimizing the first summation. This sum represents the total nonproductive time in the full sequence, beginning and ending in the idle state.

The type of structure represented by this makespan problem is often interpreted as a "traveling salesman problem." In the classical formulation, a salesman must visit clients in each of n cities on business. The salesman wishes to choose a tour that will take him to each city once and only once and that will return him to his point of origin. Given the distances between all pairs of cities, the salesman's task is to find the tour with minimum total travel distance. In the sequencing problem, s_{ij} (the setup time for job j when it immediately follows job i) corresponds to the distance between city i and city j. Of course, the literal version of the traveling salesman problem involves a symmetric distance matrix ($s_{ij} = s_{ji}$), but this need not be the case in the sequencing problem (see Table 4.2). The lack of symmetry does not, however, seem to make the traveling salesman problem significantly more difficult to solve.

In the following subsections we shall investigate various solution approaches for the traveling salesman problem. Optimizing procedures include dynamic programming and branch and bound, two of the general purpose methodologies introduced in Chapter 3. Heuristic procedures will also be treated, since there has been considerable interest in developing good heuristic techniques for the traveling salesman problem.

The following discussions deal with a given s_{ij} matrix, under the assumption that if an idle state is required in the formulation of the problem, it has already been included in the matrix. It is also convenient to use the terminology of the classical problem (and thus to refer to cities and distance rather than to jobs and setup time, for example).

4.1   A Dynamic Programming Solution

With some slight modifications the dynamic programming approach can be adapted to solve the traveling salesman problem. The important structural modification is that a solution must correspond to a complete cycle, in which the tour returns to its starting point. Let J denote a subset of the n cities and choose a city i_0 arbitrarily and designate it as the origin of the tour. Now let K denote the set of all cities, excluding i_0. The optimal tour can be interpreted as consisting of the sets $\{i_0\}$, S, $\{i\}$, J, $\{i_0\}$. In other words, the tour begins at city i_0, proceeds to the cities in set S, visits a particular city i, then proceeds to the cities in set J and finally returns to i_0. Sets S and J have no elements in common, and neither contains i or i_0. Also, if J contains k cities, then S must contain $n–k–2$ cities. With this structure, an optimal tour can be described by the principle of optimality. Consider that portion of the tour that starts at city i and returns to i_0. This portion must be the shortest possible path from city i that passes through the cities in J before reaching city i_0. (If this were not the case, the tour could not be an optimum.) Now define

$$f(i, J) = \text{the length of the shortest path from city } i \text{ passing}$$
$$\text{through the cities in } J \text{ and returning to city } i_0$$

Then the length of the optimal tour is given by

$$f(i_0, K) = \min_{j \in K} [s_{i_0, j} + f(j, K - \{j\})]$$

where in general

$$f(i, J) = \min_{j \in J} [s_{ij} + f(j, J - \{j\})]$$

and where

$$f(i, \phi) = s_{i, i_0}$$

By using these recursion relations we can construct the optimal tour by first considering sets J of size 1, then sets J of size 2, and so on until enough information has been accumulated to calculate $f(i_0, K)$. Table 4.3 displays the calculations for the 4×4 matrix of Table 4.2, yielding an optimal processing sequence (as seen previously) of 1–2–3–4–1.

This dynamic programming approach to solving the traveling salesman problem is quite similar to the general dynamic programming approach presented in Chapter 3. Perhaps the only major difference in the structure of this formulation is that the function lying at the heart of the recursion is a function of two arguments instead of one. Some of the computational differences between the two formulations are suggested by the calculations in Exercise 4.1.

4.2   A Branch and Bound Solution

Another general purpose methodology that can be adapted to the traveling salesman problem is the technique of branch and bound. In fact, one of the

Table 4.3

Let $i_0 = 1$

STAGE 1

$$f(2, \phi) = 40$$
$$f(3, \phi) = 30$$
$$f(4, \phi) = 20$$

STAGE 2

$$f(2, \{3\}) = 20 + 30 = 50 \qquad f(2, \{4\}) = 80 + 20 = 100$$
$$f(3, \{2\}) = 30 + 40 = 70 \qquad f(3, \{4\}) = 60 + 20 = 80$$
$$f(4, \{2\}) = 15 + 40 = 55 \qquad f(4, \{3\}) = 10 + 30 = 40$$

STAGE 3

$$f(2, \{3, 4\}) = \min [20 + 80, 80 + 40] = 100$$
$$f(3, \{2, 4\}) = \min [30 + 100, 60 + 55] = 115$$
$$f(4, \{2, 3\}) = \min [15 + 50, 10 + 70] = 65$$

STAGE 4

$$f(1, \{2, 3, 4\}) = \min [30 + 100, 50 + 115, 90 + 65] = 130$$

Optimal tour: 1–2–3–4–1
Distance: 130

---

earliest research studies dealing with branch and bound was carried out by Little et al. (*10*) in the solution of traveling salesman problems. The general concepts underlying the branch and bound approach were discussed in Section 5 of Chapter 3, and they can be applied in several different ways in the traveling salesman case. The specific approach developed in (*10*) is worth examining in detail because it helps illustrate the flexibility inherent in the method.

The partitioning scheme creates two subproblems at all levels, one subproblem containing a specific element of the matrix constrained to be part of the solution, and the other subproblem prohibiting that same element. For example, a partition of the original problem might require the $(1, 3)$ element to be in the tour of one subproblem and prohibit the $(1, 3)$ element in the complementary subproblem.

Lower bounds for a given s_{ij} matrix may be calculated by a method called *reduction*. Since any feasible solution contains exactly one element in each row, it is possible to subtract a constant from any row without altering the relative desirability of any feasible solution. In other words, this subtraction reduces the length of all tours by the same constant and, in particular, would not affect which of the feasible tours is optimal. In the reduction process, the minimum row element is the constant chosen for subtraction from each row.

Then, similarly, the minimum element can be subtracted from each column. The matrix that emerges has at least one zero element in every row and in every column, and the sum of the subtraction constants is a lower bound on the optimal solution. In this way, the reduction process identifies a distance that must be part of any feasible tour and that therefore is a lower bound on the optimum tour. To illustrate these steps specifically, consider the traveling salesman problem associated with the matrix in Table 4.4a.

Table 4.4a

P				
—	4	8	6	8
5	—	7	11	13
11	6	—	8	4
5	7	2	—	2
10	9	7	5	—

Table 4.4b

P (reduced)				
—	0	4	2	4
0	—	2	6	8
7	2	—	4	0
3	5	0	—	0
5	4	2	0	—

Table 4.4c

P (reduced)				
—	0^4	4	2	4
0^5	—	2	6	8
7	2	—	4	0^2
3	5	0^2	—	0^0
5	4	2	0^4	—

Reduction. By subtracting the minimum element in each row, the original matrix is reduced to the one shown in Table 4.4b. The sum of the elements subtracted is 20, which is a lower bound on the optimal solution. At this point there is at least one zero in every row and column. If this were not the case, the minimum element could be subtracted from each column that did not contain a zero.

Branching. The algorithm next partitions the problem by forcing one of the zero elements to be part of the tour on one branch and prohibiting it on the other branch. To decide which zero element to choose, one logical method is to select the zero that, when prohibited, would permit the largest possible reduction in the matrix. Therefore each zero element is labeled with the sum of the minimum element remaining in its row and the minimum element remaining in its column, as shown in Table 4.4c. Element $(2, 1)$ is chosen. The original problem is partitioned into two subproblems: P_{21}, which contains the $(2, 1)$ element, and $P_{\overline{21}}$, which prohibits the $(2, 1)$ element.

Bounding. The reduction procedure can now be applied to each subproblem. In P_{21}, since the $(2, 1)$ element will be in the solution, clearly the $(1, 2)$ element must be prohibited if the solution is to form a complete tour. In addition, elements $(2, j)$ for $j \neq 1$ and elements $(i, 1)$ for $i \neq 2$ can also be eliminated. The matrix that results (Table 4.5a) can be reduced to the matrix shown in Table 4.5b, which has a bound of 24. Meanwhile $P_{\overline{21}}$ can be reduced as shown in Table 4.6, and has a bound of 25, as anticipated.

Table 4.5a

P_{21}				
—	—	4	2	4
0*	—	—	—	—
—	2	—	4	0
—	5	0	—	0
—	4	2	0	—

Table 4.5b

P_{21}				
—	—	2	0^2	2
0*	—	—	—	—
—	0^2	—	4	0^0
—	3	0^2	—	0^0
—	2	2	0^2	—

Table 4.6

$P_{\overline{2}\overline{1}}$				
—	0^4	4	2	4
—	—	0^4	4	6
4	2	—	4	0^2
0^2	5	0^0	—	0^0
2	4	2	0^4	—

At the next stage, either subproblem could be partitioned further. Suppose the strategy is always to partition the subproblem that is closest to being fully solved (which is essentially backtracking). Under this strategy, P_{21} is partitioned next. As indicated by Table 4.5b, several zero elements are equally desirable according to the selection rule. Such ties can be broken arbitrarily. Therefore let element (5, 4) be the basis for the next partition. Thus P_{21} is partitioned into subproblems $P_{21.54}$ and $P_{21.\overline{54}}$, which can both be reduced. These two subproblems have bounds of 26 (see Tables 4.7a and

Table 4.7a

$P_{21,54}$				
—	—	0^0	—	0^0
0*	—	—	—	—
—	0^0	—	—	0^0
—	3	0^3	—	—
—	—	—	0*	—

Table 4.7b

$P_{21,\overline{54}}$				
—	—	2	0	2
0*	—	—	—	—
—	0	—	4	0
—	3	0	—	0
—	0	0	—	—

4.7b). The list of unsolved problems and their lower bounds becomes

$$P_{21.54} \quad (26)$$
$$P_{21.\overline{54}} \quad (26)$$
$$P_{\overline{2}\overline{1}} \quad (25)$$

Once again, the problem that is closest to being fully solved is partitioned. In $P_{21.54}$, the desirable zero element is (4, 3). The list becomes:

$$P_{21.54.43} \quad (26)$$
$$P_{21.54.\overline{43}} \quad (29)$$
$$P_{21.\overline{54}} \quad (26)$$
$$P_{\overline{2}\overline{1}} \quad (25)$$

The problem $P_{21.54.43}$ is, in effect, fully solved because only one feasible tour could include the elements $(2, 1)$, $(5, 4)$, and $(4, 3)$. The complete tour must be 2–1–5–4–3–2, a solution with a value of 26. The fact that a trial solution has been found with a tour of length 26 allows two other branches of the tree to be fathomed. In particular, no completion of $P_{21,54,\overline{43}}$ or of $P_{21,\overline{54}}$ can possibly improve on this trial solution, since their bounds are already at or above 26. The tree structure at this stage is shown in Figure 4.6a.

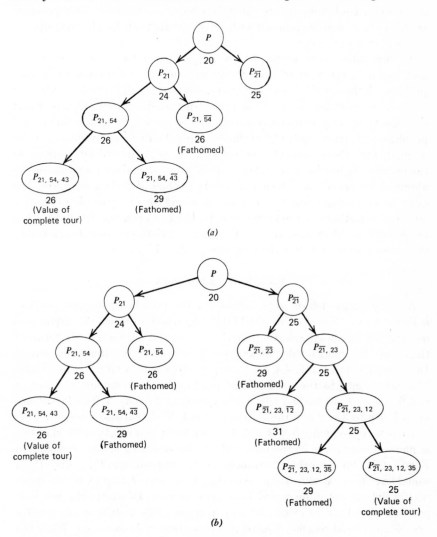

Figure 4.6

The branching tree for the example traveling salesman problem, with bounds shown below each node. (a) The tree is shown when the first complete tour has been encountered. (b) The tree is shown at the final stage.

One subproblem, $P_{\overline{21}}$, remains to be solved. Proceeding from this subproblem (Table 4.6), we can find a new trial solution with a value of 25, and the solution tree that results is shown in Figure 4.6b. At this stage the new trial solution 1–2–3–5–4–1) has a value of 25. Moreover, since all unsolved subproblems have bounds of 26 or more, no feasible solution in any of these subproblems can be better than this trial solution. Also, because the solved and unsolved subproblems are exhaustive partitions of the original problem, there can be no feasible solution with a value better than 25. The trial solution is therefore an optimum.

To summarize, it is worth interpreting the general comments on branch and bound in the light of the specific structure of the traveling salesman problem. Although the branching tree enountered in the traveling salesman problem is somewhat different from the structure illustrated in Chapter 3, it does illustrate the general characteristics listed earlier: it replaces an original problem with (two) mutually exclusive and exhaustive subproblems of the original, and these subproblems are smaller, partially solved versions of the original. Lower bounds for the original problem and all subproblems are obtained via reduction, which is a simple method of finding distances that must be part of any feasible solution. It would also be possible to employ alternative methods of obtaining bounds. For example, one could solve the assignment problem associated with the matrix[1] to obtain a lower bound that would often be better than the one produced by reduction.

4.3 Heuristic Solutions

A fairly simple heuristic procedure for the traveling salesman problem is known as the "Closest Unvisited City" algorithm, in which the sequence is constructed by always selecting the closest city not yet visited. (In terms of the sequencing model, this rule amounts to shortest setup time sequencing.) In the problem of Table 4.4, for example, suppose that city 5 is the origin. The closest city to the origin, corresponding to the minimum element in row 5, is city 4. Excluding city 5, the closest to 4 is city 3. The closest unvisited city to 3 is 2 and the closest to 2 is 1. The heuristic procedure thus constructs the sequence 5–4–3–2–1–5, which has a tour length of 26. Had this sequence been known at the outset of the backtracking scheme depicted in Figure 4.6a, the branches corresponding to subproblems $P_{21,54}$ and $P_{21,\overline{54}}$ would have been fathomed as soon as they were created, improving the speed with which an optimum would have been located. Of course the heuristic procedure need not be evaluated only in terms of its usefulness as part of a branch and bound scheme, because it is important in its own right. While the

---

[1] Here is the assignment problem. Choose n elements from the matrix, with exactly one element chosen in each row and exactly one in each column, such that their sum is a minimum. (Such a solution would not necessarily form a tour.)

closest-unvisited-city algorithm cannot guarantee optimal solutions, its importance may lie in its ability to generate good solutions rapidly in problems where the cost of implementing an optimum-seeking method is prohibitive.

Several variations of this heuristic procedure have been developed that preserve the essence of the closest unvisited city approach. The first variation involves an interpretation of "closest." If the original s_{ij} matrix is used as a basis, then absolute distances are used to identify a closest city. Alternatively, the reduced s_{ij} matrix can be used, in which case relative distances are used to identify a closest city. The second variation involves a look-ahead feature that permits a closest unvisited pair of cities to be added to the tour. Under this variation the origin is again chosen arbitrarily. Then, instead of examining the path from the origin to $(n - 1)$ other cities, this method examines the path from the origin to $(n - 1)(n - 2)$ ordered pairs of unvisited cities and adds to the tour the pair associated with minimum distance. The third variation involves several applications of the algorithm: instead of choosing the origin city once, arbitrarily, the procedure can be applied n times, each time using a different city as an origin. Then the best of the n heuristic solutions can be selected. This variation follows one of the principles recommended in Chapter 3: a heuristic procedure is often strengthened by the capacity to choose among several solutions. In short, these three variations in fact describe eight closest-unvisited-city algorithms, as listed in Table 4.8. The

Table 4.8

Algorithm	Variations
1	Absolute distances, no look-ahead, arbitrary origin
2	Absolute distances, no look-ahead, all origins
3	Absolute distances, look-ahead, arbitrary origin
4	Absolute distances, look-ahead, all origins
5	Relative distances, no look-ahead, arbitrary origin
6	Relative distances, no look-ahead, all origins
7	Relative distances, look-ahead, arbitrary origin
8	Relative distances, look-ahead, all origins

computational effectiveness of this heuristic strategy has been examined in detail by Gavett (7). His experimentation suggests that it might not be unreasonable to expect the closest-unvisited-city algorithm to produce tours whose lengths are within 10 % of optimum for $n \leq 20$, but that performance of the algorithm deteriorates if there is considerable variability in the elements of the s_{ij} matrix.

A rather different approach to the problem is suggested by the work of Karg and Thompson (*9*). The method begins with a randomly selected pair of cities, constituting a tour of length 2. Then a third city is inserted in order to minimize the resulting three-city tour; then a fourth city is inserted, and so on, until a complete tour has been constructed. Suppose, for example, that the method is applied to the problem in Table 4.4, with the cities taken in numbered order. The "seed" pair 1–2 forms a two-city tour. A three-city tour is selected by evaluating the tours 3–1–2 and 1–3–2. (The latter has the shorter tour.) A four-city tour is formed by inserting job 4 somewhere in the three-city tour. In other words, a tour is selected from among 4–1–3–2, 1–4–3–2, and 1–3–4–2. Finally, at the last stage a full tour is selected from among four candidates, producing a tour of length 26. Just as the closest-unvisited-city algorithm is sensitive to which city is designated as an origin, the Karg-Thompson approach is sensitive to which pair of cities is designated as a seed and to the order in which jobs are considered for insertion. Heuristic rules for these facets of the algorithm have not been thoroughly explored, but one way to proceed is to repeat the algorithm several times, each time beginning with a seed pair that is randomly selected.

The general purpose suboptimal methods described in Chapter 3 can also be employed in the traveling salesman problem. Indeed, the seminal paper on discrete search methods dealt extensively with the traveling salesman problem (*11*) and examined the performance of several neighborhood structures on a variety of test problems.

4.4   An Integer Programming Formulation

An integer programming approach to the traveling salesman problem is interesting to examine, even though existing computational results have indicated that the branch and bound approach seems to be a more efficient optimizing technique. However, the prospect of advances in integer programming suggests that this approach may well be a more viable alternative in the future. In addition, the traveling salesman problem helps illustrate the flexibility of linear integer programming formulations.

The major decision variable is an indicator variable, defined as follows:

$x_{ij} = 1$ if city j immediately follows city i in the tour

$x_{ij} = 0$ otherwise

The length of a tour can then be written as

$$\text{Tour length} = \sum_{i=1}^{n} \sum_{j=1}^{n} s_{ij} x_{ij} \tag{1}$$

where the x_{ij} values must represent a valid tour. In particular, only one city can immediately follow city i in a given tour, so that a feasible solution must satisfy

$$\sum_{j=1}^{n} x_{ij} = 1 \quad \text{for} \quad i = 1, 2, \ldots, n \tag{2}$$

Similarly, only one city can immediately precede city j in a given tour, requiring that

$$\sum_{i=1}^{n} x_{ij} = 1 \quad \text{for} \quad j = 1, 2, \ldots, n \tag{3}$$

Finally, a constraint must be imposed to insure that a selection of x_{ij} actually represents a feasible, complete tour. To accomplish this task, define n additional indicator variables, u_i, and require that

$$u_i - u_j + n x_{ij} \leq n - 1 \quad \text{for} \quad i \neq j \quad \text{and} \quad 1 \leq i, j \leq n \tag{4}$$

In order to demonstrate that this type of constraint provides the correct condition, first consider what happens when a set of x_{ij} corresponds to a tour of only k of the cities, where $k < n$. Suppose V denotes the set of pairs (i, j) for which $x_{ij} = 1$ in this subtour. Then the summation of (4) over the k pairs (i, j), which are elements of V, will yield

$$\sum_V u_i - \sum_V u_j + n \sum_V x_{ij} \leq \sum_V (n - 1)$$

$$nk \leq (n - 1)k$$

which is a contradiction that follows no matter how the u_i are chosen. Now it remains to show that a complete tour of all n cities will correspond to a feasible tour. In particular, consider what happens when u_i is set equal to position in sequence relative to city 1. Thus $u_1 = 1$ and $u_i = 2$ for the city that follows city 1 in the tour. In general, then, let $u_i = [i]$ relative to this arbitrary origin, city 1. It follows that $u_i - u_j \leq n - 1$, so that (4) is satisfied for all pairs (i, j) such that $x_{ij} = 0$. For the pairs on the tour, $u_i - u_j = -1$ whenever $x_{ij} = 1$, so that (4) is satisfied as a strict equality. In short, the integer programming formulation is

$$\text{Minimize} \quad \sum_{i=1}^{n} \sum_{j=1}^{n} s_{ij} x_{ij}$$

$$\text{Subject to} \quad \sum_{i=1}^{n} x_{ij} = 1 \qquad 1 \leq j \leq n$$

$$\sum_{j=1}^{n} x_{ij} = 1 \qquad 1 \leq i \leq n$$

$$u_i - u_j + n x_{ij} \leq n - 1 \qquad 1 \leq i \leq n; \, 1 \leq j \leq n, \, i \neq j$$

$$x_{ij} \geq 0 \quad \text{and integer}$$

$$u_i \geq 0$$

The dimensions of this formulation do not appear to be unreasonably large. There are n constraints of type (2), n of type (3), and $n(n-1)$ of type (4). There are $n(n-1)$ integer variables x_{ij} and n additional variables u_i. Therefore the complete formulation contains $n^2 + n$ constraints and n^2 variables. The computational features of the approach have not been reported in more than a decade, although they were not promising originally.

4.4 EXERCISES

4.1 For the dynamic programming formulation given in Section 4.1, derive a formula for (a) the number of additions and (b) the number of comparisons required for the solution of an n-city problem. Compare these with the numbers derived for the general purpose description (Exercise 3.1 of Chapter 3) for $n = 5$, 10, and 20. Which algorithm is computationally more efficient in general?

4.2 In the optimal solution to the traveling salesman problem for the matrix shown below (which includes the matrix in Table 4.4), does the optimal tour for the matrix in Table 4.4 appear intact as part of the larger optimum?

—	4	8	6	8	2
5	—	7	11	13	4
11	6	—	8	4	3
5	7	2	—	2	5
10	9	7	5	—	2
8	4	3	6	5	—

4.3 List the structural differences between the branch and bound approach of Section 4.2 and the general approach illustrated in Chapter 3.

4.4 For the traveling salesman problem in Table 4.4, draw the branching tree that emerges when a jumptracking strategy is used.

4.5 Suppose that an initial phase is added to the backtracking algorithm for the traveling salesman problem. In particular, suppose that the closest-unvisited-city algorithm is employed as an initial phase for the problem in Table 4.4. Draw the solution tree that emerges when

    (a) City 2 is chosen as the origin and Algorithm 1 of Table 4.8 is used.

    (b) Algorithm 6 of Table 4.8 is used.

5. RELATED PROBABILISTIC RESULTS

In Section 4.2 we found that when job arrivals are not simultaneous, the difference between preempt-resume and preempt-repeat revolved around the question of advance information. In the preempt-resume case, transitive optimal sequencing rules could be adapted directly, even when no information about future arrivals is available. In the preempt-repeat case, however, the decision to begin a job that might not be completed may depend on advance knowledge about job processing or arrivals during some future period. This structure suggests that somewhat different techniques are required to analyze models in which the future behavior of jobs is uncertain. The purpose of this section is to survey the major results on sequencing in probabilistic systems. Even though these results are based on rather different and more sophisticated techniques than in deterministic problems, it is encouraging to find how similar some of the probabilistic results are.

Suppose that job j has a processing time that is a random variable and that its expected value, $E[t_j]$, is known. Then when the objective is to minimize $E[\bar{F}_w]$, the optimal sequence in the static problem is given by

$$\frac{E[t_{[1]}]}{w_{[1]}} \leq \frac{E[t_{[2]}]}{w_{[2]}} \leq \cdots \leq \frac{E[t_{[n]}]}{w_{[n]}}$$

In particular, if the processing times happen to be constants, this rule obviously reduces to WSPT sequencing.

Suppose again that job j has a random processing time. When due dates are fixed, the EDD sequence minimizes

$$\max_j \{\Pr [L_j \geq 0]\}$$

that is, the maximum probability of being late. In particular, if there exists a sequence in which there is no probability that any job will be late, then EDD sequencing yields such a sequence.

Suppose that job j has a random processing time and also a random due date, having an expected value $E[d_j]$. Then when the objective is to minimize the maximum expected lateness, $\max_j \{E[L_j]\}$, the optimal sequence is given by

$$E[d_{[1]}] \leq E[d_{[2]}] \leq \cdots \leq E[d_{[n]}]$$

which is again a generalization of the deterministic result.

Finally, if job arrivals are intermittent and their arrival times are not known in advance, an appropriate model is a single-channel queue. The topic of sequencing in queues has been investigated in some studies of priority queues, but relatively few results are available. The performance measures of primary interest in queueing studies are usually mean job flowtime or mean number of jobs in the system, two measures that are intimately related by the relationships discussed in Chapter 2. In Poisson queues with no preemption allowed, it is known that SPT minimizes both mean flowtime and mean queue length and that WSPT minimizes their weighted versions. In general queues operating under a preempt-resume discipline, the optimal rule for mean flowtime and mean queue length is SRPT. In each of these situations the queueing result is an obvious extension of the deterministic single-machine result. Whether similar extensions can be developed for tardiness-oriented measures remains an open question. Details on the results listed above can be found, respectively, in references *12, 2, 4, 3, 5,* and *13.*

6. SUMMARY

Generalizations of the basic single-machine model expand its applicability but lead to new difficulties in obtaining solutions. In some cases the optimal solution to a problem involving the basic model can be directly adapted to the analogous problem involving the generalized model. At other times, however, a direct adaptation is not possible and new approaches are required.

Dynamic models, in which jobs become available intermittently, require that assumptions regarding job preemption be carefully scrutinized. If jobs can be processed in a preempt-resume mode, no idle time need ever be inserted in a schedule, and dispatching procedures can be employed. On the other hand, if the preempt-repeat mode applies, or if preemption is prohibited, then inserted idle time can be justified and look-ahead procedures can be useful in determining schedules. Moreover, even simple sequencing problems in the latter model appear to require general purpose techniques for finding optimal schedules, and the branch and bound approach appears to be quite effective whenever the corresponding preempt-resume problem is easily solved.

The generalizations of EDD sequencing and WSPT sequencing to dependent job sets suggest that optimal rules may often involve properties of job modules (feasible subsets or initial sets) rather than the properties of individual jobs. Also, the implementation of optimal sequencing rules may often be a two-phase procedure in which the sequencing phase is preceded by a labeling phase. Thus in the $T_{\max}$ problem, the first phase consists of identifying a value of d'_j for each job and, in the $\bar{F}_w$ problem with tree-structured precedence constraints, the first phase consists of calculating a value of z_j for each job.

Sequence-dependent setup times create difficulties even in the optimal solution of the makespan problem, but at least the traveling salesman problem is usually amenable to the use of branch and bound methods, or to the use of heuristic methods in large problems. Because the makespan problem has proved to be so challenging, there have been virtually no significant attempts to examine other performance measures in models with sequence-dependent setups.

While the assumptions cited in Chapter 2 may have seemed somewhat restrictive, the array of extensions considered in this chapter enrich the basic model and demonstrate that the usefulness of the model is actually quite broad. One aspect of assumption C1 that was preserved throughout, however, was the availability of only a single machine. In the next chapters, we investigate more general models in which several machines are present.

4.6. COMPUTATIONAL EXERCISES

6.1 Design and test a branch and bound algorithm for minimizing $\bar{F}$ in the dynamic single-machine problem with no preemption allowed.

6.2 Create a set of test problems in order to compare the effectiveness of each of the following heuristic procedures for solving the traveling salesman problem:

(a) The closest-unvisited-city Algorithm.
(b) The Karg–Thompson procedure.
(c) A neighborhood search procedure.
(d) A biased random sampling procedure.

For each of the four heuristic approaches examine two of the variations that exist for the algorithm.

6.3 Investigate the minimization of $\bar{F}$ in the single-machine problem with sequence-dependent setup times.

REFERENCES

1. Baker, K. R., and Su, Z. "Sequencing with Due-dates and Early Start Times to Minimize Maximum Tardiness," *Naval Research Logistics Quarterly*, Vol. 21, No. 1 (March, 1974).
2. Banerjee, B. P. "Single Facility Sequencing with Random Execution Times," *Operations Research*, Vol. 13, No. 3 (May, 1965).
3. Cobham, A. "Priority Assignment in Waiting Line Problems," *Operations Research*, Vol. 2, No. 1 (February, 1954).
4. Crabill, T. B., and Maxwell, W. L. "Single Machine Sequencing with Random Processing Times and Random Due-Dates," *Naval Research Logistics Quarterly*, Vol. 16, No. 4 (December, 1969).
5. Fife, D. W. "Scheduling with Random Arrivals and Linear Loss Functions," *Management Science*, Vol. 11, No. 3 (January, 1965).
6. Gapp, W., Mankekar, D. S., and Mitten, L. G. "Sequencing Operations to Minimize In-Process Inventory Costs," *Management Science*, Vol. 11, No. 3 (January, 1965).
7. Gavett, J. W. "Three Heuristic Rules for Sequencing Jobs to a Single Production Facility," *Management Science*, Vol. 11, No. 8 (June, 1965).
8. Horn, W. A. "Single Machine Job Sequencing with Treelike Precedence Ordering and Linear Delay Penalties," *SIAM Journal on Applied Mathematics*, Vol. 23, No. 2 (September, 1972).
9. Karg, R., and Thompson, G. L. "A Heuristic Approach to Solving Travelling Salesman Problems," *Management Science*, Vol. 10, No. 2 (January, 1964).
10. Little, J. D. C., Murty, K. G., Sweeny, D. W., and Karel, C. "An Algorithm for the Traveling Salesman Problem," *Operations Research*, Vol. 11, No. 6 (November, 1963).
11. Reiter, S., and Sherman, G. "Discrete Optimizing," *SIAM Journal*, Vol. 13, No. 3 (September, 1965).

12. Rothkopf, M. H. "Scheduling with Random Service Times," *Management Science*, Vol. 12, No. 9 (May, 1966).

13. Schrage, L. E. "A Proof of the Optimality of the Shortest Remaining Processing Time Discipline," *Operations Research*, Vol. 6, No. 3 (May–June, 1968).

14. Sidney, J. B. "One Machine Sequencing with Precedence Relations and Deferral Costs," Working Papers No. 124 and 125, Faculty of Commerce and Business Administration, University of British Columbia (April, 1972).

CHAPTER 5
PARALLEL-MACHINE MODELS

1. INTRODUCTION

According to the definition given in Chapter 1, the process of scheduling in general requires both sequencing and resource allocation decisions. When there is only a single resource, as in the single-machine model, the allocation of that resource is completely determined by sequencing decisions. Consequently there is no distinction between these two decision problems in the models covered in the foregoing chapters. To begin to appreciate this distinction we must examine multiple processor models. This chapter and the two that follow are addressed to the elementary multiple processor models: parallel machine systems, flow shop systems, and job shop systems. Section 2 of this chapter treats parallel machine problems involving identical processors and independent jobs; Section 3 treats dependent jobs.

2. PARALLEL IDENTICAL PROCESSORS AND INDEPENDENT JOBS

In scheduling problems it is often possible to take advantage of parallelism in resource structure. A simple context for investigating the effects of parallel resources is the problem of single-stage sequencing with several machines. As in the basic model, suppose there are n single-operation jobs simultaneously available at time zero. Also suppose that there are m identical machines available for processing, and that a job can be processed by at most one machine at a time. Once again, it is possible to deal with the fundamental performance measures, only this time scheduling decisions will reflect resource parallelism.

2.1 Minimizing Makespan

In the basic single-machine model, the makespan is equal to a constant for any sequence of n given jobs; therefore there was no makespan problem to consider in the single-processor case. In the multiple-processor case, however, the makespan problem is no longer trivial.

An elementary result for the makespan problem was presented by McNaughton (6) when the jobs are independent and preemption is permitted. With preemption allowed, the processing of a job may be interrupted and the remaining processing can be completed subsequently, perhaps on a different machine. The central property is that the minimum makespan, M^*, is given by

$$M^* = \max \left\{ \frac{1}{m} \sum_{j=1}^{n} t_j, \, \max_j [t_j] \right\} \qquad (1)$$

It should not be hard to see why this result might be valid, for equation 1 states that either the machines will be fully utilized throughout an optimal schedule or else the length of the longest job will determine the makespan. A method of constructing an optimal schedule follows.

ALGORITHM 5.1   McNAUGHTON'S ALGORITHM (6)
(To Minimize M with m Parallel, Identical Machines)

Step 1.   Select some job to begin on machine 1 at time zero.

Step 2.   Choose any unscheduled job and schedule it as early as possible on the same machine. Repeat this step until the machine is occupied beyond time M^* (or until all jobs are scheduled.)

Step 3.   Reassign the processing scheduled beyond M^* to the next machine instead, starting at time zero. Return to Step 2.

It is worth noting that this problem does not usually have a unique solution, and the construction method produces only one of potentially many optimal schedules. In particular, the method makes no attempt to minimize the number of preemptions. To the extent that a small setup might actually be involved with each preemption, the construction method would have to be modified to produce truly optimal schedules.

For example, consider the following job set in the case that $m = 3$ machines are available.

$$\begin{array}{c|cccccccc} \text{Job } j & 1 & 2 & 3 & 4 & 5 & 6 & 7 & 8 \\ t_j & 1 & 2 & 3 & 4 & 5 & 6 & 7 & 8 \end{array}$$

From equation 1, $M^* = 12$. The schedule in Figure 5.1 is a result of applying the construction method above to this eight-job set.

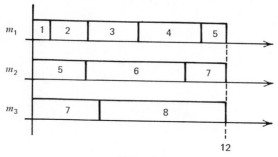

Figure 5.1

A preemptive schedule for the example problem, achieving an optimal makespan of 12.

If job preemption is prohibited, the problem of minimizing makespan is somewhat more difficult. No direct algorithm has been developed for calculating the optimal makespan or for constructing an optimal schedule. A simple yet effective heuristic procedure for constructing a schedule involves the use of longest processing time (LPT) scheduling as a dispatching mechanism.

ALGORITHM 5.2
(A Heuristic Procedure for Minimizing M)

Step 1. Construct an LPT ordering of the jobs.

Step 2. Schedule the jobs in order, each time assigning a job to the machine with the least amount of processing already assigned.

The LPT heuristic procedure cannot guarantee an optimal makespan (see Exercise 2.2). In the case of the eight-job set discussed above, the procedure yields the schedule shown in Figure 5.2, but it is possible to find a schedule with a makespan less than 13.

The efficiency of Algorithm 5.2 has been investigated as part of an experimental study reported by Kedia (5). A collection of test problems was created, and the lower bound on the optimal makespan in each problem was calculated from equation 1. Then the efficiency of Algorithm 5.2 was evaluated by calculating the ratio of the makespan obtained by the algorithm to this lower bound. The results for 18 test problems are displayed in Table 5.1. In evaluating the results, keep in mind that the efficiency ratio involves a lower bound rather than the optimum. Thus, if the ratio is 1.00, then the heuristic solution is optimal; but even when the ratio is greater than 1.00, the heuristic solution might still be optimal.

An integer programming formulation of the problem is not difficult to construct. Let y represent schedule makespan and let x_{ij} be an indicator

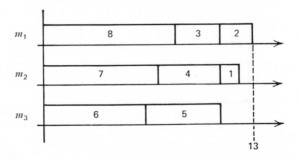

Figure 5.2
A nonpreemptive schedule resulting from the LPT heuristic procedure.

Table 5.1

Problem Size (n, m)	Range of t_j	Efficiency
(6, 3)	(1, 20)	1.00
(9, 3)	(1, 20)	1.00
(15, 3)	(1, 20)	1.00
(6, 3)	(20, 50)	1.05
(9 3)	(20, 50)	1.03
(15, 3)	(20, 50)	1.00
(8, 4)	(1, 20)	1.09
(12, 4)	(1, 20)	1.00
(20, 4)	(1, 20)	1.00
(8, 4)	(20, 50)	1.04
(12, 4)	(20, 50)	1.02
(20, 4)	(20, 50)	1.01
(10, 5)	(1, 20)	1.04
(15, 5)	(1, 20)	1.03
(25, 5)	(1, 20)	1.00
(10, 5)	(20, 50)	1.06
(15, 5)	(20, 50)	1.03
(25, 5)	(20, 50)	1.01

variable defined as follows:

$x_{ij} = 1$ if job i is assigned to machine j

$x_{ij} = 0$ otherwise

Then a feasible assignment will assign job i to only one machine, so that

$$\sum_{j=1}^{m} x_{ij} = 1 \qquad 1 \leq i \leq n$$

In addition the makespan must be at least as large as the processing time assigned to any machine, so that

$$y \geq \sum_{i=1}^{n} t_i x_{ij} \qquad 1 \leq j \leq m$$

The complete formulation is

Minimize y

Subject to $y - \sum_{i=1}^{n} t_i x_{ij} \geq 0 \qquad 1 \leq j \leq m$

$$\sum_{j=1}^{m} x_{ij} = 1 \qquad 1 \leq i \leq n$$

$$x_{ij} \geq 0 \qquad \text{and integer}$$

The formulation contains $(m + n)$ constraints in $mn + 1$ variables, but none of its computational properties have been investigated by researchers.

2.2 Minimizing Mean Flowtime and Weighted Mean Flowtime

The generalization to parallel machines of optimal sequencing properties for the basic single-machine model is fairly straightforward for $\bar{F}$ but surprisingly difficult for $\bar{F}_w$.

Consider first the problem of minimizing $\bar{F}$. Adopt the following notation:

$t_{i[j]}$ = processing time of the jth job in sequence on the ith machine

$F_{i[j]}$ = flowtime of the jth job in sequence on the ith machine

n_i = number of jobs processed by the ith machine

Then the objective function is

$$\bar{F} = \frac{1}{n} \sum_{i=1}^{m} \sum_{j=1}^{n_i} F_{i[j]} = \frac{1}{n} \sum_{i=1}^{m} \sum_{j=1}^{n_i} (n_i - j + 1) t_{i[j]}$$

As in the basic single-machine problem (see equation 1 in Chapter 2) a schedule is determined by the matching of integer coefficients $(n_i - j + 1)$ and processing times $(t_{i[j]})$, and the measure of performance corresponds to the scalar product of the coefficients vector and the processing times vector. The coefficients are

$$1, 2, \ldots, n_1, 1, 2, \ldots, n_2, \ldots, 1, 2, \ldots, n_m$$

Unlike the single-machine case, the parallel machine case allows some discretion in the choice of the coefficients, since the n_i are arbitrary, subject to $n_1 + n_2 + \cdots n_m = n$. Nevertheless, it should be clear that the scalar product cannot be minimized unless the n_i values satisfy

$$|n_i - n_k| \leq 1 \qquad \text{for all pairs } (i, k)$$

In particular, if n is an even multiple of m, it follows that the same number of jobs should be assigned to each machine: that is, $n_1 = n_2 = \cdots = n_m$. With the n_i values determined, an optimal schedule can be constructed by matching the processing times in nonincreasing order with the coefficients in nondecreasing order. In other words, the m longest jobs are assigned to m different machines, the next m longest jobs are assigned to m different machines, and so on, until all jobs are assigned. This construction can be interpreted as an m-jobs-at-a-time assignment procedure, but it should be observed that there are several optimal schedules, since the individual job-to-machine assignments are not specified at any stage of the algorithm. There is no need to consider scheduled preemptions.

For example, consider the six jobs in the following job set:

Job j	1	2	3	4	5	6
t_j	1	2	3	4	5	6

For two parallel machines the coefficients vector is $(1, 1, 2, 2, 3, 3)$. Therefore, jobs 5 and 6 are assigned to be last on different machines; then jobs 3 and 4 are assigned to different machines; and finally jobs 1 and 2 are assigned to be first on different machines. The algorithm might construct the following schedule:

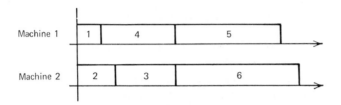

The algorithm might alternatively construct a different schedule, but one with the same optimal value of $\bar{F}$ (see Exercise 2.3).

With a little insight we can see how the m-jobs-at-a-time assignment procedure could be interpreted as a one-job-at-a-time procedure, as described by Algorithm 5.3.

ALGORITHM 5.3
(Minimizing $\bar{F}$ with Parallel Identical Machines)

Step 1.   Construct an SPT ordering of all the jobs.

Step 2.   To the machine with the least amount of processing already allocated, assign the next job on the ordered list of jobs. (Break ties arbitrarily.) Repeat until all jobs are assigned.

Except for ties, this algorithm will produce a unique schedule and, of course, it will be one of the schedules that might be produced by the m-jobs-at-a-time approach. Algorithm 5.3, however, has two special virtues. First, the algorithm is a dispatching procedure, so that scheduling decisions can be implemented in the order that they are made. Second, the algorithm can be extended in an obvious way to deterministic problems involving intermittent arrivals and to stochastic problems involving random arrivals. Neither property holds for the m-jobs-at-a-time procedure.

By contrast, no direct algorithm has been developed for constructing an optimal schedule when $\bar{F}_w$ is the criterion. Dynamic programming formulations are possible, but in this case the "curse of dimensionality" renders a dynamic programming procedure impractical for problems of even moderate size. Two theoretical properties apply to this problem. First, as should be evident, any optimal solution must have WSPT job orderings at each machine. (If this were not true, a simple pairwise interchange on one machine could improve the schedule.) Second, a lower bound on the optimum value of $\bar{F}_w$ can be computed, as shown by Eastman, Even, and Isaacs (3). Let

$B(1)$ = the minimal value of $\bar{F}_w$ for the given job set if there were only one machine (obtained via WSPT)

$B(n)$ = the minimal value of $\bar{F}_w$ for the given job set if there were n machines (obtained by assigning each job to a different machine)

Then a lower bound for m machines ($1 \leq m \leq n$) is

$$B(m) = \frac{1}{2m} [(m-1)B(1) + 2B(n)]$$

Clearly, $B = \max \{B(m), B(1)\}$ is also a valid lower bound, and may be better because of the rare occasions in which $B(m) < B(1)$.

An experimental study that compares several heuristic rules is reported in reference 1. The m-jobs-at-a-time procedure is incorporated into a heuristic procedure denoted H_m, which works in this way.

Step 1. Form a priority list of all unscheduled jobs according to some rule, R.

Step 2. Assign the first m jobs on the list to different machines. Repeat Step 2 until all jobs are scheduled and then go to Step 3.

Step 3. Apply WSPT sequencing to each machine.

The complementary heuristic procedure, called H_1, assigns one job at a time.

Step 1. Form a priority list of all unscheduled jobs according to some rule, R.

Step 2. Assign the first job on the list to the machine with the least amount of processing allocated. Repeat until all jobs have been assigned. Then go to Step 3.

Step 3. Apply WSPT sequencing to each machine.

To illustrate how these two procedures work, consider the job set shown below when $m = 5$.

Job j	1	2	3	4	5	6	7	8	9	10
t_j	5	21	16	6	26	19	50	41	32	22
w_j	4	5	3	1	4	2	5	4	3	2
t_j/w_j	1.2	4.2	5.3	6.0	6.5	9.5	10.0	10.2	10.7	11.0

Under H_m an initial ordering must be specified in Step 1. If WLPT is chosen, then the jobs are initially in the order 10–9–8– $\cdots$ –2–1. At the first stage jobs 10, 9, . . . , 6 are assigned to different machines, and at the second stage

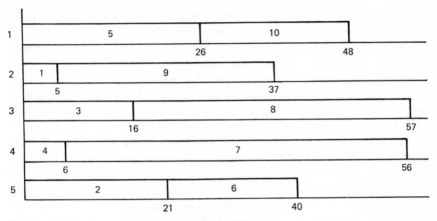

$$H_m \text{ (WLPT)}; \overline{F}_w = 32.67$$

Figure 5.3
A schedule resulting from the use of H_m with WLPT initial ordering.

Table 5.2

1.	Initial job list,			{10, 9, 8, 7, 6, 5, 4, 3, 2, 1}.

2. Assignment phase,

Stage	Processing Commitments	Jobs (w_j)	Machine Assigned
1	(0, 0, 0, 0, 0)	10 (2)	1
		9 (3)	2
		8 (4)	3
		7 (5)	4
		6 (2)	5
2	(22, 32, 41, 50, 19)	5 (4)	1
		4 (1)	4
		3 (3)	3
		2 (5)	5
		1 (4)	2

3. Reorder at each machine by WSPT.

Machine	Sequence
1	5–10
2	1–9
3	3–8
4	4–7
5	2–6

(See Figure 5.3)

the remaining jobs are assigned to different machines. Clearly, Step 2 of the procedure does not specify exactly how this second assignment should be made. If the first five assignments were actually fixed, it could be shown that the optimal assignment of the remaining jobs would be to match the largest weighting factor with the machine with the smallest amount of processing already assigned. Pursuing this rule of thumb, and subsequently applying Step 3 of the procedure, we construct the schedule displayed in Figure 5.3. (The procedure is summarized in the worksheet in Table 5.2.)

Under H_1, suppose again that the jobs are initially ordered by WLPT. The procedure then simply assigns the jobs one at a time, as described in Table 5.3, and finally reorders all jobs so that WSPT prevails on each machine. The schedule that results has a slightly smaller value of $\bar{F}_w$ than the one produced above by H_m, as shown in Figure 5.4.

The comparative study in (1) examined several variations of these heuristic procedures and concluded that their relative behavior was extremely difficult to characterize. The study found that

(a) H_1 and H_m will in general produce different schedules, and either

Table 5.3

1.	Initial job list		$\{10, 9, 8, 7, 6, 5, 4, 3, 2, 1\}$.
2.	Assignment phase.		
	Processing Commitments	Job	Machine Assigned

Processing Commitments	Job	Machine Assigned
(0, 0, 0, 0, 0)	10	1
(22, 0, 0, 0, 0)	9	2
(22, 32, 0, 0, 0)	8	3
(22, 32, 41, 0, 0)	7	4
(22, 32, 41, 50, 0)	6	5
(22, 32, 41, 50, 19)	5	5
(22, 32, 41, 50, 45)	4	1
(28, 32, 41, 50, 45)	3	1
(44, 32, 41, 50, 45)	2	2
(44, 53, 41, 50, 45)	1	3

3. Reorder at each machine by WSPT.

Machine	Sequence
1	3–4–10
2	2–9
3	1–8
4	7
5	5–6

(See Figure 5.4)

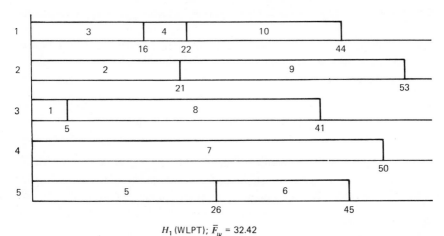

H_1 (WLPT); $\bar{F}_w$ = 32.42

Figure 5.4
A schedule resulting from the use of H_1 with WLPT initial ordering.

method will typically produce different schedules when the initial ordering R is varied;

(b) neither H_1 or H_m can guarantee optimality; and

(c) it does not appear possible to identify a "best rule" R for H_1 or for H_m.

These general conclusions aside, however, the most effective variation of the 15 procedures considered in the study was definitely H_1 used with $R =$ WSPT. Not only did this combination produce the best schedule in most of the test problems, but it also has the virtues of Algorithm 5.3. In particular, H_1 used with $R =$ WSPT is a dispatching procedure (step 3 of H_1 can be omitted) and can easily be adapted to dynamic models in both deterministic and stochastic problems. The test problems used in these comparisons contained $n = 100$ jobs and no more than $m = 6$ machines. In other words, the number of jobs was relatively large compared to the number of machines. It is still speculation whether similar behavior would be found when the number of jobs is only two or three times the number of machines. (An experimental study of the heuristic procedures in such problems is suggested in the computational exercises in Section 4.)

5.2   EXERCISES

2.1   Draw a Gantt chart of a situation in which equation 1 reduces to $M^* = \max \{t_j\}$.

2.2 Construct a schedule for the eight-job set in Figure 5.2 in which there is no preemption and $M < 13$.

2.3 The following set of six nonpreemptable jobs is to be processed by two identical machines with the objective of minimizing $\bar{F}$.

$$
\begin{array}{ccccccc}
\text{Job } j & 1 & 2 & 3 & 4 & 5 & 6 \\
t_j & 1 & 2 & 3 & 4 & 5 & 6
\end{array}
$$

(a) Construct all optimal schedules for this problem. How many are there?

(b) Suppose that a seventh job with $t_7 = 7$ is added to the job set. If job 7 is placed last on one of the machines in each of the schedules constructed in (a), are all the resulting schedules equivalent with respect to $\bar{F}$?

(c) How many optimal schedules are there for the seven-job problem?

2.4 Show that Algorithm 5.3 assigns jobs in rotation, assuming there are no ties. In other words, there is a machine numbering for which the assignment of jobs to machines is

Machine 1   jobs $[1], [m + 1], [2m + 1], \ldots$
Machine 2   jobs $[2], [m + 2], [2m + 2], \ldots$
  .
  .
  .
Machine m jobs $[m], [2m], [3m], \ldots$

2.5 Consider a static scheduling problem with n jobs and m nonidentical machines. Let t_j represent the "standard" processing time of job j and suppose that the time required to process job j on machine k will be $\alpha_k t_j$. In other words, α_k may be interpreted as a machine efficiency factor.

(a) Propose a solution approach for minimizing makespan for this model.

(b) Propose a solution approach for minimizing mean flowtime for this model.

2.6 For the 10-job five-machine problem in this section, calculate the value of the lower bound B on the optimal weighted mean flowtime.

2.7 Consider the integer programming formulation given in Section 2.1. Suppose that the integer constraints on x_{ij} are neglected. Interpret the optimal solution that results.

3. PARALLEL IDENTICAL PROCESSORS AND DEPENDENT JOBS

When the job set is dependent, the problem of minimizing makespan may be considerably more difficult. The fundamental results for this situation are based on the work of Hu (4), who presented a labeling mechanism and an associated scheduling algorithm for the makespan problem. In the simplest case, suppose that $t_j = 1$ for all jobs and that the jobs form an assembly tree (no job has more than one direct successor). A job with no successors is called a *terminal* job in such a tree. The solution algorithm contains a labeling phase followed by a scheduling phase.

ALGORITHM 5.4 HU'S ALGORITHM (4)
(To Minimize Makespan for Dependent Jobs with Equal t_j)

Labeling Phase

Step 1. Assign the label 0 to each terminal job.

Step 2. For each job j, identify the unique k for which $j \ll k$, and assign to job j the label $\alpha_j = \alpha_k + 1$.

Scheduling Phase

Step 3a. If the number of jobs without predecessors is less than or equal to m, schedule these job concurrently, leaving excess machines idle. Go to Step 4.

Step 3b. If the number of jobs without predecessors exceeds m, schedule the m jobs with the largest labels (breaking ties arbitrarily). Go to Step 4.

Step 4. Remove the scheduled jobs from the problem and return to Step 3 until all jobs are scheduled.

The labeling phase actually assigns to each job j a label equal to the length of time required to process the jobs that follow job j on the (unique) path connecting job j and a terminal job. This interpretation lies at the heart of heuristic extensions of this algorithm. The algorithm is illustrated in Figure 5.5. The various loops contain the jobs scheduled concurrently, and the loops are numbered according to the corresponding time interval.

Hu's labeling scheme appears to be effective in other more general situations. If the processing times are not equal but the jobs are preemptable, the algorithm may still be used to find a minimum makespan under certain conditions (see Exercise 3.1). If, instead, jobs are not preemptable, the algorithm cannot guarantee an optimal solution, but it will usually produce very good solutions. To deal with unequal processing times and with precedence structures more general than a tree, the labeling scheme would have to be generalized as follows:

Labeling Phase

Step 1. Assign to each terminal job a label equal to its processing time

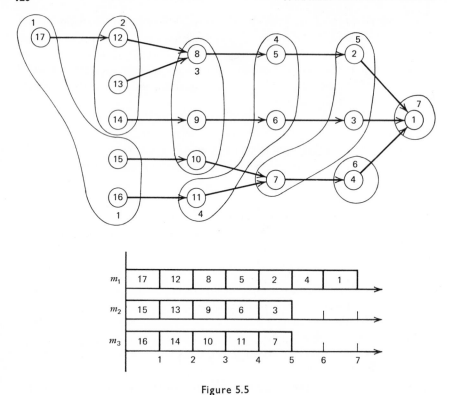

Figure 5.5

The application of Hu's algorithm to a 17-job problem with three machines, showing the Gantt chart of the schedule that results.

Step 2. Assign to job j the label α_j, where

$$\alpha_j = \max \{\alpha_i \,|\, j \ll i\} + t_j$$

In this case, again, the algorithm cannot guarantee optimal schedules but seems to generate good suboptimal schedules.

A special result concerns a dependent job set with preemptable jobs. For arbitrary precedence structures, an optimal algorithm has been developed by Muntz and Coffman (7) for the case of two identical machines. Their algorithm requires that the jobs be partitioned into several subsets, S_k, such that all jobs within a particular subset are mutually independent. That is, if $i < j$, then jobs i and j are members of different subsets. Once the jobs are assigned to subsets, precedence constraints exist only between pairs of subsets, but within each subset the jobs are independent and McNaughton's algorithm can be applied. The subsets can then be sequenced to meet precedence constraints. A method for determining subset membership begins with the generalized version of Hu's labeling algorithm, given above.

ALGORITHM 5.5   THE MUNTZ-COFFMAN ALGORITHM (7)
(To Minimize Makespan with Two Machines and Preemptable Jobs)

Labeling Phase

Step 1. Assign to each terminal job the label 0.

Step 2. Assign to job j the label $\alpha_j = \max \{\alpha_i \,|\, j \ll i\} + t_j$.

Scheduling Phase

Step 3. Let $k = 1$ and $\alpha = \max \{\alpha_j\}$.

Step 4. For jobs j such that $\alpha_j = \alpha$, assign job j to subset S_k. If more than one job is assigned to S_k, proceed to Step 6; otherwise go to Step 5.

Step 5. Consider jobs j such that $\alpha_j = \alpha - 1$. If any of these jobs either have no predecessors or else have all predecessors assigned to subsets $S_1, S_2, \ldots, S_{k-1}$, then add one such job to S_k.

Step 6. Stop if $\alpha = 1$ and schedule the subsets in numerical order, applying McNaughton's algorithm within subsets. Otherwise decrease α by 1, increase k by 1, and return to Step 4.

Unfortunately Algorithm 5.5 may not produce optimal schedules for $m > 2$, as indicated by Exercise 3.4.

This section concludes with a discussion of another parallel processor scheduling problem that also underscores the complexity of finding optimal schedules in the presence of parallel machines and dependent jobs. Recall that for independent jobs it was relatively simple to minimize makespan when preemption is allowed. The major features of the analysis are embodied in equation 1 and Algorithm 5.1, presented earlier. When the same problem is posed in the context of dependent jobs, optimization becomes quite difficult.

Muntz and Coffman (8) have presented an optimizing algorithm for this problem under the condition that the precedence structure is an assembly tree. Their analysis is aided by the concept of *processor sharing*, which allows for a given job to be assigned a resource capability, ρ, which may be less than unity. Thus, if a resource capability of $\rho < 1$ is assigned to job j, this means that the time required to complete the job will be t_j/ρ. In essence, such an assignment corresponds to allowing the job to be processed by only "part of a machine." Alternatively, when a machine is dedicated to the processing of a particular job, then the resource capability being applied is $\rho = 1$. In short, ρ can be interpreted as the rate at which a job is processed by a particular machine ($0 \leq \rho \leq 1$). If processor sharing is allowed, temporarily, then an optimal makespan can be constructed by the following algorithm, which again begins with a labeling phase that generalizes Hu's algorithm.

ALGORITHM 5.6 THE MUNTZ-COFFMAN ALGORITHM (8)

Labeling Phase

Step 1. Assign each terminal job the label 0.

Step 2. Assign job j the label $\alpha_j = \max\{\alpha_i \mid j \ll i\} + t_j$. At intermediate stages of the scheduling phase, the quantity t_j is interpreted to mean remaining processing time, if a job has previously been preempted.

Scheduling Phase

Step 3. Assign one machine to each of the jobs with maximal α_j. If there is a tie among k jobs competing for r machines $(r < k)$, then assign a processing capability of r/k to each job.

Step 4. Maintain the assignment until one of the following events occurs:

    (a) a job is completed, or

    (b) a situation arises in which there exist two jobs i and j satisfying
$\alpha_i \ge \alpha_j$, but $\rho_i < \rho_j$ under the current assignment.
In either case, return to the labeling phase, if necessary, and create a new assignment, until all processing is complete.

As an illustration of the algorithm, consider the job set in the following table when $m = 2$ (S_j denotes the set of direct successors of job j).

Job j	1	2	3	4	5
t_j	2	2	2	1	1
S_j	5	5	4	5	—

The scheduling phase begins at time $t = 0$ with schedulable jobs 1, 2, and 3. Also $\alpha_1 = 3$, $\alpha_2 = 3$, and $\alpha_3 = 4$. According to Step 3, the required assignment is $\rho_3 = 1$, $\rho_1 = \rho_2 = \frac{1}{2}$. Proceeding to Step 4, we may anticipate when when event (b) will occur, since α_1, α_2, and α_3 are functions of the time the initial assignment is maintained. In particular,

$$\alpha_3 = 4 - t \quad \text{and} \quad \alpha_1 = \alpha_2 = 3 - \frac{t}{2}$$

Condition (b) would be satisfied for $\alpha_3 \le \alpha_1$, or equivalently $t \ge 2$. However it happens that event (a) also occurs at time $t = 2$, since job 3 completes. At $t = 2$ the schedulable jobs are 1, 2, and 4, with $\alpha_1 = \alpha_2 = \alpha_4 = 1$; and Step 3 prescribes the assignment of $\rho_1 = \rho_2 = \rho_4 = \frac{2}{3}$. It is now evident that the optimal schedule will be the one shown in Figure 5.6a, for which $M^* = 4.5$. It is easy to verify that Hu's algorithm will generate a larger makespan for this problem.

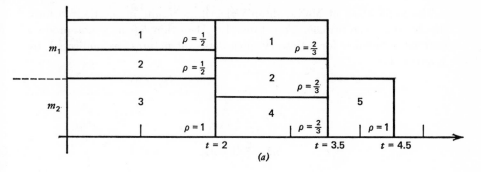

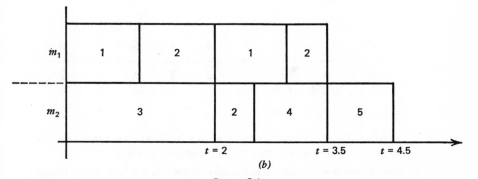

Figure 5.6

The application of Algorithm 5.6 to the example problem, (a) using processor sharing and (b) without processor sharing.

Now it remains to show that it is not necessary to rely on processor sharing. That is, it is possible to find a schedule with a makespan equal to M^* but with $\rho = 1$ for all assignments. This transformation is accomplished by identifying the intervals between assignment changes under Algorithm 5.6 and by applying McNaughton's algorithm separately to the independent jobs scheduled in each of those intervals. For instance, in order to transform the schedule in Figure 5.6a, these three subproblems must be solved by Algorithm 5.1.

Interval	Job j	t_j
[0, 2]	1	1
	2	1
	3	2
[2, 3.5]	1	1
	2	1
	4	1
[3.5, 4.5]	5	1

The application of McNaughton's algorithm results in the desired form displayed in Figure 5.6b. Unfortunately, Algorithm 5.6 may not produce optimal schedules for arbitrary precedence structures, as indicated by Exercise 3.5.

5.3. EXERCISES

3.1 Determine an optimal makespan for the following dependent job set in which all jobs are preemptable.

Job j	1	2	3	4	5	6	7	8
t_j	1	3	4	2	2	1	2	2
S_j	2, 3, 4	7, 8	5, 6	—	—	—	—	—

(S_j denotes the set of direct successors of job j.) What is the relationship between your solution and the solution displayed in Figure 5.5?

3.2 Construct counterexamples to show that Algorithm 5.4 may fail to identify an optimal makespan in the following situations:
   (a) Precedence constraints that form a tree; nonpreemptable jobs.
   (b) Arbitrary precedence structure; equal t_j.

3.3 Show how to minimize makespan for a dependent set of jobs in which the precedence structure is a branching tree and the t_j are equal.

3.4 Apply Algorithm 5.5 to the set of preemptable jobs below, in which $t_j = 1$ for all jobs and $m = 3$.

Job j	1	2	3	4	5	6	7	8	9	10	11	12
S_j	3	3	4, 5, 6	—	—	—	10	10	10	11, 12	—	—

   (a) What makespan is generated by the algorithm?
   (b) Show that a smaller makespan can be realized.

3.5 Apply Algorithm 5.6 to the problem in Exercise 3.4 to show that a suboptimal makespan results.

3.6 What approach to the mail sorting problem (See Exercise 3.9 of Chapter 4) would you suggest if two identical sorters are available?

4. SUMMARY

As noted at the outset of this chapter, problems of scheduling single-stage jobs with parallel processors contain both allocation and sequencing dimensions. The determination of optimal schedules is often rendered somewhat difficult by the need to make both kinds of decisions, and the thrust of analytic results has been aimed primarily at makespan problems for good reason: makespan problems are in fact relatively simple. Indeed, in single-machine models the makespan criterion is seldom an important consideration unless sequence-dependent setup times are involved. But from a practical viewpoint the emphasis on makespan is quite reasonable, for a sound heuristic procedure for nonpreemptive tasks is to solve the allocation problem first and then the sequencing problem. In other words, the rationale would be to distribute the processing load among machines as evenly as possible and then to determine an optimal sequence on each machine separately. Although an even distribution of the load (i.e., a minimal makespan) is not necessarily optimal, it will tend to provide very good schedules. Moreover, this two-phase method of determining a schedule is a more practicable way of managing the large combinatorial problem represented by scheduling with parallel processors.

The important makespan results are McNaughton's characterization of the optimal schedule for independent, preemptable jobs and Hu's characterization for a special class of dependent jobs. The other specialized algorithms and heuristic procedures are largely based on the concepts underlying these two fundamental results.

The minimization of mean flowtime with parallel processors involves a generalization of single-machine analysis, but the minimization of weighted mean flowtime or mean tardiness is not easily accomplished. For the weighted mean flowtime problem, it is possible to find an optimal schedule using an m-dimensional dynamic programming formulation as suggested by Rothkopf *(10)*. While Rothkopf's formulation is general enough to accommodate nonidentical machines, setup times, and certain other variations, its computational requirements are severe. Moreover, the experiments in *(1)* indicated that, at least for large problems, the rapid heuristic approach will consistently produce schedules that are within 1 or 2 % of optimum. The only analytic result for the tardiness criterion is due to Root *(9)* and provides a schedule that minimizes $\bar{T}$ when all jobs have the same due date. Recall from Theorem 2.10 that when $m = 1$, the optimal schedule in such a problem is given by SPT sequencing. Therefore, a very good schedule is likely to be obtained for $m = 1$ by using the two-phase approach suggested above: first, distribute the processing load evenly among the machines and, then, employ the SPT rule for each machine. This heuristic procedure will not guarantee optimality, but it will seldom produce a schedule that is far from optimum.

5.4 COMPUTATIONAL EXERCISES

1. Design and program a heuristic procedure for minimizing makespan, given n nonpreemptable jobs and m identical machines. Compare the efficiency of your procedure with that of Algorithm 5.2. Investigate the extent to which the results are affected by
    (a) The value of m.
    (b) The ratio n/m.
    (c) The variance of the processing times.

2. Construct a set of test problems to compare heuristic procedures H_1 and H_m for minimizing $\bar{F}_w$ with m identical machines. In particular,
    (a) Examine the effects of several different job orderings (R).
    (b) Consider test problems in which $2 \leq n/m \leq 5$.
    (c) Calculate the lower bound for each problem from the relation $\bar{F}_w \geq \max \{B(1), B(m)\}$.

REFERENCES

1. Baker, K. R., and Merten, A. G. "Scheduling with Parallel Processors and Linear Delay Costs," *Naval Research Logistics Quarterly*, Vol. 20, No. 4 (December 1973).
2. Conway, R. W., Maxwell W. L., and Miller, L. W. *Theory of Scheduling*, Addison-Wesley, Reading, Mass., 1967.
3. Eastman, W. L., Even, S., and Isaacs, I. M. "Bounds for the Optimal Scheduling of n Jobs on m Processors," *Management Science*, Vol. 11, No. 2 (November, 1964).
4. Hu, T. C. "Parallel Sequencing and Assembly Line Problems," *Operations Research*, Vol. 9, No. 6 (November, 1961).
5. Kedia, S. K. "A Job Shop Scheduling Problem with Parallel Machines," Unpublished Report, Department of Industrial Engineering, University of Michigan, 1970.
6. McNaughton, R. "Scheduling with Deadlines and Loss Functions," *Management Science*, Vol. 6, No. 1 (October, 1959).
7. Muntz, R. R., and Coffman, E. G., "Optimal Preemptive Scheduling on Two-Processor Systems," *IEEE Transactions on Computers*, Vol. 18, No. 11 (November, 1969).
8. Muntz, R. R., and Coffman, E. "Preemptive Scheduling of Real-Time Tasks on Multiprocessor Systems," *Journal of the ACM*, Vol. 17, No. 2 (April, 1970).
9. Root, J. G., "Scheduling with Deadlines and Loss Functions on k Parallel Machines," *Management Science*, Vol. 11, No. 3 (January, 1965).
10. Rothkopf, M. H., "Scheduling Independent Tasks on Parallel Processors," *Management Science*, Vol. 12, No. 5 (January, 1966).

CHAPTER 6

FLOW SHOP SCHEDULING

1. INTRODUCTION

Now that we have investigated scheduling models containing multiple processors in parallel, it is only natural to examine models with multiple processors in series. However, it is not appropriate to think in terms of serial configurations unless jobs are multistage in nature. This means that it is essential to distinguish between a job and each of the processing operations that is a part of it. For the discussion of flow shop models in this chapter, and in the more general job shop model, a job is considered to be a collection of operations in which a special precedence structure applies. In particular, each operation after the first has exactly one direct predecessor and each operation before the last has exactly one direct successor, as shown for job i below. Thus each job requires a specific sequence of operations to be carried

out for the job to be complete. This type of structure is sometimes called a *linear* precedence structure.

The shop contains m different machines, and each job consists of m operations, each of which requires a different machine. The flow shop is characterized by a flow of work that is unidirectional. Put another way, a flow shop contains a natural machine order: it is possible to number the machines so that if the jth operation of any job precedes its kth operation, then the machine required by the jth operation has a lower number than the machine required by the kth operation. The machines in a flow shop are numbered $1, 2, \ldots, m$; and the operations of job i are correspondingly numbered $(i, 1), (i, 2), \ldots, (i, m)$. Each job can be treated as if it had exactly m operations, for in cases where fewer operations exist, the corresponding processing times can be taken to be zero. Figure 6.1a represents the flow of work in a "pure" flow shop, in which all jobs require one operation on each machine. Figure 6.1b represents the flow of work in a more general flow shop. In the second case, note that jobs may require fewer than m operations, that their operations may not always require adjacent machines in the numbered order, and that the initial and terminal operations may not always occur at machines 1 and m, respectively. Nevertheless, it is sufficient to deal with the pure flow shop case to illustrate the principal traits of the model.

Within this new setting the conditions that characterize flow shop problems are similar to the conditions of the basic single-machine model.

C1. A set of n multiple-operation jobs is available for processing at time zero. (Each job requires m operations and each operation requires a different machine.)

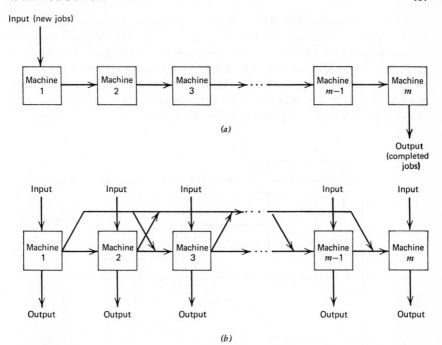

Figure 6.1

Workflow in a flow shop. The pure flow shop is depicted in (a) and the general flow shop in (b).

C2. Setup times for the operations are sequence-independent and are included in processing times.

C3. Job descriptors are known in advance.

C4. m different machines are continuously available.

C5. Individual operations are not preemptable.

One difference from the basic single-machine case is that inserted idle time may be advantageous. In the single-machine model with simultaneous arrivals it was possible to assume that the machine would never be kept idle when work was waiting. In the flow shop case, however, it may be necessary

Machine Number	Operation Times for Job 1	Operation Times for Job 2
1	1	4
2	4	1
3	4	1
4	1	4

to provide for inserted idle time to achieve optimality. For example, consider the two-job four-machine problem described on page 137. Suppose that $\bar{F}$ is the measure of performance. The two schedules shown in Figures 6.2a and 6.2b have no inserted idle time and for both, $\bar{F} = 12$. The schedule in Figure 6.2c is an optimal schedule, with $\bar{F} = 11.5$. Note that in this third schedule, machine 3 is kept idle at time $t = 5$ [when operation (1, 3) could be started] in order to await the completion of operation (2, 2).

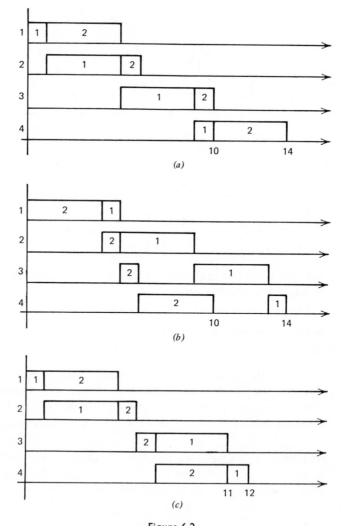

Figure 6.2
Three schedules for the example two-job problem. The schedules shown in (a) and (b) have no inserted idle time.

Recall that for one machine there was a one-to-one relation between a job sequence and a permutation of the job indices 1, 2, ..., n. To find an optimum sequence, it was necessary to examine (at least implicitly) each of the sequences corresponding to the $n!$ different permutations. Now in the flow shop problem, there are $n!$ different job sequences possible for each machine, and therefore $(n!)^m$ different schedules to be examined. Clearly, it would be helpful to be able to ignore many of these, and the extent to which the search for an optimum might be reduced is discussed in Section 2. The case $m = 2$, in which some special results apply, is examined in Section 3. For large problems, implicit enumeration methods and heuristic approaches may be most suitable, and these are explored in Sections 4 to 6. Section 7 deals with the special case in which there is no intermediate storage between machines, and Section 8 deals with general scheduling criteria.

2. PERMUTATION SCHEDULES

The example in the previous section illustrates that it may not be sufficient to consider only schedules in which the same job sequence occurs on each machine. On the other hand, it is not always necessary to consider $(n!)^m$ schedules in determining an optimum. The two dominance properties given below indicate how much of a reduction is possible in flow shop problems.

Property 6.1

With respect to any regular measure of performance, it is sufficient to consider only schedules in which the same job sequence occurs on machines 1 and 2.

It is possible to see why this property holds by considering a schedule in which the sequences on machines 1 and 2 are different. Somewhere in such a schedule it is possible to find a pair of jobs, i and j, such that operation $(i, 1)$ precedes an adjacent operation $(j, 1)$ but operation $(j, 2)$ precedes $(i, 2)$. This situation is depicted in Figure 6.3a. Now the idea is to show that the order of the jobs on machine 2 (j before i) can also be employed on machine 1 without adversely affecting the performance measure. If operations $(i, 1)$ and $(j, 1)$ are interchanged, resulting in the schedule shown in Figure 6.3b, then

    (a) with the exception of $(i, 1)$ no operation is delayed by the interchange,

    (b) operation $(i, 2)$ is not delayed by the interchange,

    (c) earlier processing of $(j, 2)$, and other operations as well, may be possible as a result of the interchange.

Therefore the interchange would not increase the completion time of any operation on the second machine or on any subsequent machine. This means that no increase in any job completion times could result from the interchange, and therefore no increase in any regular measure of performance. Since the

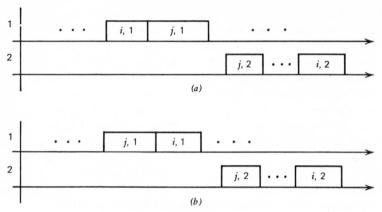

Figure 6.3
A pairwise interchange of two operations on machine 1.

same argument applies to any schedule in which job sequences differ on machines 1 and 2, the property must hold.

Property 6.2

With respect to schedule makespan as a measure of performance, it is sufficient to consider only schedules in which the same job sequence occurs on machines $m - 1$ and m.

This property can be demonstrated with an argument that resembles that given for Property 6.1. Consider a schedule in which the sequences on machines $m - 1$ and m are different. Somewhere in such a schedule it is possible to find a pair of jobs, i and j, such that operation (i, m) follows an adjacent operation (j, m), but operation $(i, m - 1)$ precedes $(j, m - 1)$, as in Figure 6.4a. As a result of the interchange of (i, m) and (j, m), shown in Figure 6.4b, it follows that:

(a) with the exception of (j, m) no operation is delayed by the interchange,
(b) operation (j, m) is completed no later than operation (i, m) in the original schedule,
(c) earlier processing of operations (i, m) and (j, m) may be possible as a result of the interchange.

Therefore the interchange would not lead to an increase in the makespan of the schedule. Again, this type of argument applies to any schedule in which job sequences differ on machines $m - 1$ and m. Therefore Property 6.2 must hold.

The implication of these two results is that in searching for an optimal schedule, it is necessary to consider different job sequences on different machines with these two general exceptions.

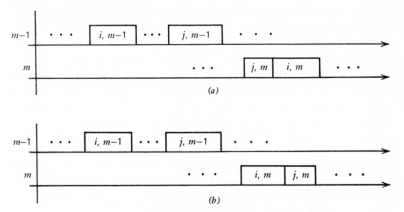

Figure 6.4
A pairwise interchange of two operations on machine m.

1. For any regular measure, it is sufficient for the same job order to occur on machines 1 and 2, so that $(n!)^{m-1}$ schedules constitute a dominant set.

2. For makespan problems, it is also sufficient for the same job order to occur on machines $m-1$ and m, so that $(n!)^{m-2}$ schedules constitute a dominant set for $m > 2$.

A permutation schedule is simply a schedule with the same job order on all machines—a schedule that is completely characterized by a single permutation of the job indices $1, 2, \ldots, n$. Another way to interpret the implications of Properties 6.1 and 6.2 is to observe that it is sufficient to consider only permutation schedules in the following cases.

1. Regular measure of performance, $m = 2$.

2. Makespan objective, $m = 2$ or $m = 3$.

Exercises 2.1 and 2.2 require counterexamples to show that no stronger general results can be obtained for permutation schedules.

Even when it is sufficient to deal only with permutation schedules, it may still be difficult to locate optima efficiently. The next section deals with the one flow shop problem that is relatively easy to solve.

6.2 EXERCISES

2.1 Construct a three-machine flow shop problem for which $\bar{F}$ is minimized only by a schedule that is not a permutation schedule.

2.2   Construct a four-machine flow shop problem for which M is minimized only by a schedule that is not a permutation schedule and that contains no inserted idle time.

2.3   Sequential crew systems consist of two or more crews following one another in a fixed sequence to complete a particular task on a unit being processed. (Such systems are commonly found in the construction of aircraft and ships, and in the maintenance of large machines.) There are a fixed number of crews who can work continuously; the first crew prepares new units upon entry into the system and the remaining crews process these units as they become available. Crews perform their assigned work in a fixed sequence with respect to each other, and units are processed by each crew in the same order as their order of entry. Show how a flow shop model can be used to describe the behavior of such a system. What is the role of permutation schedules in the analysis of this kind of system?

3.   JOHNSON'S PROBLEM

The two-machine flow shop problem with the objective of minimizing makespan is also known as Johnson's problem. The results originally obtained by Johnson (9) are now standard fundamentals in the theory of scheduling. In the formulation of this problem, job j is characterized by processing time t_{j1}, required on machine 1, and t_{j2}, required on machine 2 after the operation on machine 1 is complete. An optimal sequence can be characterized by the following rule for ordering pairs of jobs.

Theorem 6.1

(Johnson's rule) Job i precedes job j in an optimal sequence if

$$\min \{t_{i1}, t_{j2}\} \leq \min \{t_{i2}, t_{j1}\}$$

In practice, an optimal sequence is directly constructed with an adaptation of this result. The positions in sequence are filled by a one-pass mechanism that identifies, at each stage, a job that should fill either the first or last available position.

ALGORITHM 6.1
(Implementing Johnson's Rule)

Step 1.   Find $\min_i \{t_{i1}, t_{i2}\}$.

Step 2a.   If the minimum processing time requires machine 1, place the associated job in the first available position in sequence. Go to Step 3.

Step 2b. If the minimum processing time requires machine 2, place the associated job in the last available position in sequence. Go to Step 3.

Step 3. Remove the assigned job from consideration and return to Step 1 until all positions in sequence are filled. (Ties may be broken arbitrarily.)

To illustrate the algorithm, consider the five-job problem shown in Table 6.1. The accompanying worksheet shows how an optimal sequence is con-

Table 6.1

Job j	1	2	3	4	5
t_{j1}	3	5	1	6	7
t_{j2}	6	2	2	6	5

Stage	Unscheduled Jobs	Minimum t_{ik}	Assignment	Partial Schedule
1	1, 2, 3, 4, 5	t_{31}	3 = [1]	3 x x x x
2	1, 2, 4, 5	t_{22}	2 = [5]	3 x x x 2
3	1, 4, 5	t_{11}	1 = [2]	3–1 x x 2
4	4, 5	t_{52}	5 = [4]	3–1 x 5–2
5	4	$t_{41} = t_{42}$	4 = [3]	3–1–4–5–2

structed in five stages using Algorithm 6.1. At each stage, the minimum processing time among unscheduled jobs must be identified. Then Step 2 assigns one more position in sequence, and the process is repeated. The sequence that emerges is 3–1–4–5–2. The schedule produced by the algorithm has a makespan of 24, as shown in Figure 6.5.

For later reference, notice that the following algorithm, which at first sight may appear different from Algorithm 6.1, actually constructs an equivalent sequence. (It is this form of the result that can be generalized, as discussed in Section 3.2)

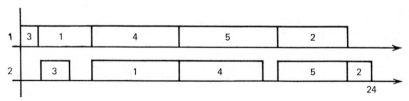

Figure 6.5
An optimal schedule for the example problem.

ALGORITHM 6.Ia
(Implementing Johnson's Rule)

Step 1.   Let $U = \{j \mid t_{j1} < t_{j2}\}$ and $V = \{j \mid t_{j1} \geq t_{j2}\}$

Step 2.   Arrange the members of set U in nondecreasing order of t_{j1}, and arrange the members of set V in nonincreasing order of t_{j2}.

Step 3.   An optimal sequence is the ordered set U followed by the ordered set V.

The next subsection deals with the proof of Johnson's rule and the following subsection discusses its important extensions.

3.1   A Proof of Johnson's Rule

The property stated in Theorem 6.1 can be demonstrated in a two-phase proof. The first phase involves an adjacent pairwise interchange, similar to those introduced in Chapter 2. The second phase shows that such an argument is valid by verifying that the ordering specified by the theorem is in fact transitive.

The operations on machine 1 can be carried out with no inserted idle time (see Figure 6.6). If $I_{[j]}$ denotes the idle time occurring on machine 2 immediately prior to the processing of job $[j]$, as in Figure 6.6, then the makespan can be written

$$M = \sum_{j=1}^{n} t_{j2} + \sum_{j=1}^{n} I_j$$

Since the first summation is a constant, an equivalent problem is to minimize the second summation. Observe that

$$I_{[1]} = t_{[1]1}$$

$$I_{[2]} = \max \{0, t_{[1]1} + t_{[2]1} - t_{[1]2} - I_{[1]}\}$$

$$I_{[3]} = \max \{0, t_{[1]1} + t_{[2]1} + t_{[3]1} - t_{[1]2} - t_{[2]2} - I_{[1]} - I_{[2]}\}$$

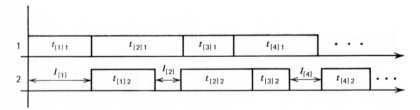

Figure 6.6
The Gantt chart for a typical schedule in a two-machine flow shop problem.

and in general

$$I_{[j]} = \max \left\{ 0, \sum_{i=1}^{j} t_{[i]1} - \sum_{i=1}^{j-1} t_{[i]2} - \sum_{i=1}^{j-1} I_{[i]} \right\}$$

Also observe that

$$I_{[1]} + I_{[2]} = \max \left\{ t_{[1]1}, t_{[1]1} + t_{[2]1} - t_{[1]2} \right\}$$

$$I_{[1]} + I_{[2]} + I_{[3]}$$
$$= \max \left\{ t_{[1]1}, t_{[1]1} + t_{[2]1} - t_{[1]2}, t_{[1]1} + t_{[2]1} + t_{[3]1} - t_{[1]2} - t_{[2]2} \right\}$$

and in general

$$\sum_{i=1}^{j} I_{[i]} = \max_{1 \le k \le j} \left\{ \sum_{i=1}^{k} t_{[i]1} - \sum_{i=1}^{k-1} t_{[i]2} \right\}$$

for convenience, let

$$Y_k = \sum_{i=1}^{k} t_{[i]1} - \sum_{i=1}^{k-1} t_{[i]2}$$

so that

$$\sum_{i=i}^{j} I_{[i]} = \max_{1 \le k \le j} \left\{ Y_k \right\}$$

and the desired objective is to minimize

$$\sum_{i=1}^{n} I_{[i]} = \max_{k} \left\{ Y_k \right\}$$

Now consider a schedule S, which does not satisfy the ordering prescribed by Theorem 6.1. This means that there exists a pair of adjacent jobs i and j, with j following i, such that

$$\min \left\{ t_{i1}, t_{j2} \right\} > \min \left\{ t_{i2}, t_{j1} \right\} \tag{1}$$

Let schedule S' denote the same schedule except with jobs i and j interchanged in sequence. Let B denote the set of jobs that precede both jobs i and j in either schedule. The inequality 1 above can be rewritten

$$\max \left\{ -t_{i1}, -t_{j2} \right\} < \max \left\{ -t_{i2}, -t_{j1} \right\} \tag{1'}$$

To both sides of (1') add the constant Q, where

$$Q = \sum_{k \in B} t_{k1} + t_{i1} + t_{j1} - \sum_{k \in B} t_{k2}$$

This addition yields

$$\max \left\{ Q - t_{i1}, Q - t_{j2} \right\} < \max \left\{ Q - t_{i2}, Q - t_{j1} \right\} \tag{2}$$

Now observe that

$$Q - t_{i1} = \sum_{k \in B} t_{k1} + t_{j1} - \sum_{k \in B} t_{k2} = Y_j(S')$$

$$Q - t_{j2} = \sum_{k \in B} t_{k1} + t_{i1} + t_{j1} - \sum_{k \in B} t_{k2} - t_{j2} = Y_i(S')$$

$$Q - t_{j1} = \sum_{k \in B} t_{k1} + t_{i1} - \sum_{k \in B} t_{k2} = Y_i(S)$$

$$Q - t_{i2} = \sum_{k \in B} t_{k1} + t_{i1} + t_{j1} - \sum_{k \in B} t_{k2} - t_{i2} = Y_j(S)$$

Hence (2) becomes

$$\max \left\{ Y_j(S'), \, Y_i(S') \right\} < \max \left\{ Y_i(S), \, Y_j(S) \right\}$$

The interchange of jobs i and j is therefore desirable in the sense that it does not increase $\max_k \{Y_k\}$ and may actually reduce it. Therefore in a sequence for which the inequality of Theorem 6.1 does not hold throughout, such a pairwise interchange will not increase the makespan and may in fact reduce it.

To complete the proof, the second phase is to demonstrate the transitivity of the job ordering. In other words, suppose $\min \{t_{i1}, t_{j2}\} \le \min \{t_{i2}, t_{j1}\}$ and $\min \{t_{j1}, t_{k2}\} \le \min \{t_{j2}, t_{k1}\}$. Then it will always be true that $\min \{t_{i1}, t_{k2}\} \le \min \{t_{i2}, t_{k1}\}$. (The details of this part of the proof are given as Exercise 3.1.)

3.2 Extensions of Johnson's Rule

For the makespan criterion and $m = 3$ it is still sufficient to consider only permutation schedules in the search for an optimum, yet it is difficult to generalize Johnson's two-machine result. In his original presentation Johnson showed that a generalization is possible when the second machine is "dominated" (i.e., when no bottleneck could possibly occur on the second machine).

1. If $\min_k \{t_{k1}\} \ge \max_k \{t_{k2}\}$, then job i precedes job j in an optimal schedule if

$$\min \{t_{i1} + t_{i2}, t_{j2} + t_{j3}\} \le \min \{t_{i2} + t_{i3}, t_{j1} + t_{j2}\}$$

2. If $\min_k \{t_{k3}\} \ge \max_k \{t_{k2}\}$ then job i precedes job j in an optimal schedule if

$$\min \{t_{i1} + t_{i2}, t_{j2} + t_{j3}\} \le \min \{t_{i2} + t_{i3}, t_{j1} + t_{j2}\}$$

In terms of applying Algorithm 6.1, these results require only that instead of seeking the minimum processing time, the first step is to seek a minimum in the form

$$\min_i \{t_{i1} + t_{i2}, t_{i2} + t_{i3}\}$$

Johnson also found that in the three-machine case, if the application of Algorithm 6.1 yields the same optimal sequence for the two-machine subproblem represented by the set $\{t_{i1}, t_{i2}\}$ and for the separate two-machine subproblem represented by the set $\{t_{i2}, t_{i3}\}$, then this sequence is optimal for the full three-machine problem.

Another type of generalization for the two-machine case involves the addition of start-lags and stop-lags, as analyzed by Mitten (*13*). In many practical situations, it may be possible to begin operation 2 before operation 1 is entirely complete. This structure may appear where jobs consist of large lots that may be split into sublots and where completed sublots may proceed to a subsequent operation without waiting for the full lot to be processed. This overlapping structure, often called lap-phasing, may also arise where the flow of work is conveyer-driven. With lap-phasing there is a specific interval a_j, called a start-lag, such that operation $j2$ can be started as soon as a_j time units after operation $j1$ begins. In particular, the strict precedence requirement of the flow shop model requires that $a_j = t_{j1}$, but lap-phasing allows $a_j < t_{j1}$. Significant transportation time between operations or inspection between operations might require $a_j > t_{j1}$. Analogously, Mitten allowed for an interval b_j, called a stop-lag such that operation $j2$ must not complete any earlier than b_j time units after operation $j1$ completes. Allowing for $a_j \geq 0$ and for all b_j, Mitten extended Johnson's rule as described in the following algorithm.

ALGORITHM 6.2
(Implementing Johnson's Rule with Start-Lags and Stop-Lags)

Step 1. Let $U = \{j | t_{j1} < t_{j2}\}$ and $V = \{j | t_{j1} \geq t_{j2}\}$.

Step 2. Define $y_j = \max \{a_j - t_{j1}, b_j - t_{j2}\}$. Arrange the members of set U in nondecreasing order of $t_{j1} + y_j$ and arrange the members of set V in nonincreasing order of $t_{j2} + y_j$.

Step 3. An optimal sequence is the ordered set U followed by the ordered set V.

Another application of this model involves a larger flow shop in which the first and last machines are the only bottleneck machines. Suppose all jobs require the first operation to be performed on machine 1 and the third operation to be performed on machine 3. If the intervening operation on each job can be performed independently of all other jobs (as if, for example, n parallel machines were available for this purpose), the intervening operation could be treated as part of a start-lag, and Mitten's result employed. Obviously, this reasoning could be extended to larger flow shops, as long as only machine 1 and machine m are bottleneck machines.

Mitten's extension has a potential drawback, however. With start-lags or stop-lags in the model, it is not possible to guarantee that there exists an optimal schedule that is a permutation schedule. Therefore Mitten's result holds only for permutation schedules, and it must be recognized that the best permutation schedule may not be an optimal schedule.

6.3 EXERCISES

3.1   Show that Johnson's rule is transitive.

3.2   In the two-machine problem with start-lags and stop-lags, suppose that $a_j = b_j$ for all jobs. Show that Algorithm 6.2 is equivalent to scheduling according to the rule:

Job i precedes job j in an optimal sequence if

$$\min \{t_{i1} + y_i, t_{j2} + y_j\} \leq \min \{t_{i2} + y_i, t_{j1} + y_j\}$$

In this situation how can Algorithm 6.1 be adapted to produce optimal schedules?

3.3   A manufacturer of charm bracelets has five jobs to schedule for a leading customer. Each job requires a stamping operation followed by a finishing operation, which can begin on an item immediately after its stamping is complete. The table below shows operation times per item (in minutes) for each job in the order. In addition, preparations for each job at the stamping facility require a setup before processing begins, as described in the table. Find a schedule that completes all five jobs as soon as possible.

| | | Operation Times per Item | | |
Job	Items in Lot	Stamping	Finishing	Setup Time
1	20	2	8	100
2	25	2	5	250
3	100	1	2	60
4	50	4	2.5	60
5	40	3	6	80

4. BRANCH AND BOUND ALGORITHMS FOR MAKESPAN PROBLEMS

Except for the very special cases mentioned in the previous section, the makespan problem with $m = 3$ cannot be solved more efficiently than by controlled enumeration. Nevertheless, branch and bound methods have been employed with some success. For larger flow shop problems, the same branch and bound approaches have also been used to find optimal permutation schedules. Even though permutation schedules are not a dominant set for makespan problems when $m \geq 4$, it is intuitively plausible that the best permutation schedule should be at least very close to the true optimum.

4.1   The Ignall–Schrage Algorithm

The basic branch and bound procedure was developed by Ignall and Schrage (*8*), and independently by Lomnicki (*10*). The underlying branching tree has the same structure as the tree shown in Figure 3.3, except that σ represents a partial permutation occurring at the beginning of the sequence instead of at the end. In other words, the job sequence is constructed in a forward direction (instead of a backward direction) in proceeding down the branching tree. For each node on the tree, a lower bound on the makespan associated with any completion of the corresponding partial sequence σ is obtained by considering the work remaining on each machine. To illustrate the procedure for $m = 3$, let σ' denote the set of jobs that are not contained in the partial permutation σ. For a given partial sequence σ, let

$q_1 =$ the latest completion time on machine 1 among jobs in σ (hence the earliest time at which some job $j \in \sigma'$ could begin processing).

$q_2 =$ the latest completion time on machine 2 among jobs in σ.

$q_3 =$ the latest completion time on machine 3 among jobs in σ.

The amount of processing yet required of machine 1 is

$$\sum_{j \in \sigma'} t_{j1}$$

Moreover, suppose that a particular job k is last in sequence. After job k completes on machine 1, an interval of at least $(t_{k2} + t_{k3})$ must elapse before the whole schedule can possibly be complete, as depicted in Figure 6.7a. In the most favorable situation, the last job

(1)   encounters no delay between the completion of one operation and the start of its direct successor, and

(2)   has the minimal sum $(t_{j2} + t_{j3})$ among jobs $j \in \sigma'$.

Hence one lower bound on the makespan is

$$b_1 = q_1 + \sum_{j \in \sigma'} t_{j1} + \min_{j \in \sigma'} \{t_{j2} + t_{j3}\}$$

Similar reasoning applied to the processing yet required of machine 2 (Figure 6.7b) yields a second lower bound:

$$b_2 = q_2 + \sum_{j \in \sigma'} t_{j2} + \min_{j \in \sigma'} \{t_{j3}\}$$

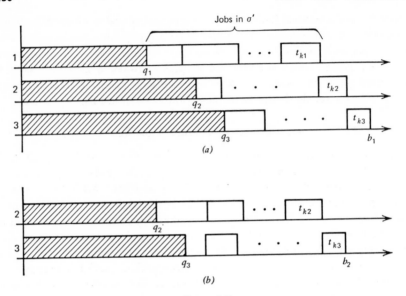

Figure 6.7

The structure of a flow shop schedule for the purposes of calculating lower bounds on makespan for a given partial sequence. The shaded areas represent machine time consumed by the jobs assigned to the partial sequence.

Finally, a lower bound based on the processing yet required of machine 3 is

$$b_3 = q_3 + \sum_{j \in \sigma'} t_{j3}$$

If we employ these calculations, the lower bound proposed by Ignall and Schrage is

$$B = \max \{b_1, b_2, b_3\}$$

The branch and bound procedure described in (8) is essentially Algorithm 3.2, with jumptracking. Furthermore, the algorithm employs a dominance property to eliminate certain partial sequences from consideration.

Property 6.3

Suppose partial sequences $\sigma^{(1)}$ and $\sigma^{(2)}$ contain the same jobs (in different order). If $q_2^{(1)} \leq q_2^{(2)}$ and $q_3^{(1)} \leq q_3^{(2)}$, then $\sigma^{(1)}$ dominates $\sigma^{(2)}$, and $\sigma^{(2)}$ need not be considered any further in the search for an optimum.

In the algorithm, a subproblem corresponding to a dominated node can be discarded from the active list whenever it is found. Although Ignall and Schrage included the dominance check in their algorithm, they did not address the specific question of whether the time spent in making dominance checks seemed worth the branching that was eliminated or the storage space saved. In any event, the dominance check may not be a crucial part of the algorithm.

To illustrate the calculations, consider the four-job three-machine flow shop problem described in Table 6.2. The first node generated by the branch and bound algorithm might well correspond to the subproblem P_1^1, for which job 1 is assigned the first position in sequence and $\sigma' = \{2, 3, 4\}$. For this partial sequence: $q_1 = t_{11} = 3$, $q_2 = t_{11} + t_{12} = 7$, and $q_3 = t_{11} + t_{12} + t_{13} = 17$. The lower bound calculations are

$$b_1 = 3 + 28 + 6 = 37$$

$$b_2 = 7 + 22 + 2 = 31$$

$$b_3 = 17 + 20 = 37$$

$$B = \max \{37, 31, 37\} = 37$$

The computations required to locate an optimum are tabulated in Table 6.2,

Table 6.2

Job j	1	2	3	4
t_{j1}	3	11	7	10
t_{j2}	4	1	9	12
t_{j3}	10	5	13	2

Partial Sequence	(q_1, q_2, q_3)	(b_1, b_2, b_3)	B
1	(3, 7, 17)	(37, 31, 37)	37
2	(11, 12, 17)	(45, 39, 42)	45
3	(7, 16, 29)	(37, 35, 46)	46
4	(10, 22, 24)	(37, 41, 52)	52
12	(14, 15, 20)	(45, 38, 35)	45
13	(10, 19, 30)	(37, 34, 37)	37
14	(13, 25, 27)	(37, 40, 45)	45
132	(21, 22, 35)	(45, 36, 37)	45
134	(20, 32, 34)	(36, 38, 39)	39

and the associated branching tree is displayed in Figure 6.8. It is interesting to note that although the conditions for Johnson's extension to the three-machine problem both fail, his rule ($i < j$ if $\min \{t_{i1} + t_{i2}, t_{j2} + t_{j3}\} \le \min \{t_{i2} + t_{i3}, t_{j1} + t_{j2}\}$) does construct an optimal sequence, 1–3–4–2.

The solution in Table 6.2 is also a case for which the jumptracking algorithm creates only the minimum number of nodes en route to an optimum.

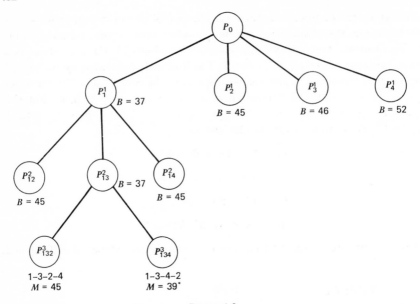

Figure 6.8

The branching tree for a branch and bound solution of the flow shop problem in Table 6.2.

To the extent that they investigated the performance of the algorithm on test problems, Ignall and Schrage found that frequently the minimum number of nodes was sufficient to locate an optimum, at least for $m = 3$ and $n \leq 10$. In these cases a backtracking version of the algorithm would also have generated the minimum number of nodes.

Finally, observe that the method can easily be extended to $m > 3$, in order to find the best permutation schedule (see Exercise 4.1). For this situation, however, Brown and Lomnicki (3) found that the algorithm was far less likely to generate exactly the minimum number of nodes in the branching tree.

4.2   Modifications of the Basic Algorithm

A variety of extensions and refinements have been developed for the branch and bound procedure. The major modifications are summarized in the following paragraphs.

Modification 1: Refined Bounds.   In their original paper, Ignall and Schrage noted that their bounds b_2 and b_3 could be strengthened slightly. The use of q_2 in the calculation of b_2 ignores the possibility that the starting time of job j on machine 2 may be constrained by commitments on machine 1. Hence, in the calculation of b_2, it is possible to replace q_2 with

$$q_2' = \max \left\{ q_2, q_1 + \min_{j \in \sigma'} [t_{j1}] \right\}$$

Similarly, the use of q_3 in the calculation of b_3 ignores the possibility that the starting time of job j on machine 3 may be constrained by commitments on the earlier machines. Hence, in the calculation of b_3, it is possible to replace q_3 with

$$q_3' = \max \left\{ q_3, q_2 + \min_{j \in \sigma'} [t_{j2}], q_1 + \min_{j \in \sigma'} [t_{j1} + t_{j2}] \right\}$$

The form of the algorithm originally tested by Ignall and Schrage contained these refinements.

Modification 2: Job-based Bounds. McMahon and Burton (*11*) referred to the lower bound B as a *machine-based* bound, in that the bound is determined from unsatisfied requirements on the three machines. A complementary approach is to use a *job-based* bound, which is determined from unsatisfied requirements for unscheduled jobs. Let job k represent some unscheduled job. An amount of time $(t_{k1} + t_{k2} + t_{k3})$ must still be added to the schedule, at or after time q_1. In addition, time might also be spent processing other jobs $j \in \sigma'$ that either precede or follow job k in sequence. To construct the most favorable case for minimum makespan, let J_1 denote the set of jobs $j \in \sigma'$, excluding job k, for which $t_{j1} \leq t_{j3}$ and let J_2 denote the set of jobs $j \in \sigma'$, excluding job k, for which $t_{j1} > t_{j3}$. Now suppose that all jobs in J_1 precede job k in sequence and that all jobs in J_2 follow job k. Following the schedule displayed in Figure 6.9a, the makespan must satisfy

$$\geq q_1 + (t_{k1} + t_{k2} + t_{k3}) + \sum_{j \in J_1} t_{j1} + \sum_{j \in J_2} t_{j3}$$

But an inequality for this form could be written for each job $k \in \sigma'$. Therefore another lower bound is

$$b_4 = q_1 + \max_{k \in \sigma'} \left\{ t_{k1} + t_{k2} + t_{k3} + \sum_{\substack{j \in \sigma' \\ j \neq k}} \min [t_{j1}, t_{j3}] \right\}$$

Another job-based bound is developed by applying similar reasoning to commitments on machines 2 and 3 (see Figure 6.9b), leading to a bound of

$$b_5 = q_2' + \max_{k \in \sigma'} \left\{ t_{k2} + t_{k3} + \sum_{\substack{j \in \sigma' \\ j \neq k}} \min [t_{j2}, t_{j3}] \right\}$$

Finally, the lower bound associated with any node in the branching tree is

$$B' = \max \{B, b_4, b_5\}$$

Obviously, $B' \geq B$. This means that the combination of machine-based and job-based bounds represented by B' will lead to a more efficient search of the branching tree in the sense that fewer nodes will be created. Furthermore, the experimental work reported in (*11*) indicates the savings in calculation time due to this search efficiency more than compensates for the

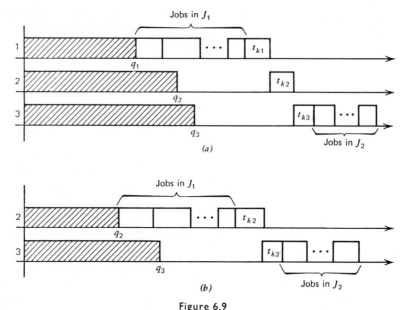

Figure 6.9
The structure of a flow shop schedule for the purposes of calculating job-based bounds.

added calculation time associated with obtaining the composite bounds B'.

It was noted in the introduction to branch and bound methods (Chapter 3) that the decision to use stronger bounds involves recognition of a trade-off between time spent computing bounds and time spent searching the branching tree. The McMahon–Burton contribution is representative of results that occur in other scheduling problems as well: in large combinatorial problems, the increased effort required to obtain strong bounds frequently tends to be offset by a greater savings in reduced tree searching.

Modification 3: Dominant Machine. Along with any given flow shop problem, it is possible to construct a "reversed" problem that is equivalent with respect to makespan. The reversed problem simply assumes that the operations must be processed in the machine order 3–2–1 instead of 1–2–3. For a given set of processing times, however, the optimal makespan for the reversed problem is identical to that of the original problem and, of course, the optimal sequence for the reversed problem is the reverse of that for the original problem. This being the case, it is natural to ask under what conditions the reversed problem can be solved more efficiently than the original.

McMahon and Burton proposed one answer to this question based on the concept of a dominant machine. Machine 3 is said to *dominate* machine 1 if

$$\sum_{j=1}^{n} t_{j3} > \sum_{j=1}^{n} t_{j1}$$

and vice versa. They argued that when machine 3 is dominant, the idle time on machine 3 is largely determined somewhat earlier in the job sequence than when machine 1 is dominant. Since minimizing makespan corresponds to minimizing idle time on machine 3, they concluded that lower bounds tend to be more efficient when machine 3 is dominant. Therefore they proposed that the reversed problem be solved whenever machine 1 is dominant. In their experimental investigation, McMahon and Burton found this guideline to be very reliable, even though machine 1–dominant problems could occasionally be solved more rapidly than their reversed versions.

In addition to the two modifications already discussed, McMahon and Burton investigated some minor tie-breaking rules for the branch and bound algorithm. The importance of their research contribution is not merely that they proposed clever modifications (in fact, Modifications 2 and 3 were proposed earlier by other authors). The primary significance of their contribution is that they tested and evaluated their proposals and, thus, substantiated the value of the modifications. Tables 6.3 and 6.4 display some

Table 6.3

	Mean Number of Nodes		Mean Solution Time	
n	Bound B	Bound B'	Bound B	Bound B'
4	12.1	9.4	0.030	0.024
5	22.2	16.0	0.065	0.045
6	43.5	26.6	0.197	0.089
7	77.1	38.7	0.898	0.160
8	137.1	71.8	1.744	0.409
9	148.8	89.7	2.449	0.635
10	143.9	90.9	3.313	0.631

of their results. Table 6.3 compares the use of machine-based bounds with the use of composite bounds in terms of the mean number of nodes created and mean solution time in 50 test problems for each of several problem sizes. The computer times are in seconds on a CDC 3600 computer. Table 6.4 reflects the dominant machine properties by showing that the solution method tended to be more efficient when machine 3 was dominant than when machine 1 was dominant. For moderate-sized problems ($n \geq 8$), the dominant machine property had a dramatic effect. In machine 1–dominant problems, the branching process became very lengthy, whereas in the reversed problem the branching process did not get out of hand. Therefore, the dominant

Table 6.4

	Mean Number of Nodes		Mean Solution Time	
n	Machine 1 Dominant	Machine 3 Dominant	Machine 1 Dominant	Machine 3 Dominant
4	10.6	9.4	0.028	0.024
5	18.4	15.9	0.054	0.045
6	35.1	26.5	0.141	0.088
7	114.4	37.7	1.898	0.155
8	345.1*	63.9	4.586*	0.335
9	632.5*	82.7	30.301*	0.575
10	1036.8*	81.3	382.750*	0.571

* Algorithm terminated on some problems prior to finding an optimal schedule (3000 node limit).

machine property appears to be very effective in insulating the algorithm from the increased computational demands that might be anticipated as the problem size is increased.

6.4   EXERCISES

4.1 Suppose that the Ignall–Schrage algorithm were to be used for finding the best permutation schedule when $m > 3$. Show how the lower bounds B would be calculated for general m.

4.2 Propose a "dominant machine" modification for problems in which $m > 3$.

4.3 Consider the following four-job three-machine problem.

Job j	1	2	3	4
t_{j1}	13	7	26	2
t_{j2}	3	12	9	6
t_{j3}	12	16	7	1

(a) Find the minimum makespan using the basic Ignall–Schrage algorithm (Section 4.1). Count the nodes generated by the branching process.

(b) Find the minimum makespan using the modified algorithm (Section 4.2). What reduction is achieved in the extent of the branching process?

4.4 Find the minimum makespan in this situation.

Job j	1	2	3	4	5	6
t_{j1}	6	12	4	3	6	2
t_{j2}	7	2	6	11	8	14
t_{j3}	3	3	8	7	10	12

5. DOMINANCE PROPERTIES FOR MAKESPAN PROBLEMS

We have seen that the role of dominance properties is to limit the search for an optimum to as small a set as possible. In addition, the use of dominance properties can enhance the efficiency of combinatorial optimization algorithms, provided that the effort required to check dominance conditions is not too extensive. This principle was exploited in the hybrid algorithm for the single-machine tardiness problem discussed in Section 4 of Chapter 3, and it has also been applied in the solution of flow shop problems.

Let σ denote a partial permutation (i.e., a partial sequence of the jobs) and let σi denote the partial permutation in which i is appended to the end of σ. Also, let $q(\sigma, k)$ denote the maximum completion time on machine k for the partial sequence σ. These quantities are usually obtained recursively from the relation

$$q(\sigma i, k) = \max \{q(\sigma i, k - 1), q(\sigma, k)\} + t_{ik} \qquad \text{for } k = 1, 2, \ldots, m$$

where, for completeness, we take $q(\sigma, 0) = q(\phi, k) = 0$.

A simple dominance property for flow shop problems has already been introduced as Property 6.3. It is fairly straightforward to employ this property as an elimination condition in the search for an optimal schedule, as illustrated in the example problem given below. At stage k, all undominated partial sequences of size k are generated and Property 6.3 is applied to pairs

Job j	1	2	3	4
t_{j1}	4	3	6	5
t_{j2}	6	7	4	3
t_{j3}	6	9	2	1

of partial sequences containing the same jobs. Then the undominated partial sequences that remain are used to form partial sequences at stage $k + 1$. Table 6.5 shows the calculations that are needed for the example problem given at the bottom of page 157. Note that with no dominance checks at all, an enumeration method would construct 64 partial sequences in a four-job problem. The use of Property 6.3 in this problem, however, requires only 32 partial sequences to be constructed.

Table 6.5

Stage	σ	$q(\sigma, 1)$	$q(\sigma, 2)$	$q(\sigma, 3)$	Dominated by
1	1	4	10	16	—
	2	3	10	19	—
	3	6	10	12	—
	4	5	8	9	—
2	12	7	17	26	21
	13	10	14	18	—
	14	9	13	17	—
	21	7	16	25	—
	23	9	14	21	—
	24	8	13	20	—
	31	10	16	22	13
	32	9	17	26	23
	34	11	14	15	—
	41	9	15	21	14
	42	8	15	24	24
	43	11	15	17	34
3	132	13	21	30	213
	134	15	18	19	—
	142	12	20	29	214
	143	15	19	21	134
	213	13	20	27	—
	214	12	19	26	—
	231	13	20	27	213
	234	14	17	22	—
	241	12	19	26	214
	243	14	18	22	234
	341	15	21	27	134
	342	14	21	30	234
4	1342			34	
	2134			28	
	2143			28	
	2341			30	

Suppose now that π and π' represent two partial sequences containing different jobs and excluding the jobs in a given partial sequence σij. Then another form of a dominance property might be

$$\text{If [relation] then } q(\sigma ij\pi\pi', m) \leq q(\sigma j\pi i\pi', m) \tag{3}$$

Such a result indicates that job i dominates job j with respect to σ. In other words, all sequences that begin with the partial sequence σj can be eliminated from consideration in the search for an optimal schedule. Various researchers have proposed elimination conditions of this sort, and their successes and failures have been surveyed by McMahon (12) and by Szwarc (16), who provided the dominance property given below. Define Δ_k as follows.

$$\Delta_k = q(\sigma ij, k) - q(\sigma j, k)$$

Property 6.4

If $\Delta_{k-1} \leq \Delta_k \leq t_{ik}$ for all k, $2 \leq k \leq m$, then

$$q(\sigma ij\pi\pi', m) \leq q(\sigma j\pi i\pi', m)$$

so that job i dominates job j with respect to σ.

The proof of this result is somewhat complicated and is not included here. Details can be found in (16). In a subsequent investigation (17) Szwarc was also able to demonstrate that Property 6.4 exhibits some optimal characteristics in the class of all dominance conditions of the form in (3). Moreover, he was able to find other equivalent conditions that provide exactly the same elimination criterion as Property 6.4. A list of all of these equivalent dominance relations is given below.

1. $\Delta_{k-1} \leq \Delta_k \leq t_{ik}$ $\qquad\qquad 1 \leq k \leq m$

2. $\Delta_{k-1} \leq t_{ik}$ and $\Delta_k \leq t_{ik}$ $\qquad 1 \leq k \leq m$

3. $\max \{\Delta_1, \Delta_2, \ldots, \Delta_k\} \leq t_{ik}$ $\qquad 1 \leq k \leq m$

4. $\Delta_k \leq \min \{t_{ik}, \ldots, t_{im}\}$ $\qquad\quad 1 \leq k \leq m$

5. $\Delta_{k-1} \leq \Delta_k \leq \min \{t_{ik}, \ldots, t_{im}\}$ $\quad 1 \leq k \leq m$

Only one of these five forms need ever be used in a solution algorithm, and the choice should be based on convenience (for a computerized version of the method).

While several authors have worked on theoretical aspects of this approach to the problem, the design of a computerized algorithm has been discussed thoroughly only in references 2 and 15. The basic procedure, employing only Property 6.4, is suggested by the algorithm shown below.

ALGORITHM 6.3
(Generating Undominated Sequences for the Flow Shop Problem)

Step 1.   For a given partial sequence σ ($\sigma = \phi$ at the outset), let the jobs not contained in σ be the initial candidate set for next sequence position. Let i be one such job.

Step 2.   Choose $j \neq i$ to be some other job in the candidate set.

Step 3.   Compare σij and σj using Property 6.4, to determine whether job i dominates job j with respect to σ. If job i dominates job j, remove job j from the candidate set and then go to Step 4.

Step 4.   Repeat Step 2 for all other jobs j in the candidate set.

Step 5.   Repeat Step 1 for all jobs i initially in the candidate set.

Step 6.   All jobs i remaining in the candidate set after executing the loop in Step 5 are used to form augmented partial sequences, σi. For each augmented partial sequence, return to Step 1 and repeat.

The solution of the example problem given above by Algorithm 6.3 leads to the calculations shown in Table 6.6. At stage 1, all four one-job partial sequences are created. Then two-job partial sequences are examined in an attempt to find jobs that are dominated in first position. Thus when Property 6.4 is applied to the partial sequence 13, we find that job 3 is dominated in first position. (Notice that the partial sequence 13 was actually constructed, even though it was subsequently discovered that job 1 is also dominated in first position. This means that certain partial sequences can be constructed and discarded at the same stage: these are indicated by asterisks in the table.) In all, only 23 partial sequences are enumerated en route to finding an optimum. If Property 6.3 is included in the dominance checks at each stage, this number can be reduced to 17 (see Exercise 5.2).

An alternative form of a dominance property is

$$\text{If [relation], then } q(\sigma ij\pi\pi', m) \leq q(\sigma i\pi\pi' j, m) \qquad (4)$$

which states that with respect to the initial partial sequence σi, any sequence that assigned job j to the last position need not be considered in the search for an optimum. Using this rationale Szwarc (*17*) derived an additional dominance property.

Property 6.5

If $\max \{\Delta_1, \Delta_2, \ldots, \Delta_m\} \leq t_{im}$ then $q(\sigma ij\pi\pi', m) \leq q(\sigma i\pi\pi' j, m)$ so that job j is dominated in the last position with respect to σi.

Since this result provides a different elimination criterion than Property 6.4, Szwarc recommended that the two properties be employed in tandem when implementing an elimination algorithm.

Table 6.6

Stage	σ	$q(\sigma, 1)$	$q(\sigma, 2)$	$q(\sigma, 3)$	Dominated by
1	1	4	10	16	21
	2	3	10	19	—
	3	6	10	12	13
	4	5	8	9	—
2	12	7	17	26	*
	13	10	14	18	*
	14	9	13	17	*
	21	7	16	25	—
	23	9	14	21	213
	24	8	13	20	214
	41	9	15	21	421
	42	8	15	24	—
	43	11	15	17	413
3	213	13	20	27	—
	214	12	19	26	—
	412	12	22	31	*
	413	15	19	23	*
	421	12	21	30	—
	423	14	19	26	—
4	2134			28	
	2143			28	
	4231			32	
	4231			32	

Notice the difference between the dominance properties stated above and the dominance properties that were used in the hybrid algorithm in Section 4 of Chapter 3. The latter results involved general dominance relations that were conditioned on incomplete information about the set of jobs preceding job j and the set following job j. The flow shop dominance results are not as strong because the dominance properties involve a more restrictive condition. For example, suppose $\sigma^{(1)}$ and $\sigma^{(2)}$ are different partial sequences containing the same jobs. If job i dominates job j with respect to $\sigma^{(1)}$, it does not follow that job i necessarily dominates job j with respect to $\sigma^{(2)}$. In addition, suppose π is a nonempty partial sequence so that $\sigma\pi$ is an extended partial sequence beginning with σ. If job i dominates job j with respect to σ, it does not follow that job i dominates job j with respect to $\sigma\pi$. Nevertheless, in evaluating the potential of dominance properties to reduce the search for an optimum, remember that even though the dominance relations might be restricted in their ability to eliminate several partial sequences at once, this drawback can be offset if a large number of dominance conditions can be obtained.

Perhaps the most substantial modification of Algorithm 6.3 involves exploiting the symmetry of the makespan problem. As discussed in Section 4.2, an optimal makespan can always be found by solving a reversed problem, in which the precedence structure of the original problem is inverted. A comprehensive algorithm should attempt to identify dominance conditions in both directions as it proceeds to enumerate sequences. This means that while Property 6.4 can certainly be used to identify jobs that are dominated in the first unassigned position in sequence, it can also be used to identify jobs that are dominated in the last unassigned position in sequence. The symmetric dominance check involves an application of Property 6.4 to an initial partial sequence for the reversed problem. Similarly, Property 6.5 can be used not only to identify jobs that are dominated in the last sequence position, but also jobs that are dominated in the first sequence position. The symmetric elimination strategy suggested by this approach is similar to the hybrid algorithm described in Chapter 3, but in spite of its promise for improved efficiency, there has yet been no experimental study of its computational behavior.

6.5 EXERCISES

5.1 Prove that the five inequalities listed for Property 6.4 are equivalent. *Hint.* At some stage it should be helpful to use the fact that

$$\min\{A\text{--}C,\ B\text{--}D\} \leq \max\{A,\ B\} - \max\{C,\ D\} \leq \max\{A\text{--}C,\ B\text{--}D\}$$

5.2 Verify that when Property 6.3 is incorporated into Algorithm 6.3, the example problem is solved with the construction of only 17 partial sequences.

5.3 Apply elimination methods to find the minimum makespan.

job j	1	2	3	4
t_{j1}	1	3	5	2
t_{j2}	5	5	2	7
t_{j3}	6	2	3	5

5.4 Prove that in order for job i to dominate job j by Property 6.4, it is necessary to have

$$t_{i1} \leq t_{ik} \qquad 2 \leq k \leq m$$

5.5   What are the implications of the result stated in Exercise 5.4 for carrying out Algorithm 6.3 efficiently?

6.   HEURISTIC APPROACHES

The branch and bound approach and the elimination approach discussed in the previous sections have two inevitable disadvantages, which are typical of implicit enumeration methods. First, the computational requirements will be severe for large problems. Second, even for relatively small problems, there is no guarantee that the solution can be obtained quickly, since the extent of the partial enumeration depends on the data in the problem. Heuristic algorithms avoid these two drawbacks: they can obtain solutions to large problems with limited computational effort, and their computational requirements are predictable for problems of a given size. The drawback of heuristic approaches is, of course, that they do not guarantee optimality; and in some instances it may even be difficult to judge their effectiveness. The three heuristics described in this section are representative of quick, sub-optimal solution techniques for the makespan problem.

The guideline suggested by Palmer (*14*) can be stated qualitatively as follows: give priority to jobs having the strongest tendency to progress from short times to long times in the sequence of operations. While there might be many ways of implementing this precept, Palmer proposed the calculation of a slope index, s_j, for each job.

$$s_j = (m - 1)t_{jm} + (m - 3)t_{j,m-1} + (m - 5)t_{j,m-2} + \cdots$$
$$- (m - 3)t_{j2} - (m - 1)t_{j1}$$

Then a permutation schedule is constructed using the job ordering

$$s_{[1]} \geq s_{[2]} \geq \cdots \geq s_{[n]} \tag{5}$$

For $m = 2$, Palmer's heuristic sequences the jobs in nonincreasing order of $(t_{j2} - t_{j1})$. This method is slightly different than Johnson's rule and will not guarantee an optimum. For the job set of Table 6.1, however, the heuristic yields the sequence 1–3–4–5–2. Although this is different from the sequence constructed by Johnson's rule, it still has an optimal makespan. In the job set of Table 6.2, Palmer's heuristic yields the optimal sequence 1–3–4–2.

Gupta (*6*) sought a transitive job ordering in the form of (5) that would produce good schedules. He noted that when Johnson's rule is optimal in the three-machine case, it is in the form of (5) where

$$s_j = \frac{e_j}{\min \{t_{j1} + t_{j2}, t_{j2} + t_{j3}\}}$$

where

$$e_j = \begin{cases} 1 & \text{if} \quad t_{j1} < t_{j2} \\ -1 & \text{if} \quad t_{j1} \geq t_{j2} \end{cases}$$

Generalizing from this structure, Gupta proposed that for $m > 2$, the job index to be calculated is

$$s_j = \frac{e_j}{\min_{1 \leq k \leq m-1} \{t_{jk} + t_{j,k+1}\}}$$

where

$$e_j = \begin{cases} 1 & \text{if} \quad t_{j1} < t_{jm} \\ -1 & \text{if} \quad t_{j1} \geq t_{jm} \end{cases}$$

Thereafter the jobs are sequenced according to (5). Gupta compared this heuristic to Palmer's extensively and found it to generate better schedules than Palmer's in a substantial majority of cases. (For the problems in Tables 6.1 and 6.2, Gupta's heuristic also produces an optimum.) In addition, Gupta (6) has investigated a set of other heuristics that are also based on schedule construction via transitive rules.

Perhaps the most significant heuristic method for makespan problems is the method of Campbell, Dudek, and Smith (CDS) (4). Its strength lies in two properties: (1) it uses Johnson's rule in a heuristic fashion, and (2) it generally creates several schedules from which a "best" schedule can be chosen.

The CDS algorithm corresponds to a multistage use of Johnson's rule applied to a new problem, derived from the original, with processing times t'_{j1} and t'_{j2}. At stage 1,

$$t'_{j1} = t_{j1} \quad \text{and} \quad t'_{j2} = t_{jm}$$

In other words, Johnson's rule is applied to the first and mth operations and intermediate operations are ignored. At stage 2,

$$t'_{j1} = t_{j1} + t_{j2} \quad \text{and} \quad t'_{j2} = t_{jm} + t_{j,m-1}$$

That is, Johnson's rule is applied to the sums of the first two and last two operation processing times. In general at stage i,

$$t'_{j1} = \sum_{k=1}^{i} t_{jk} \quad \text{and} \quad t'_{j2} = \sum_{k=1}^{i} t_{j,m-k+1}$$

For each stage i ($i = 1, 2, \ldots, m - 1$), the job order obtained is used to calculate a makespan for the original problem. After $m - 1$ stages, the best makespan among the $m - 1$ schedules is identified. (Some of the $m - 1$ sequences may be identical.) To deal with ties at any stage, one approach might be to evaluate the makespan for all alternatives at a given stage. In the original presentation, the authors propose breaking ties between pairs of jobs by using the ordering of the two jobs in the previous stage (or referring to a future stage when necessary).

Campbell, Dudek, and Smith tested their algorithm extensively and examined its performance as compared to Palmer's heuristic in several problems. They found that the CDS algorithm was generally more effective, for both small and large problems. In addition, the computer times required were of the same order of magnitude for $n \leq 20$. Only in somewhat larger problems would the question of trading-off solution value for computing time arise.

To illustrate the three heuristic methods, consider the five-job three-machine problem shown in the table below. Palmer's method for $m = 3$ sets

Job J	1	2	3	4	5
t_{j1}	6	4	3	9	5
t_{j2}	8	1	9	5	6
t_{j3}	2	1	5	8	6

the slope index to $s_j = 2t_{j3} - 2t_{j1}$. Thus

$$s_1 = -8 \qquad s_2 = -6 \qquad s_3 = 4 \qquad s_4 = -2 \qquad s_5 = 2$$

The sequence in (5) yields the job ordering 3–5–4–2–1, for which $M = 37$. With Gupta's heuristic

$$s_1 = -\tfrac{1}{10} \qquad s_2 = -\tfrac{1}{2} \qquad s_3 = \tfrac{1}{12} \qquad s_4 = -\tfrac{1}{13} \qquad s_5 = \tfrac{1}{11}$$

The sequence (5) yields the job ordering 5–3–4–1–2, for which $M = 36$. Thirdly, the CDS heuristic yields the job ordering 3–5–4–1–2 at both stages, and for this sequence, $M = 35$.

Further experimentation with these three heuristics is suggested in Exercise 9.4.

6.6   EXERCISES

6.1   What might be an advantage of a heuristic method that employs a transitive ordering, as in formula 5?

6.2   Find the makespan generated by each of the three heuristic methods for the following problem.

Job J	1	2	3	4
t_{j1}	4	3	1	3
t_{j2}	3	7	2	4
t_{j3}	7	2	4	3
t_{j4}	8	5	7	2

6.3   What is the optimal makespan for the example problem in this section?

7. FLOW SHOPS WITHOUT INTERMEDIATE QUEUES

In many practical situations once the processing of a job begins, subsequent processing must be carried out with no delays in the operation sequence. In other words, no queues are allowed to form at any machine. Such a requirement is frequently encountered in the metal processing industries, particularly where metal is rolled while it is hot. Delays between operations result in cooling that makes the rolling operation prohibitively difficult.

Consider the problem of minimizing makespan when no delays are permitted (18). Again, for simplicity, an optimal permutation schedule is sought, even though the set of permutation schedules is not dominant in a theoretical sense. Suppose that jobs i and j are adjacent in sequence and that job i precedes job j. Figure 6.10a shows the delays that would be incurred in the processing of job j if the two jobs were released to a shop at the same time and job i encountered no delays. In the figure, I_{jh} denotes the idle time or delay incurred by job j prior to its operation on machine h. To process job j without any delays so that it will be completed at the same time, the idle time need only be incurred at the start, as shown by the rearrangement in Figure 6.10b. Now suppose that job j is followed in sequence by job k. Notice that the delays incurred in the processing of job k do not depend on what happened before job j in sequence but only on the operation times of job j itself, when it is processed without delay, as in Figure 6.10b. Let D_{ij} denote the total delay (measured from the start of job i) incurred by job j when it follows job i in sequence. That is,

$$D_{ij} = I_{j1} + I_{j2} + \cdots + I_{jm}$$

Similarly define D_{jk} to be the total delay (measured from the start of job j) incurred by job k when it follows job j in sequence. If the schedule consisted

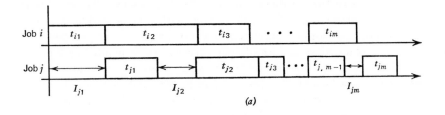

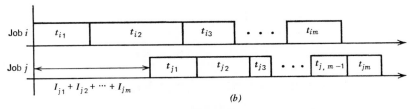

(a)

(b)

Figure 6.10

The timing of individual operations on successive jobs i and j. The rearrangement in (b) avoids delays on job j at any machine after the first, without delaying the final completion of job j.

of only these three jobs, then an expression for the makespan of the schedule associated with the sequence ijk (see Figure 6.11) is simply

$$M = D_{ij} + D_{jk} + \sum_{h=1}^{m} t_{kh}$$

In general, an expression for the makespan is

$$M = \sum_{j=1}^{n-1} D_{[j],[j+1]} + \sum_{h=1}^{m} t_{[n]h}$$

Thus, the makespan is the sum of two quantities: (1) a sum of sequence-dependent delay terms and (2) the total processing time of the last job in

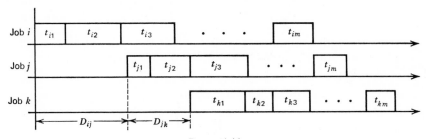

Figure 6.11

The timing of individual operations for three jobs, when no intermediate delays are permitted.

sequence. The structure of this expression closely resembles the criterion in the traveling salesman problem and, in fact, with a little modification this makespan problem can be formulated as a traveling salesman problem.

In the traveling salesman formulation, each city corresponds to a job, and the intercity distances correspond to the delay pairs D_{ij}. In addition, one dummy city must be added to the problem (corresponding to an idle state) to which the distance from city i is $\sum_{h=1}^{m} t_{ih}$, and from which the distance to all other cities is zero, as shown in Table 6.7.

Table 6.7

—	D_{12}	D_{13} $\cdots$	D_{1n}	$\sum_{k=1}^{m} t_{1k}$
D_{21}	—	D_{23} $\cdots$	D_{2n}	$\sum_{k=1}^{m} t_{2k}$
.				
.				
.				
D_{n1}	D_{n2}	D_{n3} $\cdots$	—	$\sum_{k=1}^{m} t_{nk}$
0	0	0 $\cdots$	0	—

As an example, suppose the problem contains four jobs and five machines with the processing times tabulated below. It is then possible to verify that

Job j	1	2	3	4
t_{j1}	3	1	4	2
t_{j2}	4	3	2	9
t_{j3}	6	5	1	8
t_{j4}	8	7	0	7
t_{j5}	2	6	5	3

the appropriate traveling salesman problem to solve is associated with the following distance matrix:

—	12	16	5	23
3	—	15	2	22
4	5	—	4	12
13	17	22	—	29
0	0	0	0	—

Suppose the closest-unvisited-city algorithm (see Chapter 4) is used to find a solution to this problem. If city 1 is chosen as an origin, then the procedure constructs the sequence 1-4-2-3, with a makespan of 49. Exercise 7.2 asks whether this is the optimal makespan.

6.7 EXERCISES

7.1 Solve the example problem in this section by using the other heuristic methods introduced in Chapter 4 for the traveling salesman problem.

7.2 What is the optimal makespan in the example problem?

8. OTHER PERFORMANCE MEASURES

Even though so much research has been devoted to flow shop scheduling, relatively few results exist for performance measures other than makespan. Perhaps the most extensive investigation of a specialized solution algorithm was carried out by Ignall and Schrage (8) for mean flowtime. They devised a branch and bound procedure for determining the best permutation schedule and tested their procedure on job sets with $m = 2$, for which permutation schedules are dominant. Their computational results were somewhat discouraging, and they concluded that the branch and bound approach is less successful in the mean flowtime problem when $m = 2$ than it is in the makespan problem when $m = 3$. More recently, Gupta (6) has proposed and tested a collection of heuristic procedures for flow shop problems. His primary goal was the development of heuristic approaches to the mean flowtime problem, but it is interesting to note that heuristic procedures that seemed effective at minimizing mean flowtime also were fairly effective at minimizing makespan. Nevertheless, none of the mean flowtime-oriented methods could match the CDS procedure in makespan problems.

It is also possible to attack mean flowtime problems with integer programming formulations. In fact the main advantage of an integer programming approach is that it can accommodate a variety of scheduling criteria. The particular formulation described below (for $m \geq 3$) is fairly economical in terms of its use of decision variables, although it does not appear to be computationally practical on any but the smallest problem sizes, and it comprises only permutation schedules.

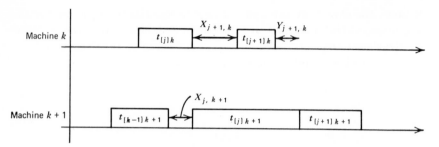

Figure 6.12
Notation for the integer programming formulation.

Let z_{ij} be an indicator variable defined in the following way:

$$z_{ij} = 1 \quad \text{if job } i \text{ is assigned position } j \text{ in sequence}$$
$$= 0 \quad \text{otherwise}$$

Therefore a feasible solution to the problem requires that

$$\sum_{i=1}^{n} z_{ij} = 1 \tag{6}$$

$$\sum_{j=1}^{n} z_{ij} = 1 \tag{7}$$

$X_{jk} = $ idle time on machine k just prior to the start of the job in sequence position j, for $k = 2, 3, \ldots, m$

$Y_{jk} = $ idle time of the job in sequence position j between its completion on machine k and its start on machine $(k + 1)$, for $k = 1, 2, \ldots, m - 1$

These two variables are depicted in Figure 6.12. Notice at this point that the processing time of the job in sequence position j on machine k can be written

$$\sum_{i=1}^{n} t_{ik} z_{ij}$$

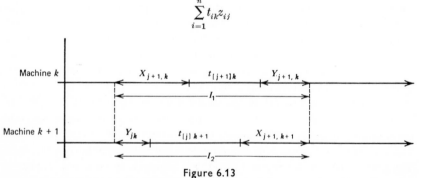

Figure 6.13
The principal consistency constraint of the integer programming formulation ($I_1 = I_2$), displayed on a Gantt chart.

Now by reference to Figure 6.13, we can see that the variables X_{jk} and Y_{jk} are consistent (i.e., feasible) if the two intervals I_1 and I_2 shown in the figure are constrained to be equal. Feasibility, therefore, requires that

$$X_{j+1,k} + \sum_{i=1}^{n} t_{ik} z_{i,j+1} + Y_{j+1,k} = Y_{j,k} + \sum_{i=1}^{n} t_{i,k+1} z_{ij} + X_{j+1,k+1} \qquad (8)$$

Notice that makespan is equal to the total idle time on machine m plus the total processing time on machine m. Since the latter is a constant in any schedule, the makespan can be written as $\sum_{j=1}^{n} X_{jm}$, and the minimization of makespan is formulated as follows.

Minimize $\sum_{j=1}^{n} X_{jm}$

Subject to

$$X_{j+1,k} + \sum_{i=1}^{n} t_{ik} z_{i,j+1} + Y_{j+1,k} - Y_{j,k} - \sum_{i=1}^{n} t_{i,k+1} z_{ij} - X_{j+1,k+1} = 0,$$

$$1 \leq k \leq m - 1$$
$$1 \leq j \leq n - 1$$

$$\sum_{i=1}^{n} z_{ij} = 1 \qquad 1 \leq j \leq n$$

$$\sum_{j=1}^{n} z_{ij} = 1 \qquad 1 \leq i \leq n$$

$$X_{jk} \geq 0 \qquad Y_{jk} \geq 0 \qquad \text{and} \qquad z_{ij} = 0 \qquad \text{or} \qquad 1$$

where $X_{j1} = 0$, since it is not necessary to schedule idle time on the first machine, and $Y_{jm} = 0$ by definition. The number of constraints in the formulation is $2n + (n-1)(m-1)$, and the number of variables is $n^2 + n(2m-2)$ or $n^2 + 2mn - 2n$. For a small problem containing $n = 4$ jobs and $m = 3$ machines, the integer programming formulation contains 14 constraints and 32 variables, and for a moderate-sized problem with $n = 10$ and $m = 5$, the integer programming formulation is 56 by 180. Although these problem sizes are considered fairly large given the capabilities of integer programming codes, one important advantage of the formulation is that it can accommodate other performance measures without many changes (see Exercise 8.3). A more general integer programming approach, which can accommodate nonpermutation schedules, is presented in the next chapter.

Gupta and Dudek (7) reported an experimental study of a comprehensive performance measure in flow shop problems. They proposed a criterion that included several types of costs normally related to scheduling decisions. The performance measure was a total cost function consisting of in-process inventory costs, tardiness penalty costs, machine idle costs, and sequence-dependent setup costs. The authors performed a sensitivity analysis by evaluating the schedules produced by a solution method that optimizes with respect to only one or two components of the true total cost function. Among the suboptimal procedures they investigated, the best was a method that focused on both mean flowtime and weighted mean tardiness. However, they also observed that scheduling to minimize makespan was not a particularly good method for minimizing total costs. While these conclusions are not startling, the significance of the work is that it may signal a departure of flow shop studies from the makespan orientation that has become so traditional.

6.8 EXERCISES

8.1 What are the dimensions of the integer programming formulation for the minimization of M in the following types of problems:
  (a) 4 jobs, 3 machines.
  (b) 4 jobs, 4 machines.
  (c) 5 jobs, 4 machines.
  (d) 20 jobs, 10 machines.

8.2 Write out the complete set of constraints for the integer programming formulation for minimizing M with the job set given in Exercise 4.3.

8.3 Develop linear integer programming formulations for minimizing $\bar{F}$ and $\bar{T}$ in a flow shop problem.

8.4 Consider a flow shop problem in which the m machines are rented to perform a collection of jobs, and suppose that the pertinent measure of performance is total machine rental cost. Let h_k denote the cost associated with renting machine k for one time period, where h_k is incurred from time 0 (when all machines are rented) until machine k is no longer needed. Construct an objective function for determining an optimal schedule and discuss methods of producing a schedule.

9. SUMMARY

In the development of scheduling models more general than single-machine models, the flow shop represents the most direct extension to multiple-resource situations. In the area of flow shop problems, scheduling theory has been strongly influenced by Johnson's early work, very possibly because it is the only optimal scheduling rule applicable to a large class of flow shop problems. One disadvantage of this influence might be the disproportionate attention that researchers have paid to the makespan problem, since that was the focus of Johnson's result. In view of the many intriguing and practical variations in the single-machine model, it is remarkable that no similar progress has been made with other performance measures.

On the other hand, the pivotal influence of Johnson's work has had some definite advantages. First, by emphasizing the properties of permutation schedules, he focused flow shop research on problems of manageable size. Multiple-resource problems are certainly more difficult than single-resource problems. In a sense, the multiple-resource structure potentially represents a situation in which each resource is itself associated with a combinatorial problem and in which these several problems are closely interrelated. In such a case, it is an acceptable simplification to deal only with a manageable set of alternatives. In the flow shop model, the problem of finding a best permutation schedule is no larger than related single-machine problems, and it might be anticipated that implicit enumeration methods would often be appropriate, except for large job sets.

A second advantage of the Johnson influence is that the two-machine analysis seems to have captured the essence of larger problems. Thus where Johnson's rule provided a basis for the development of a heuristic approach to larger problems (as in the Gupta and CDS procedures) it was remarkably successful.

In general, solutions to flow shop problems appear to require either combinatorial techniques that take advantage of special problem structures or else clever heuristic methods. Given the reliance on these two approaches, it is critically important to recognize the trade-offs involved. The effectiveness of any solution method can be evaluated only on relative terms, on the basis of the availability of computational resources and the acceptability of suboptimal results.

6.9   COMPUTATIONAL EXERCISES

9.1   Write a computer program to solve the n-job m-machine makespan problem using the basic Ignall–Schrage branch and bound algorithm (with jumptracking). Generate a set of test problems and compare the performance of the basic algorithm to a modified version that incorporates the ideas of Section 4.2.

9.2   Compare the most efficient jumptracking algorithm (Exercise 9.1) with an efficient backtracking algorithm that uses a heuristic procedure to obtain a good initial solution. Investigate, where appropriate, the modifications discussed in Section 4.2.

9.3   Write a computer program to find an optimal makespan by elimination methods. On a set of test problems, evaluate the computational implications of using Dominance Properties 6.3 and 6.5 as well as the effects of exploiting symmetry. Evaluate elimination as an optimization strategy as compared to branch and bound.

9.4   Construct a set of test problems to compare the performance of the heuristic methods described in Section 6. Evaluate all schedules with respect to $\bar{F}$ as well as with respect to makespan.

9.5   Propose and test some heuristic procedures for minimizing $\bar{F}$ in flow shop problems.

9.6   Design and test heuristic procedures for minimizing $\bar{F}$ in the flow shop without intermediate queues.

9.7   Design and test an optimizing algorithm for minimizing $\bar{F}$ in the flow shop without intermediate queues. Hence evaluate the efficiency of the heuristic procedures developed in Exercise 9.6.

REFERENCES

1. Ashour, S. "An Experimental Investigation and Comparative Evaluation of Flow Shop Scheduling Techniques," *Operations Research*, Vol. 18, No. 3 (May, 1970).
2. Bagga, P. C., and Chakravati, N. K. "Optimal m-Stage Production Schedule," *CORS Journal*, Vol. 6, No. 2 (July, 1968).
3. Brown, A., and Lomnicki, Z. "Some Applications of the Branch and Bound Algorithm to the Machine Scheduling Problem," *Operational Research Quarterly*, Vol. 17, No. 2 (June, 1966).
4. Campbell, H. G., Dudek, R. A., and Smith, M. L. "A Heuristic Algorithm for the n Job m Machine Sequencing Problem," *Management Science*, Vol. 16, No. 10 (June, 1970).
5. Gupta, J. N. D. "A Functional Heuristic Algorithm for the Flow Shop Scheduling Problem," *Operational Research Quarterly*, Vol. 22, No. 1 (March, 1971).
6. Gupta, J. N. D. "Heuristic Algorithms for Multistage Flow Shop Problem," *AIIE Transactions*, Vol. 4, No. 1 (March, 1972).
7. Gupta, J. N. D., and Dudek, R. A. "Optimality Criteria for Flow Shop Schedules," *AIIE Transactions*, Vol. 3, No. 3 (September, 1971).
8. Ignall, E., and Schrage, L. E. "Application of the Branch and Bound Technique to Some Flow Shop Scheduling Problems," *Operations Research*, Vol. 13, No. 3 (May, 1965).
9. Johnson, S. M. "Optimal Two- and Three-Stage Production Schedules with Setup Times Included," *Naval Research Logistics Quarterly*, Vol. 1, No. 1 (March, 1954).
10. Lomnicki, Z. "A Branch-and-Bound Algorithm for the Exact Solution of the Three-Machine Scheduling Problem," *Operational Research Quarterly*, Vol. 16, No. 1 (March, 1965).

11. McMahon, G. B., and Burton, P. G. "Flow-Shop Scheduling with the Branch and Bound Method," *Operations Research*, Vol. 15, No. 3 (May, 1967).

12. McMahon, G. B. "Optimal Production Schedules for Flow Shops," *CORS Journal*, Vol. 7, No. 2 (July, 1969).

13. Mitten, L. G., "Sequencing *n* Jobs on Two Machines with Arbitrary Time Lags," *Management Science*, Vol. 5, No. 3 (April, 1959).

14. Palmer, D. S. "Sequencing Jobs Through a Multi-Stage Process in the Minimum Total Time—A Quick Method of Obtaining a Near Optimum," *Operational Research Quarterly*, Vol. 16, No. 1 March, 1965).

15. Smith, R. D., and Dudek, R. A. "A General Algorithm for Solution of the *n*-Job M-Machine Sequencing Problem of the Flow Shop," *Operations Research*, Vol. 15, No. 1 (January, 1967) and Errata, Vol. 17, No. 4 (July, 1969).

16. Szwarc, W. "Elimination Methods in the $m \times n$ Sequencing Problem," *Naval Research Logistics Quarterly*, Vol. 18, No. 3 (September, 1971).

17. Szwarc, W. "Optimal Elimination Methods in the $m \times n$ Flow Shop Scheduling Problem," *Operations Research*, Vol. 21, No. 6 (November–December, 1973).

18. Wismer, D. A. "Solution of the Flow Shop Scheduling Problem with No Intermediate Queues," *Operations Research*, Vol. 20, No. 3 (May, 1972).

CHAPTER 7
JOB SHOP SCHEDULING

1. INTRODUCTION

The classical job shop scheduling problem differs from the flow shop problem in one important respect: the flow of work is not unidirectional. The elements of a problem are a set of machines and a collection of jobs to be scheduled. Each job consists of several operations with the same linear precedence structure as in the flow shop model. Although it is possible to allow any number of operations in a given job, the most common formulation of the job shop problem specifies that each job has exactly m operations, one on each machine. It is conceptually no more difficult to deal with general cases in which a job may require processing by the same machine more than once in its operation sequence. Because the workflow in a job shop is not unidirectional, each machine in the shop can be characterized by the input and output flows of work shown in Figure 7.1. Unlike the flow shop model, there is no initial machine that performs only the first operation of a job, nor is there a terminal machine that performs only the last operation of a job.

In the flow shop, operation k of any job is performed by machine k, and there was really no need to distinguish between operation number and machine number. In the job shop case it is more appropriate to describe an operation with a triplet (i, j, k) in order to denote the fact that operation j of

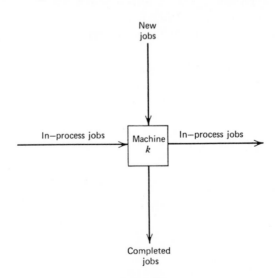

Figure 7.1
Work flow at a typical machine in a job shop.

178

job i requires machine k. Otherwise, the job shop model is based on the same fundamental assumptions that were specified for the flow shop model in Chapter 6.

A graphical description of the job shop problem involves the jobs and a Gantt chart to be filled in. The graphical job description in Figure 7.2a consists of a collection of blocks, each of which is identified by a job-operation-machine triplet. The length of the block is equal to the processing time of the associated operation, using the scale of the Gantt chart. The sequential numbering of operations for a given job is a means of indicating the linear operation sequence. If the operation blocks are placed as compactly as possible on the Gantt chart in some arbitrary fashion as in Figure 7.2b, the chart describes the workload for each machine but is unlikely to represent a valid schedule. A feasible schedule is shown in Figure 7.3a. A schedule is a feasible resolution of the resource constraints when no two operations ever occupy the same machine simultaneously. A schedule is also a feasible resolution of the logical constraints when all operations of each given job can be placed on one time axis in precedence order and without overlap. A graphical display of this property is shown in Figure 7.3b.

A tabular representation of the data for this example problem is shown in Tables 7.1a and 7.1b. The first table consists of operation processing times and the second consists of operation machine assignments. The set of machine

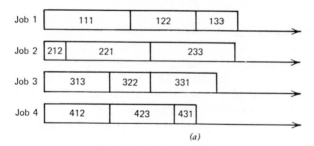

(a)

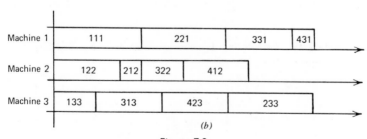

(b)

Figure 7.2

Graphical descriptions of the job shop problem. In (a) a job-by-job description of the work is given, while in (b) a machine-by-machine description is given.

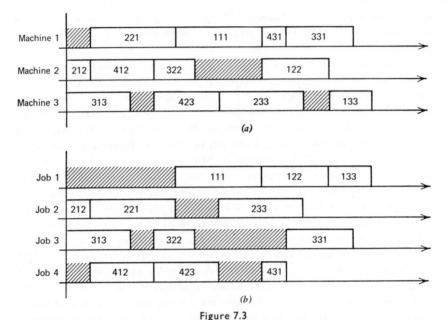

Figure 7.3

Two views of a feasible job shop schedule: (*a*) the Gantt chart and (*b*) the job-by-job description.

assignments for a given job constitute a *routing*. For example, job 2 has a machine routing of 2–1–3.

To complete the problem statement, of course, a measure of performance must be specified. The problem is then one of constructing a schedule (graphically, this means placing operation blocks on the Gantt chart) that is feasible and that optimizes the performance measure.

Recall that in the flow shop problem there appeared at first glance to be $(n!)^m$ schedules to examine in the search for an optimum. Certain theoretical properties allowed this number to be reduced in special cases. Moreover, it was possible to argue that for large problems the subset of permutation

Table 7.1*a* Processing Times

		Operation		
		1	2	3
	1	4	3	2
Job	2	1	4	4
	3	3	2	3
	4	3	3	1

Table 7.1*b* Routing

		Operation		
		1	2	3
	1	1	2	3
Job	2	2	1	3
	3	3	2	1
	4	2	3	1

schedules was likely to contain very good solutions even if it could not be guaranteed to contain an optimum. In a sense, the first problem in dealing with the job shop is to locate a similar "very good" subset of the feasible solutions for more detailed examination. This subset should be straightforward to construct and should be as small as possible. Section 2 discusses this subset of schedules, and Section 3 describes how to generate these schedules systematically. This generation procedure suggests a branch and bound approach to small problems, which is explored in Section 4, as well as heuristic approaches to large problems, which are discussed in Section 5. Integer programming formulations for general performance measures are introduced in Section 6.

2. TYPES OF SCHEDULES

In principle, there are an infinite number of feasible schedules for any job shop problem, because an arbitrary amount of idle time can be inserted at any machine between adjacent pairs of operations. It should be clear, however, that once the operation sequence is specified for each machine, this kind of idle time cannot be helpful for any regular measure of performance. Rather, it is desirable that the operations be processed as compactly as possible. Superfluous idle time exists in a schedule if some operation can be started earlier in time without altering the operation sequences on any machine. Adjusting the start time of some operation in this way is equivalent to moving an operation block to the left on the Gantt chart while preserving the operation sequences. This type of adjustment is thus called a *local left-shift*, or a limited left-shift. Given an operation sequence for each machine, there is only one schedule in which no local left-shift can be made. The set of all schedules in which no local left-shift can be made is called the set of *semiactive* schedules and is equivalent to the set of all schedules that contain none of the superfluous idle time described above. This set dominates the set of all schedules, which means that it is sufficient to consider only semiactive schedules to optimize any regular measure of performance.

The number of semiactive schedules is at least finite, although it may well be quite large. The exact number is usually difficult to determine. For the classical job shop problem, in which each job has exactly one operation on each machine, each machine must process n operations. The number of possible sequences is therefore $n!$ for each machine. If the sequences on each machine were entirely independent, there would be $(n!)^m$ semiactive schedules. However, the effect of the precedence structure and machine routing for each job is usually to render some of these combinations of sequences infeasible. For example, consider the case $n = 2$ and $m = 2$, where the jobs have the

Table 7.2

	Operation	
	1	2
Job 1	1	2
2	2	1

different routings shown in Table 7.2. Although $(n!)^m = 4$ in this case, the reader should find it possible to construct only three feasible semiactive schedules.

A network interpretation of this structure is quite useful. The two-job example is represented by the simple precedence relationships shown in

(a)

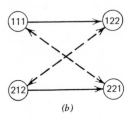

(b)

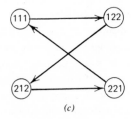

(c)

Figure 7.4

Network interpretations of the logical constraints in job shop models.

Figure 7.4a. The construction of a schedule will resolve the question of whether operation (1, 1, 1) precedes (2, 2, 1) on machine 1 and whether (1, 2, 2) precedes (2, 1, 2) on machine 2. In network terms, these unresolved aspects of sequence are represented by *disjunctive arcs*, drawn as unoriented arrows (dotted lines) in Figure 7.4b. The disjunctive arcs represent precedence relations that cannot be determined before a schedule is constructed. However, once a sequence is determined for machine 1, the disjunctive arc connecting nodes (1, 1, 1) and (2, 2, 1) will be replaced by the usual (oriented) precedence arrow, or *conjunctive* arc. Similarly, the choice of a sequence for machine 2 will resolve the disjunctive arc between (1, 2, 2) and (2, 1, 2). Now the only restriction governing the use of these disjunctive arcs is that a resolution must not form a cycle (or loop) in the network. Of the four potential resolutions of the network in Figure 7.4b, only the one shown in Figure 7.4c contains a loop and cannot be interpreted as representing a valid schedule (there is no initial operation in the network).

This type of reasoning applies to larger versions of the job shop problem. For instance, the two-job example is contained in the four-job, four-machine problem of Table 7.1, so that the number of semiactive schedules in that problem must certainly be smaller than $(4!)^4$. The main point is simply that the number of semiactive schedules is finite. The size of the exact number is only of academic interest, since its only practical use would be "to demonstrate the enormous size of the problem and to discourage attempts at enumeration" (*6*, p. 110). Moreover, it is possible to find a dominant subset within the set of semiactive schedules.

In a semiactive schedule the start time of a particular operation is constrained either by the processing of a different job on the same machine or by the processing of the directly preceding operation on a different machine. In the former case, where the completion of an earlier operation on the same machine is constraining, it may still be possible to find obvious means of improvement. Suppose, in the example of Table 7.1, that the job sequence 4–3–2–1 is used at each machine. The associated semiactive schedule is displayed in Figure 7.5a. While no local left-shifts are possible in this schedule, a better schedule can obviously be devised. For instance, it is possible to start operation (1, 1, 1) earlier than at time 18 without delaying any other operation. Indeed, operation (1, 1, 1) can be started at time 0, and all three operations of job 1 can be started earlier without delaying any of the other operations. On the Gantt chart, such an alteration would correspond to shifting operation (1, 1, 1) to the left and beyond other operations already scheduled on machine 1. This type of adjustment—in which some operation is begun earlier without delaying any other operation—is called a *global left-shift*, or simply a left-shift. The set of all schedules in which no global left-shift can be made is called the set of *active* schedules, and is clearly a subset of the set of semiactive schedules.

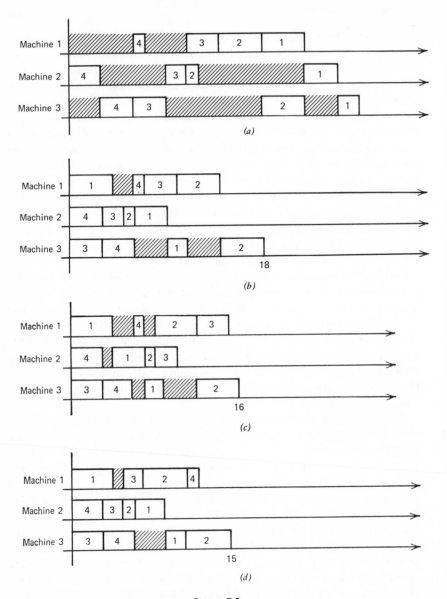

Figure 7.5
The effect of left-shifts in altering a given semiactive schedule (*a*) and rendering it more compact, as in (*b*), (*c*), or (*d*).

Just as the set of semiactive schedules dominates the set of all schedules, so the set of active schedules dominates the set of semiactive schedules. In other words, in optimizing any regular measure of performance it is sufficient to consider only active schedules. Evidently the number of active schedules is a function of both the routings and the processing times in a given problem, whereas the number of semiactive schedules is a function of only the routings. While one semiactive schedule corresponds to each feasible combination of machine sequences, as discussed above, many semiactive schedules can often be compacted into the same active schedule through a series of left-shifts.

It should also be observed that several different active schedules can be constructed by a series of left-shifts starting with a given semiactive schedule. For example, suppose the operations in Figure 7.5a are left-shifted as far as possible, in the job order 3–2–1 (the operations of job 4 cannot be left-shifted at all). The active schedule that emerges is shown in Figure 7.5b and has a makespan of 18. Alternatively, suppose the operations in Figure 7.5a are left-shifted as far as possible, but in the job order 1–2–3. The active schedule that results is shown in Figure 7.5c and has a makespan of 16.

Another way to look at the role of semiactive and active schedules is with the use of a Venn diagram. The large rectangle in Figure 7.6 represents the (infinite) set of all schedules. The interior of the region labeled $S–A$ represents the finite set of semiactive schedules. Wholly contained within that set is the set of active schedules, represented by the region labeled A. The asterisk represents some optimal schedule, placed to indicate that at least one optimum must lie in the active subset.

The number of active schedules still tends to be large, and it is sometimes convenient to focus on an even smaller subset called the *nondelay* schedules. In a nondelay schedule no machine is kept idle at a time when it could begin processing some operation. For example, in Figure 7.5b, notice that machine 1 remains idle at time 5 when it could start on operation $(3, 3, 1)$. Therefore the schedule shown is not a nondelay schedule. If the job order on

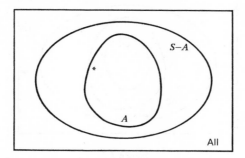

Figure 7.6
A Venn diagram of the semiactive (S-A) and active (A) schedules.

machine 1 were changed to 1–3–2–4 the associated semiactive schedule would also be active and nondelay (see Figure 7.5*d*). By examining the idle intervals in Figure 7.5*c*, it can also be determined that the schedule shown is not a nondelay schedule. This particular schedule should suggest that it may not be simple to construct a nondelay schedule from some given active schedule.

All nondelay schedules are active schedules since no left-shifting would be possible. On the other hand many active schedules may not be nondelay schedules. This means that the number of nondelay schedules can be significantly less than the number of active schedules. The dilemma is that there is no guarantee that the nondelay subset will contain an optimum. The Venn diagram of Figure 7.6 is extended to include nondelay schedules in Figure 7.7. Figure 7.7*a* depicts a situation in which at least one optimal schedule is a nondelay schedule, while in Figure 7.7*b* no optimal schedule is a nondelay schedule.

In summary, the active schedules are generally the smallest dominant set in the job shop problem. The nondelay schedules are smaller in number but are not dominant. Nevertheless, as will be discussed subsequently, the best

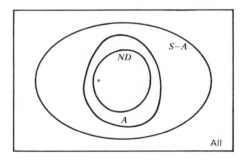

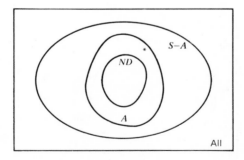

Figure 7.7

Venn diagrams illustrating the relation of nondelay (*ND*) schedules to active and semiactive schedules.

nondelay schedule can usually be expected to provide a very good solution, if not an optimum. In a sense, the role of the nondelay schedules is similar to that of the permutation schedules in large flow shop problems: although the set is not always dominant, it can usually produce a solution close to the optimum.

This treatment of schedule classifications only lays the groundwork for dealing with job shop problems. The next phase is the development of systematic procedures for the generation of schedules. Thereafter, a variety of solution algorithms can be designed, adapting the generating procedures to the needs of specific problems.

7.2 EXERCISES

2.1 Devise a regular measure of performance (and supply additional data, if necessary) for which the active schedule in Figure 7.5*b* is better than the nondelay schedule in Figure 7.5*d*.

2.2 A flow shop problem can be viewed as a special case of the job shop problem. Sketch the network diagram for a disjunctive graph model of a flow shop schedule (compare Figure 7.4). What can be said about the number of semi-active schedules in a flow shop problem?

2.3 Treating the flow shop problem as a special case of the job shop problem, sketch the Venn diagrams that relate active and nondelay schedules in the flow shop case. Is there any situation in which the best nondelay schedule is guaranteed to be optimal?

3. SCHEDULE GENERATION

Procedures for generating schedules are fundamental to a variety of solution techniques for job shop problems. Because this role is so vital, it is desirable for schedule generation procedures to be logical in design and efficient in implementation.

Generation procedures, like the schedules they generate, can be classified. Depending on the way that operation start times are determined, a generating procedure can be classified as a *single-pass* mechanism or an *adjusting* mechanism. In a single-pass procedure the start time of an operation is permanently fixed the first time it is assigned; therefore a full schedule can be generated with a single pass through the list of operations. In an adjusting procedure, a start time may be reassigned after subsequent operations are added to the schedule. It is often argued that manual solutions to a job shop problem—based on manipulations of a Gantt chart—are most apt to be adjusting procedures. Nevertheless, manual techniques actually used in practice might be intricate and difficult to generalize, so that single-pass structures pervade experimental and theoretical results. Conway, Maxwell, and Miller (6) make the following observation on this subject.

"One might initially suppose that the restrictions placed on single-pass procedures would make some schedules inaccessible to this type of generation, so that adjusting procedures would be theoretically preferable. Strictly speaking, this is not the case, since for any schedule at all there is a corresponding single-pass procedure capable of producing it. It follows that for any active schedule there is a single-pass procedure. However, while this implies that the class of single-pass procedures is sufficient, it does not necessarily imply that it is desirable to restrict attention to this class. An optimal single-pass generation procedure assuredly exists for a particular problem, but it may have neither rhyme nor reason, and no similarity to an optimal procedure for any other problem. It may be easier to search among adjusting procedures than to pursue a patternless single-pass procedure."

An important class of procedures for generating schedules is the class of *dispatching* procedures. As defined in more simple problems (see Chapters 4 and 5), a dispatching procedure is one in which the actual decisions affecting a given machine can be implemented in the same order that they are made. In practice, this means that scheduling decisions need not be made all at once, but only as they are needed. In the job shop problem a scheduling decision is usually necessary whenever a machine becomes idle. The decision is either to leave such a machine idle or else to begin processing one of the operations that might be waiting for it. With a dispatching procedure, this type of decision need not be made in advance in order that the latest shop data can be taken into account. For this reason, dispatching procedures are rather common in actual practice, where they can easily be adapted to dynamic job arrivals, machine breakdowns, or other factors that affect shop status over time.

Dispatching procedures are single-pass procedures in two respects. Not only do they make one pass through the list of operations, assigning an irrevocable starting time to each, but they also make one pass in time from the beginning of the schedule to the end. They construct the schedule left to right on the Gantt chart. A different kind of single-pass approach, for example, is a job-at-a-time procedure. This type of mechanism makes a single pass through the operations, job by job. It schedules all the operations of a given job before proceeding to schedule the operations of other jobs. Such an approach makes one pass through the list of operations, although it will likely make several passes in time through the schedule.

Most schedule generation procedures treat operations in an order consistent with the precedence relations of the problem. In other words, no operation is considered until all of its predecessors have been scheduled. Once all the predecessors of operation (i, j, k) are scheduled, the operation is said to be *schedulable*, regardless of the actual time at which the next scheduling decision is required. Generation procedures operate with a set of schedulable operations at each stage, and this set is determined simply from precedence structure. The number of stages for a one-pass procedure is equal to the number of operations, or nm. At each stage, the operations that have already been assigned starting times make up a *partial schedule*. Given a partial schedule for any job shop problem, a unique corresponding set of schedulable operations may be constructed. Let

PS_t = a partial schedule containing t scheduled operations

S_t = the set of schedulable operations at stage t, corresponding to a given PS_t

σ_j = the earliest time at which operation $j \in S_t$ could be started[1]

ϕ_j = the earliest time at which operation $j \in S_t$ could be completed

For a given active partial schedule, the potential start time σ_j is determined by the completion time of the direct predecessor of operation j and the latest completion time on the machine required by operation j. The larger of these two quantities is σ_j. The potential finish time ϕ_j is simply $\sigma_j + t_j$, where t_j is the processing time of operation j.

A systematic approach to generating active schedules was first proposed by Giffler and Thompson ($\mathcal{8}$). The procedure works as follows.

ALGORITHM 7.1
(Active Schedule Generation)

Step 1. Let $t = 0$ and begin with PS_t as the null partial schedule. Initially, S_t includes all operations with no predecessors.

Step 2. Determine $\phi^* = \min_{j \in S_t} \{\phi_j\}$ and the machine m^* on which ϕ^* could be realized.

Step 3. For each operation $j \in S_t$ that requires machine m^* and for which $\sigma_j < \phi^*$, create a new partial schedule in which operation j is added to PS_t and started at time σ_j.

Step 4. For each new partial schedule PS_{t+1}, created in Step 3, update the data set as follows:
   (a) Remove operation j from S_t.
   (b) Form S_{t+1} by adding the direct successor of operation j to S_t.
   (c) Increment t by one.

Step 5. Return to Step 2 for each PS_{t+1} created in Step 3, and continue in this manner until all active schedules have been generated.

[1] For convenience we are using the single subscript j rather than a triplet, as an operation index.

The key condition in Algorithm 7.1 that yields active schedules is the inequality $\sigma_j < \phi^*$, employed in Step 3. Once ϕ^* is determined, it will be impossible to add to PS_t any operation that will complete prior to ϕ^*. In addition, any schedule that contained PS_t and that left machine m^* idle through time ϕ^* would not be an active schedule, because some schedulable operation could be left–shifted entirely into that idle interval, by definition of ϕ^*. For the next scheduling decision, then, machine m^* must be assigned some processing prior to ϕ^*. The possibilities to be explored are clearly operations requiring machine m^* for which $\sigma_j < \phi^*$. If m^* is not unique, Step 3 must be expanded to apply to every operation that requires the use of one of the machines associated with ϕ^*.

To illustrate how Algorithm 7.1 generates partial schedules recursively, consider the example problem of Table 7.1. Suppose that stage 7 is initiated with PS_6, the particular partial schedule shown in Figure 7.8. It follows that

$$S_6 = \{(1, 2, 2), (2, 2, 1), (3, 3, 1), (4, 3, 1)\}$$
$$\phi^* = \min \{\phi_{122}, \phi_{221}, \phi_{331}, \phi_{431}\} = \min \{9, 10, 8, 7\} = 7$$
$$m^* = 1$$

For machine 1: $\sigma_{221} = 6$, $\sigma_{331} = 5$, and $\sigma_{431} = 6$. Since each of these three potential start times are less than ϕ^*, three active partial schedules can be formed for stage 8. These correspond to the following.

1. Start $(2, 2, 1)$ at time 6; $S_7 = \{(1, 2, 2), (2, 3, 3), (3, 3, 1), (4, 3, 1)\}$,
2. Start $(3, 3, 1)$ at time 5; $S_7 = \{(1, 2, 2), (2, 2, 1), (4, 3, 1)\}$,
3. Start $(4, 3, 1)$ at time 6; $S_7 = \{(1, 2, 2), (2, 2, 1), (3, 3, 1)\}$.

Note that the third partial schedule on this list is contained in the full schedule shown in Figure 7.5b.

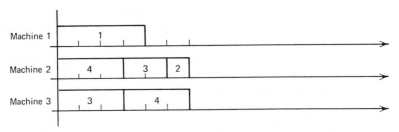

Figure 7.8
A partial schedule for the example problem.

The structure of the generation procedure can easily be adapted so that only nondelay schedules are generated. The crucial factors in Algorithm 7.1 to be changed appear in Steps 2 and 3. The complete procedure is shown below.

ALGORITHM 7.2
(Nondelay Schedule Generation)

Step 1.   Let $t = 0$ and begin with PS_t as the null partial schedule. Initially S_t includes all operations with no predecessors.

Step 2.   Determine $\sigma^* = \min_{j \in S_t} \{\sigma_j\}$ and the machine m^* on which σ^* could be realized.

Step 3.   For each operation $j \in S_t$ that requires machine m^* and for which $\sigma_j = \sigma^*$, create a new partial schedule in which operation j is added to PS_t and started at time σ_j.

Step 4.   For each new partial schedule PS_{t+1}, created in Step 3, update the data set as follows:
  (a) Remove operation j from S_t.
  (b) Form S_{t+1} by adding the direct successor of operation j to S_t.
  (c) Increment t by one.

Step 5.   Return to Step 2 for each PS_{t+1} created in Step 3, and continue in this fashion until all nondelay schedules have been generated.

The number of schedules generated by Algorithm 7.2 will usually be smaller than the number generated by Algorithm 7.1. This property follows from the fact that $\sigma^* < \phi^*$ for a given partial schedule; therefore the number of operations with $\sigma_j = \sigma^*$ will be less than or equal to the number with $\sigma_j < \phi^*$.

To indicate how this difference arises, consider the application of Algorithm 7.2 at Stage 7 to the example in Figure 7.8. Once again,

$$S_6 = \{(1, 2, 2), (2, 2, 1), (3, 3, 1), (4, 3, 1)\}$$

But in this case,

$$\sigma^* = \min \{\sigma_{122}, \sigma_{221}, \sigma_{331}, \sigma_{431}\} = \{6, 6, 5, 6\} = 5$$
$$m^* = 1$$

For machine 1, only $\sigma_{221} = 5$ and, therefore, only one partial schedule is to be generated at the next stage:

Start $(3, 3, 1)$ at time 5; $S_7 = \{(1, 2, 2), (2, 2, 1), (4, 3, 1)\}$

This was one of the alternatives that emerged when Algorithm 7.1 was applied, but the other alternatives did not lead to nondelay schedules and do not appear this time.

The σ^* values determined at the various stages represent the points in time at which scheduling decisions are made—at each σ^* a machine is committed to start a specific operation. Since σ^* values form a nondecreasing sequence, Algorithm 7.2 is quite obviously a dispatching procedure. For

Algorithm 7.1, the decision points for each machine form an increasing sequence; therefore it is also a dispatching procedure.

The generation procedure on which Algorithms 7.1 and 7.2 are based is a tree-structured approach to schedule generation. The nodes in the tree correspond to partial schedules, and each time a new operation is placed in a partial schedule the algorithm proceeds from one level to the next. If the tree is constructed in its entirety, then all active schedules are enumerated under Algorithm 7.1 and all nondelay schedules are enumerated under Algorithm 7.2. Given this tree-structured mechanism, a possible approach might be to curtail enumeration with a branch and bound procedure, as discussed in the next section. Furthermore, the design of several effective heuristic procedures is based on the same approach to schedule generation.

7.3 EXERCISES

3.1 (a) Propose a general rule appropriate in makespan problems for generating a schedule using a job-at-a-time procedure.

   (b) Propose a job-at-a-time rule that is suited to mean flowtime problems.

   (c) Using the two procedures proposed in (a) and (b), construct active schedules for the numerical example in Table 7.1. Calculate M and $\bar{F}$ for both schedules.

3.2 Generate all active schedules and all nondelay schedules for the following problem:

Processing Times				Routings		
	Operation				Operation	
	1	2			1	2
1	1	3		1	1	2
Job 2	2	1		Job 2	2	1
3	2	2		3	1	2

(*Note.* In this problem $(n!)^m = 36$, but there are considerably fewer active schedules.)

3.3   Describe how Algorithms 7.1 and 7.2 can be extended to accommodate
(a) Precedence relations among different jobs.
(b) Different job ready times.

3.4   In a more general formulation, each machine in the job shop is replaced by
two identical machines that can operate in parallel though not on the same
operation. In other words the shop consists of m machine groups, each group
consists of two identical machines, and each job consists of m operations (one
for each machine group). What alterations are required in Algorithms 7.1
and 7.2 to generate all active or nondelay schedules?

4.   A BRANCH AND BOUND APPROACH

Given the tree-structured procedure for generating all active schedules,
it is only natural to investigate branch and bound approaches to finding a
solution in the job shop problem. As mentioned at the end of the previous
section, the nodes in the tree correspond to partial schedules. Therefore the
effectiveness of any branch and bound method will depend on whether good
lower bounds can be computed for partial schedules. As in the branch and
bound methods examined in earlier chapters, the efficiency of a particular
bound will often depend on the data in a given problem as well as on the
measure of performance.

The only measure of performance that has received substantial attention
in job shop research is the makespan objective. The basic work in this area
was carried out by Brooks and White (4). More recently, refinements of
analogous techniques have been developed in the context of the more
general model that arises in resource-constrained scheduling. These refinements will be treated comprehensively in Chapter 10, and for the purposes
of the job shop discussion, the coverage is limited to the Brooks–White
method.

One of the more significant insights in the branch and bound approach to
the flow shop problem was the recognition of the complementary roles played
by jobs and machines in the calculation of lower bounds. Analogously, the
Brooks–White method is based on the calculation of a job-based bound and
a machine-based bound.

The calculation of a job-based bound assumes that there is no resource
conflict when the remaining processing for all jobs is scheduled as compactly
as possible. This calculation is based on a given partial schedule, PS_t, and
an associated set of schedulable operations, S_t. At any stage, there will be
one operation in the set S_t for each job not yet completed. For operation j in
the set S_t, let σ_j denote the earliest time at which its processing could be
started and let R_j denote the unscheduled processing for the job corresponding to operation j. Then, in order to accommodate this particular job, the

length of the schedule must be at least $\sigma_j + R_j$. Therefore the form of the job-based lower bound will be

$$b_1 = \max_{j \epsilon S_t} \{\sigma_j + R_j\}$$

A complementary machine-based bound assumes that there is no logical (precedence) conflict when the remaining processing for all machines is scheduled as compactly as possible. This calculation is also based on a given partial schedule PS_t, in which the latest completion of an operation on machine k occurs at time f_k. Let M_k denote the unscheduled processing that will require machine k. Then in order to accommodate the load on machine k, the length of the schedule must be at least $f_k + M_k$. Therefore the form of the machine-based lower bound will be

$$b_2 = \max_{1 \le k \le m} \{f_k + M_k\}$$

The final lower bound is then $B = \max \{b_1, b_2\}$.

The machine-based bound can be improved slightly with a little added calculation. The time f_k can be replaced by the earliest time at which some unscheduled operation could begin on machine k. If this time is denoted f_k', then the form of the lower bound is

$$b_2' = \max_{1 \le k \le m} \{f_k' + \quad _k\}$$

Since $f_k' \ge f_k$, it follows that b_2' is a better lower bound than b_2. The problem is that f_k' is more difficult to obtain. The earliest time at which operation $j \in S_t$ could begin on machine k is simply σ_j, if operation j requires machine k. In addition, there may be some unscheduled operation not in S_t that requires machine k and that could start on machine k before operation j. In particular, this condition might arise if operation j_2 requires machine k when a predecessor operation j_1 is still in S_t. For this situation, the earliest time at which operation j_2 could start on machine k (if $j_1 \ll j_2$) is $\sigma_{j_2} = \sigma_{j_1} + t_{j_1}$, and it is certainly possible that $\sigma_{j_2} < \sigma_j$. This means that the determination of f_k' requires examination of not only the operations in set S_t, but potentially several of their successors as well. Nevertheless, the improvement in the lower bound may well be worth this effort.

Returning to the example problem introduced earlier in this chapter, suppose that the lower bounds are to be calculated for the partial schedule in Figure 7.8. Recall that

$$S_6 = \{(1, 2, 2), (2, 2, 1), (3, 3, 1), (4, 3, 1)\}$$

The calculation of σ_j and R_j is required for each operation in S_6. Hence

$$\sigma_{122} = 6 \qquad \sigma_{221} = 6 \qquad \sigma_{331} = 5 \qquad \sigma_{431} = 6$$
$$R_{122} = 5 \qquad R_{221} = 8 \qquad R_{331} = 3 \qquad R_{431} = 1$$

Therefore the job-based bound is

$$b_1 = \max_{j \in S_2} \{\sigma_j + R_j\} = \max \{11, 14, 8, 7\} = 14$$

For the machine-based bound

$$f_1 = 4 \qquad f_2 = 6 \qquad f_3 = 6$$

$$M_1 = 8 \qquad M_2 = 3 \qquad M_3 = 6$$

Hence

$$b_2 = \max_k \{f_k + M_k\} = \max \{12, 9, 12\} = 12$$

In this case b_2' is slightly better than b_2:

$$f_1' = 5 \qquad f_2' = 6 \qquad f_3' = 8$$

$$b_2' = \max_k \{f_k' + M_k\} = \max \{13, 9, 14\} = 14$$

Finally, the lower bound on a completion of this partial schedule is

$$B = \max \{b_1, b_2'\} = 14$$

Notice that the full schedule in Figure 7.5d does not achieve this bound because that operation $(2, 2, 1)$ is not added to this partial schedule at the next stage.

The two types of bounds presented here can be used for curtailing enumeration in the tree of active schedules. For large problems, computational requirements may make it prohibitively expensive to find the optimal solution from the tree of active schedules. It may then be a legitimate alternative to determine the best nondelay schedule. Although this is a less demanding computational task, remember that the nondelay subset may not contain an optimum. Sometimes, even controlled enumeration procedures applied to the nondelay tree may be impractical, and in such cases it is necessary to consider heuristic methods, such as those described in the next section.

5. HEURISTIC PROCEDURES

The enumeration tree of Algorithm 7.1 is the basis for an optimum-seeking approach in schedule generation. For large problems, the vast computational effort required may render such an approach infeasible, even when the enumeration is curtailed by a branch and bound scheme. At the other extreme, a suboptimal approach that generates only one complete schedule might entail a light computational effort even in very large problems. Other heuristic approaches lie somewhere between these two computational extremes.

5.1   Priority Dispatching Rules

In Step 3 of Algorithms 7.1 and 7.2, the generation procedure may create several branches in the tree of partial schedules. For a given partial schedule the algorithm essentially identifies all processing conflicts at a given machine. In the case of active schedule generation, conflicts arise on machine m^* for every operation with $\sigma_j < \phi^*$. In the case of nondelay schedule generation, conflicts arise on machine m^* for every operation with $\sigma_j = \sigma^*$. An enumeration procedure must resolve these conflicts in all possible ways at each stage. It does this by selecting one operation at a time from among the conflicting operations, each time creating a new partial schedule. By contrast, a heuristic procedure that is designed to generate only one full schedule need resolve a conflict in only one way in the course of constructing a schedule. This means that the procedure must specify a priority rule for selecting one operation from among the conflicting operations. For a given priority rule R, Algorithm 7.1 can be adapted as a heuristic procedure by altering Step 3 as follows.

ALGORITHM 7.3
(Heuristic Schedule Generation)

Step 1.   Let $t = 0$ and begin with PS_t as the null partial schedule. Initially S_t includes all operations with no predecessors.

Step 2.   Determine $\phi^* = \min_{j \in S_t} \{\phi_j\}$ and the machine m^* on which ϕ^* could be realized.

Step 3.   For each operation $j \in S_t$ that requires machine m^* and for which $\sigma_j < \phi^*$, calculate a priority index according to a specific priority rule. Find the operation with the smallest index and add this operation to PS_t as early as possible, thus creating only one partial schedule, PS_{t+1}, for the next stage.

Step 4.   For the new partial schedule, PS_{t+1}, created in Step 3, update the data set as follows:
(a) Remove operation j from S_t,
(b) Form S_{t+1} by adding the direct successor of operation j to S_t.
(c) Increment t by one.

Step 5.   Return to Step 2 for the PS_{t+1} created in Steps 3 and 4 until a complete schedule is generated.

Similarly, Algorithm 7.2 can be adapted by inserting the same Step 3, only with the condition $\sigma_j < \phi^*$ replaced by the condition $\sigma_j = \sigma^*$. The two heuristic algorithms that are devised in this way—one for active dispatching and the other for nondelay dispatching—will often construct different schedules. The remaining problem is to identify an effective priority rule.

To suggest the kinds of information that can be used effectively, the following list consists of some of the priority rules examined in a study carried out by Jeremiah, Lalchandani, and Schrage (*12*).

SPT (Shortest Processing Time): Select the operation with the minimum processing time.

FCFS (First Come First Served): Select the operation that entered S_t earliest.

MWKR (Most Work Remaining): Select the operation associated with the job having the most work remaining to be processed.

MOPNR (Most Operations Remaining): Select the operation that has the largest number of successor operations.

LWKR (Least Work Remaining): Select the operation associated with the job having the least work remaining to be processed.

RANDOM (Random): Select the operation at random.

This study examined a variety of factors involving heuristic dispatching.[1] In makespan problems there was no single priority rule that dominated the others, although the most successful rules were often those favoring jobs with much processing remaining. The MWKR rule and some of its variations—in which the concept of "most work" was redefined—most often produced the best makespan found. In addition, the SPT rule produced best schedules in a few test problems. Perhaps the most significant result of the makespan study was that nondelay dispatching was a better basis for heuristic schedule generation than active dispatching. For example, in 20 test problems containing 10 jobs and four machines, the active dispatching algorithm produced a better schedule than the nondelay dispatching algorithm only twice.

The study also investigated mean flowtime as a measure of performance. Again, no single priority rule was found that was clearly dominant, although SPT and LWKR were usually more effective than the other rules. Once again, nondelay dispatching performed better than active dispatching, and more convincingly than in the makespan study. In 20 test problems containing 10 jobs and four machines, nondelay dispatching with the SPT rule always produced a lower mean flowtime than the best active dispatching algorithm, frequently improving on the active schedule by 20%.

These experiments demonstrate that schedule generation based on priority dispatching rules is a practicable method of obtaining suboptimal solutions to job shop problems. The results support the use of the set of nondelay schedules as a basis for schedule generation, rather than the set of active schedules. For makespan problems, the most suitable priority

---

[1] The highlights of the study are summarized by Conway, Maxwell and Miller (*6*, p. 121ff).

assignments seem to favor jobs with a heavy unprocessed workload (and that may be quantified several ways), while for mean flowtime problems, the most suitable assignments seem to favor jobs with a light unprocessed workload.

To illustrate the calculations involved in priority dispatching rules, suppose that MWKR is applied to the nondelay schedules for the example problem given earlier in Table 7.1. The construction of a complete schedule for this problem requires 12 stages because there are 12 operations. At each stage, it is necessary to identify the jobs in S_t and to keep track of the times that the machines are available for processing. These times were denoted f_k in Section 4. Also, recall that R_j denotes the work remaining on the job associated with operation j.

Stage 1. Initially the vector of f_k values is $\{0, 0, 0\}$ since no processing has been assigned and the schedulable operations are those without predecessors so that

$$S_0 = \{(1, 1, 1), (2, 1, 2), (3, 1, 3), (4, 1, 2)\}$$

The associated value of σ^* is zero, since $\sigma_{111} = \sigma_{212} = \sigma_{313} = \sigma_{412} = 0$. Furthermore $\sigma_j = \sigma^*$ for all $j \in S_0$. Therefore the priority rule must be invoked to select among all four operations:

$$R_1 = 9 \qquad R_2 = 9 \qquad R_3 = 8 \qquad R_4 = 7$$

The priority rule does not resolve the conflict uniquely in this case, and a tie-breaking rule is needed. Suppose that SPT is used as a tie breaker. Then the conflict is resolved in favor of $(2, 1, 2)$, since $t_{212} < t_{111}$. This means that PS_1 consists of operation $(2, 1, 2)$ started at time 0.

Stage 2. $f_1 = 0 \qquad f_2 = 1 \qquad f_3 = 0$
$S_1 = \{(1, 1, 1), (2, 2, 1), (3, 1, 3), (4, 1, 2)\}$
$\sigma_{111} = 0 \qquad \sigma_{221} = 1 \qquad \sigma_{313} = 0 \qquad \sigma_{412} = 1$
$\sigma^* = \min\{\sigma_{111}, \sigma_{221}, \sigma_{313}, \sigma_{412}\} = 0$
At this stage $\sigma_j = \sigma^*$ for only two operations in S_t. Thus the priority rule must be invoked to choose between $(1, 1, 1)$ and $(3, 1, 3)$:

$$R_1 = 9 > R_3 = 8$$

The conflict is resolved in favor of $(1, 1, 1)$ which is added to PS_1 starting at time 0, to form PS_2.

Stage 3. $f_1 = 0 \qquad f_2 = 1 \qquad f_3 = 3$
$S_2 = \{(1, 2, 2), (2, 2, 1), (3, 1, 3), (4, 1, 2)\}$
$\begin{matrix} \sigma_{122} \\ = 0 \end{matrix} \qquad \sigma_{221} = 1 \qquad \begin{matrix} \sigma_{313} \\ = 3 \end{matrix} \qquad \sigma_{412} = 1$
$\sigma^* = 0$
At this stage $\sigma_j = \sigma^*$ for only one operation, and the priority rule does not have to be used. It should be expected that this condition will occur far more frequently in the tree of nondelay schedules than in the tree of active schedules.

The complete set of calculations is shown in Table 7.3. The schedule that

Table 7.3

Stage	(f_1, f_2, f_3)	$j \in S_{t-1}$	σ_j	MWKR Priority
1	(0, 0, 0)	111	0	9
		212	0	9*
		313	0	8
		412	0	7
2	(0, 1, 0)	111	0	9*
		221	1	—
		313	0	8
		412	1	—
3	(4, 1, 0)	122	4	—
		221	1	—
		313	0	8*
		412	1	—
4	(4, 1, 3)	122	4	—
		221	4	—
		322	3	—
		412	1	7*
5	(4, 4, 3)	122	4	5
		221	4	8*
		322	4	5
		423	4	4
6	(8, 4, 3)	122	4	5
		233	8	—
		322	4	5*
		423	4	4
7	(8, 6, 3)	122	6	—
		233	8	—
		331	8	—
		423	4	4*
8	(8, 6, 7)	122	6	5*
		233	8	—
		331	8	—
		431	8	—
9	(8, 9, 7)	133	9	—
		233	8	4*
		331	8	3
		431	8	1
10	(8, 9, 12)	133	12	—
		331	8	3*
		431	8	1
11	(11, 9, 12)	133	12	—
		431	11	1*
12	(12, 9, 12)	133	12	2*

199

emerges (Figure 7.9) has a makespan of 14 and a mean flowtime of 11.75. In the course of the computations, the tie-breaking rule is applied once more, at stage 6; and the priority rule itself is invoked in only six of the 12 stages.

A rather different approach to the generation of a single schedule with a dispatching procedure is based on the branch and bound solution. A back-tracking mechanism (see Chapter 3) begins by pursuing the branching tree to a terminal branch as directly as possible. Having thus obtained a feasible solution, the mechanism usually proceeds to find an optimum by attempting to fathom other branches. If however, the algorithm is terminated after the first feasible solution is obtained, the abbreviated algorithm is called branch and bound *without backtracking*. The usual procedure in obtaining the first complete solution is to branch at each level from the node with the minimum lower bound. Thus a heuristic procedure using branch and bound without backtracking is identical to the priority dispatching heuristic except for Step 3, which would read as follows.

Step 3. For each operation $j \in S_t$ that requires machine m^* and for which $\sigma < \phi^*$ create a new partial schedule PS_{t+1} by starting operation j at time σ_j. For each of these partial schedules calculate a lower bound. Identify the partial schedule with the minimum lower bound and consider only this PS_{t+1} at Step 4.

In a sense this procedure is but a variation of the priority dispatching heuristic. Instead of a straightforward priority index, this algorithm employs a lower bound calculation that depends both on the operation selected from S_t and on the partial schedule that already exists. An analogous Step 3 exists, of course, for nondelay dispatching.

5.2 Sampling Procedures

At the beginning of the discussion of heuristic procedures two computational extremes were identified: complete or implicit enumeration in the search for an optimum and priority dispatching rules for the construction of a single schedule. Even when the enumerative approach is impractical for the solution of large problems, the construction of only a single schedule by priority dispatching may still be a very brief computational task. In such situations, it might be reasonable to think in terms of repeating the procedure by which a single schedule is obtained, but with some simple variations. In this way, the best of several schedules can be selected. (Compare the philosophy of the CDS heuristic in flow shop problems discussed in Chapter 6.)

To view this repeating method as a sampling approach, think of an enumeration procedure as an examination of an entire population (e.g., the population of all active schedules in a given problem). In the same sense,

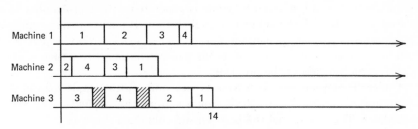

Figure 7.9
A complete schedule produced by the MWKR heuristic procedure.

a priority dispatching procedure is one that examines just one member of the population. An intermediate procedure would examine a given number of schedules in the population: it would essentially take a sample from the population. The general philosophy of this approach was introduced in Section 7 of Chapter 3 in the context of the single-machine model. The same ideas can be applied in job shop models.

The first significant experimentation with sampling procedures for job shop problems was reported by Giffler, Thompson, and Van Ness (9), who used random samples from the population of active schedules. Whereas a priority dispatching rule always resolves a given conflict in the same way, a sampling procedure resolves a given conflict randomly. In particular, after identifying the conflicting operations, the sampling procedure chooses among them by using a random mechanism that assigns to each operation an equal probability of being chosen. If there are k conflicting operations at some stage, then any particular operation will be selected in Step 3 with a probability of $1/k$. This selection having been made, a unique PS_{t+1} is carried to the next level, where another equally likely mechanism is used to resolve any conflict that arises. The sampling algorithm that emerges can produce a single schedule virtually as rapidly as the priority dispatching algorithm. In addition, when the sampling algorithm is repeated several times, a collection of different schedules will usually be generated, as long as the random mechanism resolves conflicts differently in each repetition.

As discussed in Chapter 3, it is difficult to draw quantitative conclusions about the best schedule in the sample. The function $1 - (1 - p)^N$ represents the theoretical probability that the sampling procedure would locate an optimum and, if the value of p were known, it would be at least possible to choose a sample size on the basis of trading off sampling costs and the value of $1 - (1 - p)^N$. Giffler, Thompson, and Van Ness presented a table of values of this function for various p and N, but they were not able to learn much about what p might be. To make matters fairly difficult, they noted that making equally likely choices among resolutions in the generation algorithm is not the same as making equally likely choices among the schedules in the population. Instead, a given schedule is generated with a probability that varies inversely with the number of conflicts in it. It might further seem that good schedules tend to contain few conflicts, so that they would have relatively high probabilities of being generated, but even this relation depends on the data of the problem.

Giffler, Thompson, and Van Ness experimented with sample sizes of 200, adapting Algorithm 7.1 to draw samples from the population of active schedules. They compared the best schedule obtained this way (with makespan as the criterion) to the schedule obtained from Algorithm 7.3 with the SPT priority rule. Broadly speaking, there was no clear preference for one approach over the other on the basis of the makespan values observed. However, this result is of little value for two reasons. First, as discussed above in Section 5.1, a more appropriate priority rule for solution of the makespan problem is MWKR, or some variation. Second, the set of active schedules does not appear to be the best population to use.

Bakhru and Rao (1) used sampling procedures to examine the difference between the active and nondelay populations. They took samples of size 50 and found rather convincing evidence that the nondelay population is preferable for sampling. Table 7.4 summarizes some of their results and indicates that while the set of nondelay schedules is not guaranteed to contain an optimal schedule, it is nevertheless a more desirable basis for sampling than the set of active schedules.

5.3 Probabilistic Dispatching Procedures

The sampling approach described in the previous section lies between the computational extremes of generating all schedules and generating only one, and the technique of probabilistic dispatching is a variation on the same theme. In the class of repetitive but nonexhaustive generation procedures, random sampling itself may be viewed at one end of the spectrum. At the other end is a repetition of Algorithm 7.3 several times with a different priority rule each time. In a makespan problem, for example, this might mean obtaining a schedule using MWKR, then another schedule using MOPNR, then another using SPT, and so on. This would certainly be a rational approach, although if computing capability allowed for 200 repetitions, it might take a fair amount of ingenuity to devise 200 distinct priority rules that are appropriate to the makespan problem. While this approach has not been pursued literally, a closely related method would be to identify a family of appropriate rules that are distinct only in terms of a single parameter. Then the algorithm could be repeated for several parametric values and the best schedule chosen.

A similar approach is to employ a family of rules in a way that combines the philosophies of priority dispatching rules and random sampling. Even

Table 7.4

Problem		Value of Best in Active Sample	Value of Best in Nondelay Sample
(Makespan)	1	76	71
	2	83	78
	3	86	82
	4	68	64
	5	74	70
	6	95	85
	7	69	66
	8	76	73
	9	82	75
	10	67	62
	11	84	86
(Mean Flowtime)	1	61.9	59.1
	2	61.5	61.3
	3	62.8	69.2
	4	51.7	49.0
	5	56.0	54.1
	6	67.7	65.2
	7	51.8	51.0
	8	57.4	55.0
	9	60.0	58.9
	10	52.6	51.3
	11	61.4	61.0

with a good priority rule, occasional departures from strict application of the rule might be helpful. On the other hand, when sampling is employed, there is no reason to be satisfied with equally likely ways of resolving conflicts if the random selections can be biased toward a reliable priority rule as outlined in Chapter 3. A graphical interpretation of this approach is shown in Figure 7.10. A sampling procedure based on equally likely ways of resolving conflicts will generate a distribution of schedule values, represented by the frequency distribution labeled E. On the other hand, a priority dispatching rule resolves conflicts uniquely and will generate only one schedule, represented by the single point labeled R. Although there is usually some probability that the sampling procedure will be better than the priority rule in any particular instance (represented by the lefthand tail of the E distribution), a sampling procedure based on biased random ways of resolving conflicts might generate a more useful distribution of schedule values (labeled B). This type of approach can be viewed as a sampling scheme biased toward

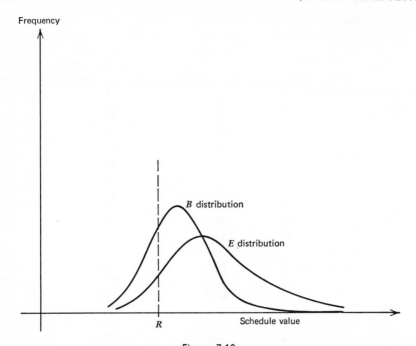

Figure 7.10

The hypothetical behavior of schedule values generated by priority rule (R), equally
likely sampling mechanisms (E), and biased sampling mechanisms (B).

priority dispatching or as priority dispatching that includes a probabilistic
mechanism. It is from the latter view that the technique derives the name
probabilistic dispatching.

To construct a probabilistic dispatching procedure, Algorithm 7.3 need be
altered only in Step 3. As in the sampling procedure, a choice among conflicting operations is made using a random mechanism, but one that assigns
selection probability α_j to operation j. The operations are first ranked by
the given priority rule and then the α_j's are assigned in order, with the first
operation being assigned the largest α_j, the next operation being assigned
the second largest α_j, and so on. (In most of the work on probabilistic
dispatching, the α_j values form a geometric distribution as described in
Chapter 3.)

Some of the results from the experiments of Jeremiah, Lalchandani, and
Schrage (12) are typical of the behavior of probabilistic dispatching. Table
7.5 displays the results for 10 similar makespan problems, comparing three
representative heuristic procedures for generating active schedules. Note
that among the three procedures the priority dispatching rule generates a
best schedule only once, while the probabilistic dispatching version generates

Table 7.5

Problem Number	Schedule Value from Priority Dispatching (MWKR)	Best Schedule from Random Sampling	Best Schedule from Probabilistic Dispatching (MWKR)
1	164	188	160*
2	219	214	213*
3	205	235	196*
4	164*	180	164*
5	195	191*	195
6	193	170*	170*
7	193	191	185*
8	243	249	237*
9	210	218	204*
10	248	210*	216

a best schedule in eight of the 10 problems. Similar results were reported by Nugent (13).

In general, it appears that where it is feasible to solve a job shop problem by selecting the best from a sample of schedules, probabilistic dispatching is more effective than random sampling. At least, this conclusion has been drawn from the research work that has examined makespan and mean flowtime problems. In both cases there is sufficient experimental data to point to one or two suitable priority rules. In a somewhat different case, such as mean tardiness problems, the choice between probabilistic dispatching and random sampling may not be as clear-cut without some idea of which priority rule is suitable. Furthermore, probabilistic dispatching, like random sampling, suffers from the lack of quantitative knowledge about the best schedule in the sample and the related implications for selecting a sample size. In this sense, it is really difficult to know whether the improvement of probabilistic dispatching over priority dispatching is worth the added computational burden. Conway, Maxwell, and Miller (6) conclude, for instance, that probabilistic dispatching will provide only diminishing returns in larger problems.

7.5 EXERCISES

5.1 Starting with the partial schedule shown in Figure 7.8, generate a complete schedule using branch and bound without backtracking. Explore two versions of the branching tree: one for active schedules and one for nondelay schedules. Calculate the makespan in both cases.

5.2 Generate a solution to the makespan problem in Exercise 3.2 by using branch and bound without backtracking.

5.3 Propose a parametric family of priority dispatching rules for generating solutions to mean flowtime problems. Demonstrate how it works on the example in Table 7.1.

5.4 Propose a set of priority dispatching rules for generating solutions to mean tardiness problems.

6. AN INTEGER PROGRAMMING APPROACH

The determination of an optimal job shop schedule can be formulated as an integer programming problem if it is desired to use a general purpose solution approach. As in other models the integer programming approach can accommodate a variety of performance measures, but its computational demands may often be severe. This section describes one specialized type of integer programming structure that is potentially useful in solving job shop problems.

The formulation relies on indicator variables to specify operation sequence. Let x_{ik} denote the completion time of job i on machine k (i.e., the completion time of the particular operation of job i that requires machine k). The x_{ik} are decision variables and their values will essentially determine a schedule. In order to write inequalities representing precedence constraints, suppose that operation j of job i requires machine k and operation $(j - 1)$ of job i requires machine h. Then in order for a set of x_{ik} to be feasible, it is necessary to have

$$x_{ik} - t_{ijk} \geq x_{ih} \qquad 1 \leq j \leq m, 1 \leq i \leq n \qquad (1)$$

where for the first operation $(j = 1)$ the constraint is simply

$$x_{ik} - t_{i1k} \geq 0 \qquad 1 \leq i \leq n \qquad (2)$$

In addition it is necessary to employ a large number of constraints to assure that no two operations are processed simultaneously by the same machine. Suppose, for example, that job i precedes job p on machine k, which means that operation (i, j, k) is completed before operation (p, q, k) begins. Then it is necessary to have

$$x_{pk} - t_{pqk} \geq x_{ik}$$

On the other hand, if job p precedes job i on machine k, then it is necessary to have

$$x_{ik} - t_{ijk} \geq x_{pk}$$

These are usually called *disjunctive constraints* because one or the other must hold. (Compare the concept of disjunctive arcs, introduced in Section 2.) In order to accommodate these constraints in the formulation, we define an indicator variable y_{ipk} as follows:

$$y_{ipk} = 1 \quad \text{if job } i \text{ precedes job } p \text{ on machine } k$$

$$= 0 \quad \text{otherwise}$$

Then the constraints become

$$x_{pk} - x_{ik} + H(1 - y_{ipk}) \geq t_{pqk} \tag{3}$$

$$x_{ik} - x_{pk} + H y_{ipk} \geq t_{ijk} \tag{4}$$

where H represents a very large positive number. For the mean flowtime problem the entire formulation is

Minimize $\quad \sum_{i=1}^{n} x_{ik_i}$

Subject to $\quad x_{ik} - t_{ijk} \geq x_{ih} \quad$ for $\quad (i, j-1, h) \ll (i, j, k)$

$$x_{pk} - x_{ik} + H(1 - y_{ipk}) \geq t_{pqk} \quad 1 \leq i, p \leq n, 1 \leq k \leq m$$

$$x_{ik} - x_{pk} + H y_{ipk} \geq t_{ijk} \quad 1 \leq i, p \leq n, 1 \leq k \leq m$$

$$x_{ik} \geq 0 \qquad y_{ipk} = 0 \text{ or } 1$$

where k_i denotes the machine at which the last operation of job i is scheduled. There are mn constraints of similar to inequalities 1 or 2, and there are $mn(n-1)$ of type 3 or 4, or a total of mn^2 constraints. There are mn x_{ik} variables and $mn(n-1)/2$ y_{ipk} variables, since y_{pik} need not be defined if y_{ipk} is in the formulation. The total number of variables is therefore $mn(n+1)/2$. For a small problem containing $n = 4$ jobs and $m = 3$ machines, this formulation requires 48 constraints and 15 variables, while a 10-job, five-machine formulation is 500 by 275. When we consider the size of these formulations, it is interesting to compare the flow shop formulation discussed in Section 8 of Chapter 6. Although that earlier formulation is more economical in terms of number of constraints, it considers only permutation schedules. The formulation given above can be applied to flow shop problems without limiting its scope to only permutation schedules, but the size of the integer programming problem that results will usually be substantially larger.

Greenberg (*10*) developed a specialized computer code for solving this integer programming problem by branch and bound. In Greenberg's formulation, the constraints 3 and 4 are omitted initially and the remaining problem is solved as a linear program. If there are no machine conflicts in the resulting solution, then it represents an optimal schedule. If there is some conflict, say between jobs i and p on machine k, then two subproblems are solved. One subproblem contains the additional constraint

$$x_{pk} - t_{pqk} \geq x_{ik}$$

and the other subproblem contains instead the constraint

$$x_{ik} - t_{ijk} \geq x_{pk}$$

Both of these subproblems can then be solved as linear programs, for there are still no integer variables in the formulation. The branching process continues in this way, each time branching from an infeasible solution to two subproblems containing an additional inequality taken from the appropriate pair of disjunctive constraints. Whenever an infeasible solution is obtained, the value of the objective function in the corresponding linear program can be used as a lower bound. Thus, the branch and bound scheme solves a linear programming problem for each node in the branching tree as a means of solving the overall integer programming problem.

The graph-theoretic model based on the disjunctive constraints has been pursued by a number of researchers (2, 3, 5, 7, 11). The disjunctive graph approach allows some flexibility in the way that a branching tree is generated and has the potential for greater computational efficiency. In particular, the approach based on generation of active partial schedules resolves machine conflicts (i.e., disjunctive arcs) that occur early in the schedule before resolving the conflicts that appear later. By contrast, the approach suggested by Greenberg's formulation can resolve conflicts in any order, and this flexibility may allow the solution to be determined more rapidly. However, no thorough investigation of this potential has yet been reported. What might be even more significant is that a refinement of a lower bound calculation can make any of the formulations appear to be more efficient. The present state of research in scheduling leaves unsettled the question of which formulation and which lower bounds are most productive. Actually, this may not be a pressing question, for the capabilities of an available computer and the skills of the programmer may well dictate which approach is desirable.

7.6   EXERCISES

6.1   Use the constraint set (1) to (4) to develop an integer programming formulation of the flow shop problem.

6.2   Develop an integer programming formulation for the minimization of makespan for the data in Tables 7.1.

6.3   If Greenberg's branch and bound scheme is used to solve a job shop problem, what is the maximum number of levels that can occur in the branching tree?

7. SUMMARY

As a context for solving sequencing problems the job shop model is highly complicated. Compared to the basic single-machine model, which in its own right yields complex combinatorial problems, the job shop has the added features of several machines and logical constraints.

The treatment of the job shop model in Sections 2 to 6 suggests a general approach to large combinatorial problems. The first stage in this approach is an examination of the set of feasible solutions with a view to finding the smallest possible dominant subset. The next stage is the design and development of systematic methods for finding optimal solutions by enumeration and implicit enumeration. Section 3 emphasized procedures that iteratively augmented partial schedules mainly because the existing research has relied extensively on such approaches, but increased attention to mathematical programming and graph theoretic formulations, such as those in Section 6, may open the way for equally significant achievements using other techniques. The third stage involves the recognition that even efficient implicit enumeration methods may be impractical for large problems. In this situation the tree structure of the enumeration device is a natural place to start in the development of heuristic procedures. The three heuristic techniques discussed in this chapter represent general philosophies for the suboptimal solution of large and complex scheduling problems. The use of priority rules to resolve conflicts is an effective heuristic procedure when the priority rule is appropriately chosen and can be employed as a manual dispatching rule in practice. Random sampling appears to be a simple but powerful technique for resolving conflicts. The use of a substantial sample size is quite effective in obtaining good solutions, although the computational effort involved is considerably larger than in the use of a single priority dispatching rule. Probabilistic dispatching, or biased sampling, is a combination of these two heuristic approaches that seems to be capable of retaining the efficient nature of both. The actual use of probabilistic dispatching requires the setting of more parameters than in the other approaches, but when this is handled well, the technique appears to be capable of better performance. In both sampling approaches, an area still to be explored is the quantitative relationship between sample size and solution efficiency.

The general approach exemplified by this discussion of the job shop problem is a natural way to treat the more general models of project scheduling and will be utilized in Chapter 10.

7.7. COMPUTATIONAL EXERCISES

The following experiments require the use of computer programs for generating schedules using heuristic procedures. Programs are required for

      I. Priority Dispatching

     II. Random Sampling

   III. Probabilistic Dispatching

7.1   Generate several data sets and compare procedures I and II for makespan problems. For procedure I use MWKR with nondelay schedules and for procedure II use sample sizes of 200.

7.2   Repeat Exercise 7.1 using SPT in procedure I and sample sizes of 50 in procedure II.

7.3   Repeat Exercise 7.1 using the following family of priority rules in procedure I:

For operation $j \in S_t$ calculate $p_1 =$ priority index under MWKR and calculate $p_2 =$ priority index under SPT. Employ a final priority index of $p_1/p_2{}^{\alpha}$.

Test the procedure with several values of α.

7.4   Repeat Exercise 7.1 using branch and bound without backtracking in procedure I.

7.5   Compare the best version of procedure I found in Exercises 7.1 to 7.4 with procedure III.

7.6   (See Exercise 5.4). Compare procedure I and procedure III for a set of tardiness problems. Hence evaluate the priority dispatching rules proposed in Exercise 5.4.

REFERENCES

1. Bakhru, A. N., and Rao, M. R., "An Experimental Investigation of Job-Shop Scheduling," Research Report, Department of Industrial Engineering, Cornell University, 1964. (See also *6*, Chapter 6.)
2. Balas, E., "Machine Sequencing via Disjunctive Graphs: An Implicit Enumeration Algorithm," *Operations Research*, Vol. 17, No. 6 (November, 1969).
3. Balas, E. "Machine Sequencing: Disjunctive Graphs and Degree Contrained Subgraphs," *Naval Research Logistics Quarterly*, Vol. 17, No. 1. (March, 1970).
4. Brooks, G. H., and White, C. R., "An Algorithm for Finding Optimal or Near-optimal Solutions to the Production Scheduling Problem," *Journal of Industrial Engineering*, Vol. 16, No. 1 (January, 1965).
5. Charlton, J. M., and Death, C. C., "A Generalized Machine-Scheduling Algorithm," *Operational Research Quarterly*, Vol. 21, No. 1 (March, 1970).
6. Conway, R. W., Maxwell, W. L., and Miller, L. W., *Theory of Scheduling*, Addison-Wesley, Reading, Mass., 1967.
7. Florian, M., Trepant, P., and McMahon, G., "An Implicit Enumeration Algorithm for the Machine Sequencing Problem," *Management Science*, Vol. 17, No. 12 (August, 1971).
8. Giffler, B., and Thompson, G. L., "Algorithms for Solving Production Scheduling Problems," *Operations Research*, Vol. 8, No. 4 (July, 1960).
9. Giffler, B., Thompson, G. L., and Van Ness, V., "Numerical Experience with the Linear and Monte Carlo Algorithms for Solving Production Scheduling Problems," in Muth and Thompson, Eds., *Industrial Scheduling*, Prentice-Hall, Englewood Cliffs, N. J., 1963.
10. Greenberg, H., "A Branch and Bound Solution to the General Scheduling Problem," *Operations Research*, Vol. 16, No. 2 (March, 1968).

11. Heck, H. W., and Roberts, S. D., "Sequencing and Scheduling via Disjunctive Graphs," *Proc. AIIE Institute National Conference* (May, 1971).
12. Jeremiah, B., Lalchandani, A., and Schrage, L., "Heuristic Rules Toward Optimal Scheduling," Research Report, Department of Industrial Engineering, Cornell University, 1964. (See also *6*, Chapter 6.)
13. Nugent, C. N., "On Sampling Approaches to the Solution of the n-by-m Static Sequencing Problem," Ph.D. thesis, Cornell University, September, 1964.

CHAPTER 8

SIMULATION STUDIES OF THE DYNAMIC JOB SHOP

1. INTRODUCTION

One of the most thoroughly studied and widely applied areas of scheduling research involves the dynamic version of the job shop model. In the dynamic model, jobs arrive at the shop randomly over time, so that the shop itself behaves like a network of queues. In this context, scheduling is generally carried out by means of dispatching decisions: at the time a machine becomes free a decision must be made regarding what it should do next. These scheduling decisions are unavoidable in the operation of such a system, and, since research has demonstrated substantial differences among dispatching procedures, it makes sense to seek out the decision rules that promote good performance.

The effects of dispatching procedures in queueing networks are very difficult to describe by means of analytic techniques. Nevertheless the study of scheduling in dynamic job shops has made considerable progress with the use of computer simulation models. The rationale for using simulation methods in job shop studies is not different from the rationale for simulation in dealing with any other complex system: short of testing alternative policies in the actual system, there is no way to anticipate fully how different operating procedures will affect system behavior. Experimentation with a computer simulation model has made it possible to compare alternative dispatching rules, test broad conjectures about scheduling procedures, and generally develop greater insight into job shop operation.

The purpose of this chapter is to convey the flavor of job shop simulation experiments. Section 2 examines the typical elements in simulation work, and the following sections highlight some of the major results. The reader interested in a more comprehensive treatment of the subject should consult the survey material in references *5, 9, 10,* and *15* and the bibliography in each.

2. ELEMENTS OF SIMULATION MODELS

The literature on the dynamic job shop model includes simulations of both actual and hypothetical systems. The hypothetical shops, in particular, have typically consisted of a small number of machines, usually less than 10. Models of actual shops have sometimes contained 100 or even 1000 machines, but there is no evidence that the number of machines has a crucial influence on the relative performance of scheduling rules. Aside from the question of scale, there are several other issues in the building of a model. To a certain extent it is desirable for the model to be somewhat simplified in order to focus on the effects of scheduling and also to permit generalizations of the experimental results. On the other hand, if the model is too simple it may be difficult to argue persuasively that the conclusions will apply under other, more realistic conditions. The successful work in this area exemplifies a convincing blend of simple structure and complex detail, and the following list of model assumptions typifies many of the simulation studies.

1. Jobs consist of strictly ordered operation sequences.
2. A given operation can be performed by only one type of machine.
3. There is only one machine of each type in the shop.
4. Processing times as well as due dates are known in advance.
5. Setup times are sequence independent.
6. Once an operation is begun on a machine, it must not be interrupted.
7. An operation may not begin until its predecessors are complete.
8. Each machine can process only one operation at a time.
9. Each machine is continuously available for production.

The first five of these assumptions have frequently been relaxed in simulation experiments, either to achieve a better representation of reality in the simulation of an actual shop or else to examine the effects of alternative assumptions on basic results. The remaining assumptions are virtually standard in job shop studies.

The input to the simulation model is a job file that describes the entire set of jobs appearing at the shop over the course of the simulation. The jobs arrive randomly over time, and most often the assumption is that the intervals between job arrivals have an exponential distribution. In addition, the most common assumption is that operation processing times are also samples from an exponential distribution. Alternatives to both these probabilistic assumptions have been investigated, with little indication that the nature of the arrival process or the service process is critical in comparing scheduling rules. To complete the description of an arriving job, it is necessary to specify the number of its operations, which may vary among jobs or remain fixed, and its machine routing. In the so-called *closed job shop*, each job must have one of a number of specified routings, representing a fixed line of products. By contrast, the *open job shop* accommodates virtually any possible machine routing, as might be found with custom-ordered products. Finally, an aggregate description of the machine routings is contained in a routing matrix, R, in which element r_{ij} represents the proportion of jobs that proceed to machine j after completion of an operation on machine i. (Values of r_{0j} indicate the destinations of jobs upon arrival to the shop and $r_{i,m+1}$ indicates the proportion of jobs that leave the shop after an operation on machine i. Thus the matrix has $m + 1$ rows and columns if there are m machines.) The two extreme cases are the *pure job shop*, in which these proportions are equally distributed, and the *pure flow shop*, in which there is only one routing.

Table 8.1

A	1	2	3	4	L
Arrive	—	1/4	1/4	1/4	1/4	—
1	—	—	1/4	1/4	1/4	1/4
2	—	1/4	—	1/4	1/4	1/4
3	—	1/4	1/4	—	1/4	1/4
4	—	1/4	1/4	1/4	—	1/4
Leave	—	—	—	—	—	—

Table 8.2

A	1	2	3	4	L
Arrive	—	1	0	0	0	—
1	—	—	1	0	0	0
2	—	0	—	1	0	0
3	—	0	0	—	1	0
4	—	0	0	0	—	1
Leave	—	—	—	—	—	—

Routing matrices for these two cases are displayed in Tables 8.1 and 8.2, respectively, for a four-machine shop.

The output of the simulation is a set of statistics that describe the behavior of the model over the simulated interval of operation. Usually, the experiment is aimed at characterizing system performance in the long run, after the system reaches a "steady state." Therefore there is usually a warm-up period after which performance data is gathered. Probably the most important feature of the experimentation is the maintenance of a reproducible job file. That way the simulation can be repeated several times using the same input each time and varying only the scheduling rules in order to focus on their differences. Nevertheless it is still important to deal with the statistical nature of such results, and investigators have employed various forms of statistical analysis in an effort to support their conclusions as convincingly as possible.

Detailed scheduling decisions in a job shop environment are usually determined by means of dispatching rules. At the completion of any operation a machine becomes free, and the dispatching rule must specify what the machine should do next. One of the options, of course, is to keep the machine idle for a certain period, but most dispatching rules immediately assign work to the machine as long as there are operations waiting to be processed. This assignment is based on priorities determined for each of the waiting jobs. Two types of classifications are important in describing priority rules. First a rule is *local* if priority assignment is based only on information about the jobs represented in the individual machine queue. Here are two examples of local rules.

   SPT (Shortest Processing Time): highest priority is given to the waiting operation with the shortest imminent operation time.

   LWKR (Least Work Remaining): highest priority is given to the waiting operation associated with the job having the least amount of total processing remaining to be done.

(Notice that LWKR can be interpreted as a generalization of single-stage SPT sequencing to the job shop case.) By contrast, a rule is *global* if it utilizes information from other machines in addition to the one at which the queue has formed. Examples of global rules include the following.

   AWINQ (Anticipated Work in Next Queue): highest priority is given to the waiting operation whose direct successor operation will encounter the queue with the least work waiting. This includes work that has not yet arrived there, but that is anticipated to arrive before the direct successor operation can begin.

   FOFO (First Off First On): highest priority is given to the operation that could be completed earliest. If this operation is not yet in the queue, the machine remains idle until it arrives.

Although it is easy to hypothesize that global rules ought to be more effective than local rules, it is not easy to determine which global rules are good. Moreover, the information base required for global rules may be so extensive as to preclude implementation in many shop systems. The simulation studies have largely examined local rules.

   A second classification of dispatching rules involves the dynamics of the information base. A rule is *static* if its relative assignment of priorities does not change over time and *dynamic* otherwise. It is necessary, however, to elaborate somewhat on this distinction. The simplest set of static rules provides that each operation of a given job has the same priority. For example,

   FASFS (First Arrival at the Shop First Served): highest priority is given to the job that arrived at the shop earliest.

   TWORK (Total Work): highest priority is given to the job with the least total processing requirement on all operations.

   EDD (Earliest Due Date): highest priority is given to the job with the earliest due date.

Certain rules, including SPT and LWKR, are static with respect to a particular operation, but dynamic with respect to a particular job in the sense that individual operations of the same job acquire different relative priorities. Here are other examples.

FCFS (First Come First Served): highest priority is given to the waiting operation that arrived at the queue first.

MST (Minimum Slack Time): highest priority is given to the waiting operation corresponding to the job with minimum slack time. Slack time is equal to the difference between the due date and the time the job could be completed if there were no delays. Essentially, MST assigns a priority equal to the difference between the due date and work remaining on the job.

OPNDD (Operation Due Date): highest priority is given to the waiting operation with the earliest operation due date. An operation due date is determined by dividing the interval between the job due date and its shop arrival time into as many subintervals as there are operations. The end of each subinterval represents a due date for the corresponding operation.

A dynamic version of OPNDD results if the shop arrival time is replaced by the current (dispatching) time. Furthermore, slack-oriented versions can be developed by incorporating remaining work into the priority calculation. Two other dynamic rules are listed below.

S/OPN (Slack per Operation): highest priority is given to the waiting operation corresponding to the job with the minimum ratio of slack time to remaining operations.

TSPT (Truncated SPT): highest priority is given to the waiting operation with the shortest imminent operation time (as under SPT) except when an operation in the queue has waited in this queue more than W time units. Operations with queue times larger than W are given overriding priority and are dispatched under FCFS.

It is not difficult to devise a plausible dispatching rule, as the foregoing examples should demonstrate. In some situations the rationale for using a particular rule may be that it helps relieve congestion in the shop, while in other instances the motivating factor may be the need to meet order due dates. The major value of simulation research is that it has been able to examine a wide variety of alternative rules and to identify a few simple but effective rules for each situation. The following sections suggest the tenor of these simulation studies.

3. REDUCING MEAN FLOWTIME

The most commonly used measure of shop congestion has been mean job flowtime. An equivalent measure is mean number of jobs in the system, because the flowtime–inventory relationship described in Chapter 2 also pertains to the dynamic job shop. Because SPT is known to minimize $\bar{F}$ in single-machine problems,[1] it is natural to expect that shortest-first strategies would perform well in the job shop situation. Therefore it is not surprising to find that the major comparative studies (*1, 7, 13, 19*) have found that SPT minimizes $\bar{F}$ among the dozen or so simple dispatching rules that are frequently considered.

Conway (*7*) performed a more elaborate study, using mean number of jobs in the system, $\bar{J}$, as a performance measure. Conway simulated a pure job shop containing nine machines and operating under the assumptions listed in the previous section. The experiments gathered statistics on about 9000 jobs and reported results for over 30 rules. Table 8.3 reproduces some of those

Table 8.3

Dispatching Rule	$\bar{J}$
Simple rules	
FASFS	57.51
FCFS	58.87
SPT	23.25
LWKR	47.52
AWINQ	34.03
Combination Rules	
SPT, LWKR ($\alpha = 0.985$)	22.98
SPT, AWINQ ($\alpha = 0.96$)	22.67

results, dramatizing the effectiveness of the SPT rule. Note that even the global rule AWINQ was not able to match the performance of SPT, although both performed substantially better than FASFS, which essentially ignores job traits and shop status in determining priorities. In order to find a rule that performed better than SPT, Conway investigated the performance of several combination rules, two of which appear in Table 8.3. A combination of SPT and LWKR was constructed by computing job priorities under each and then taking a weighted sum of the two values (weighting the SPT priority value by α and the LWKR priority value by $1 - \alpha$). A parametric set of combination rules is generated by different values of the weighting parameter α. Conway's experiments showed that the proper choice of α could yield a slight improvement over SPT, but a poor choice of α could lead

---

[1] See Sections 2.3 and 4.5.

to worse performance. Similarly, a combination rule could be constructed by weighting the SPT priority value with the AWINQ value, and in Conway's study this rule produced the smallest J.

The effectiveness of combination rules has limited practical value, for several reasons. First, any combination rule requires the specification of a weighting parameter, and it would take considerable effort to find an "optimal" value of α for a given situation. The range of desirable α values might well be quite sensitive to shop utilization and certain job parameters. Moreover, the added benefits of using a combination rule—and a global rule as well, if AWINQ is involved—are marginal at best compared to the performance under SPT. Since the pure SPT rule is so much easier to implement, and since it accounts for nearly all of the good performance of the combination rules, it is considered the best rule for all practical purposes where the objective is to minimize mean flowtime.

As mentioned earlier, several studies have drawn the same conclusions about SPT. One of the most thorough comparative studies was carried out by Nanot (*17*), who investigated the behavior of several dispatching rules under a variety of shop conditions. He simulated the behavior of shops with 2, 4, and 8 machines, shops with low, medium, and high workloads, and shops with and without the routing matrix of a pure job shop. Under all of these conditions SPT was consistently the most effective rule for minimizing mean flowtime.

Conway also studied whether the SPT rule was sensitive to the reliability of processing time information in situations where priority assignments must employ estimates of processing times. His experimentation was motivated by the fact that in practice it is not always possible in advance to have completely reliable information about operation processing times. Instead, an estimate of each processing time is available, but the actual time is often subject to some uncertainty. Therefore Conway concluded that the quality of the estimates could be described in terms of their precision. In his model the actual times were uniformly distributed random variables ranging from a specified proportion β below the estimate to the same proportion above the estimate. For example, if a particular operation had an estimated time of 10 hours and the quality parameter β was set at 0.2 then the actual time was equally likely to be any value between 8 and 12 hours. Of course, the case $\beta = 0$ corresponds to the implementation of SPT with perfect information. As shown in Table 8.4, the SPT rule is remarkably insensitive to this kind of uncertainty. Even when the estimate is allowed to be off by 100% (corresponding to $\beta = 1.0$) the deterioration in performance is very slight, suggesting that SPT can still be effective when the quality of available information is relatively poor.

Table 8.4 also displays the result of simulating the behavior of a two-class rule under which "short" jobs were placed in a high priority class and "long"

Table 8.4

Dispatching Rule	$\bar{J}$
SPT ($\beta = 0$)	23.25
SPT ($\beta = 0.1$)	22.23
SPT ($\beta = 1.0$)	27.13
2CLASS	35.29
FCFS	58.87

jobs were placed in a low priority class. The dispatching rule selected jobs in the queue from the high priority class whenever they were available and from the low priority class only when no high priority jobs were present. Within classes, however, dispatching was simply based on a first-come-first-served priority. The dividing line between short and long was arbitrarily taken as the mean of the processing time distribution. The significance of this rule is that it requires only a two-way classification of jobs, which is rather a coarse method of discrimination compared to SPT. Even though the performance of the two-class rule does not approach that of SPT, the use of a short-long distinction accounts for a significant improvement over a rule such as FCFS, which is completely blind to job characteristics. It is possible to envision a family of similar rules with three classes, four classes, and so on. In this family, a larger number of classes represents a finer discrimination among tasks until in the limiting case SPT represents perfect short-long discrimination. The two-class rule is the simplest rule in this family. However, although it is the least demanding in terms of the quality of information required, it nevertheless accounts for about two-thirds of the benefit that SPT itself achieves over FCFS.

The mechanism by which SPT reduces mean flowtime should not be difficult to understand. By giving priority to short tasks, it accelerates the progress of several short jobs at the expense of a few long jobs. On the whole the average flowtime is reduced, but long jobs tend to encounter very long waiting times. In other words, the turnaround is good for most of the jobs but extremely poor for the few long jobs that are assigned low priorities. Several suggestions for ameliorating this aspect of performance have been proposed, but all involve sacrificing some of the benefits of SPT with respect to aggregate behavior. Conway first investigated TSPT, under which SPT is the normal dispatching mode, but operations receive special priority once their waiting time in a given queue exceeds a certain value, W. The parametric behavior of this rule is described in Table 8.5. In Conway's study, the average waiting time per operation observed under FCFS was 7.27 and under SPT was only 2.78. Therefore truncation at $W = 32$ still allows individual

Table 8.5

Dispatching Rule	$\bar{J}$
Truncated SPT	
TSPT (W = ∞)	23.25 (SPT)
TSPT (W = 32)	32.85
TSPT (W = 16)	44.20
TSPT (W = 8)	53.50
TSPT (W = 4)	55.67
TSPT (W = 0)	58.87 (FCFS)
Relief SPT	
RSPT (J = 1)	23.25 (SPT)
RSPT (J = 5)	29.49
RSPT (J = 9)	38.67
RSPT (J = ∞)	58.87 (FCFS)

waiting times to be far above average, yet any earlier truncation appears to sacrifice most of the benefits of SPT. A second suggestion involves the use of SPT in a relief role (RSPT). Under this rule the normal dispatching mode is FCFS, but when the length of an individual queue grows too long, the local dispatching mechanism switches over to SPT. In particular, when the length of any queue reaches a certain number J, then priorities within that queue are reassigned according to SPT. However, once the queue length drops below J the dispatching rule reverts to FCFS. Since FCFS is the normal dispatching mode, long jobs do not typically encounter excessive delays. Long jobs are sometimes delayed temporarily, however, while SPT provides relief to individual machines facing severe congestion. The mean queue length under pure FCFS was 6.54 and under SPT was 2.58. Therefore a queue length parameter of $J = 9$ allows machine queues to grow beyond their mean length before FCFS dispatching is suspended. At the same time the flowtime performance at $J = 9$ was able to retain over half the benefit of SPT sequencing.

Compromise mechanisms such as TSPT and RSPT are necessary in systems that will not tolerate the few very long flowtimes that are produced by SPT. Nevertheless it is important to recognize that different mechanisms will exhibit different performance trade-offs. In the case of TSPT and RSPT, the data in Table 8.5 suggest that RSPT is much more effective at preserving much of the mean flowtime performance of pure SPT while meeting the objections raised about long jobs. Therefore any departure from a desirable pure rule should be thoroughly explored in order to avoid losing the advantages the pure rule achieves.

4. MEETING DUE DATES

When the scheduling objective involves meeting job due dates, the most significant performance measures are likely to be tardiness-based criteria, such as the proportion of jobs tardy or mean job tardiness. In such instances it becomes relevant to consider dispatching strategies that employ due-date information, as exemplified by many of the rules described in Section 2 above. In addition, the attainment of good tardiness performance appears to be a much more complex problem than the minimization of mean flowtime, for several factors can affect comparative performance.

To begin with, consider the distribution of job latenesses. Since lateness is just the algebraic difference between the completion time and a (given) due date, it can be expected that the mean of this distribution will be minimized by SPT. Nevertheless, it is not only the lateness mean that accounts for good tardiness performance, but also the lateness variance. A collection of hypothetical lateness distributions is shown in Figure 8.1 in order to depict a variety of means and variances. The distribution in Figure 8.1a represents the behavior of an arbitrary dispatching procedure that ignores both processing time and due-date information. Figure 8.1b represents the behavior of SPT, which tends to minimize mean lateness while allowing some low priority jobs to become quite tardy. Figure 8.1c represents the behavior of a minimum variance type of rule, one that attempts to schedule jobs for completion as close to their due dates as possible. While the low variance is achieved at the expense of an increased mean, the trade-off may still be desirable unless the mean increases so much that a large proportion of jobs become tardy (Figure 8.1d).

A comparative simulation study carried out by Conway (8) provides more specific information about these results. The study was primarily concerned with proportion of jobs tardy as a performance measure, and the comparison involved several rules that seem to represent priority settings found in actual shops. The rule FCFS exhibits the kind of behavior that might be expected from a procedure that is oriented to neither the lateness mean nor the lateness variance. In a shop operating under a moderately heavy load (Conway's experiments involved utilizations of 88.4 %) FCFS can result in a large proportion of jobs tardy, as shown in Table 8.6. By comparison the SPT rule was able to achieve a small proportion of jobs tardy because of its extremely low lateness mean, which offsets its relatively high lateness variance. Among the rules that use due-date information, it was surprising to find the OPNDD rule exhibiting an enormous lateness variance, for which there seems to be no explanation. The rule S/OPN exhibited the lowest variance, which accounts for its extremely good performance.

As in his flowtime experiments, Conway examined various combination rules in an attempt to find a rule capable of even better performance. He

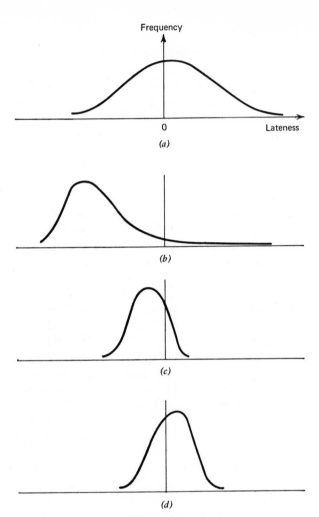

Figure 8.1
The lateness behavior of some hypothetical dispatching rules.

Table 8.6

Dispatching Rule	Lateness Mean	Lateness Variance	Jobs Tardy (Percentage)
FCFS	−4.5	1686	44.8
SPT	−44.9	2878	5.0
EDD	−15.5	432	17.8
OPNDD	−9.9	14560	10.4
MST	−13.1	433	22.0
S/OPN	−12.8	226	3.7

discovered that an equal weighting of SPT and S/OPN priorities in combination yielded a percentage of jobs tardy of only 1.5. This type of behavior should not be surprising, since the combination rule is made up of mean-oriented and variance-oriented components. Nevertheless, the practical value of a combination rule is again open to question, since a weighting factor must be supplied. It can be expected that system performance is somewhat sensitive to the parametric weighting factor, and although equal weightings performed well in the Conway study, it is difficult to believe equal weightings would always be best. On the other hand, the logic of combining the processing time-oriented and slack time-oriented rules is quite persuasive. This logic has led researchers to investigate analogous combinations in models involving both scheduling and inventory performance (3, 4).

Conway's investigation continued in two other directions that suggest how difficult it is to draw general conclusions about the relative performance of dispatching rules. One question involved the manner in which job due dates are set. For the experiment reported in Table 8.6, the time between arrival time and due date was roughly proportional to the total work (TWK) required by the associated job. An alternative was to assign a due date in proportion to the number of operations (NOP) required by the associated job. The TWK and NOP modes represent the kind of due date structure that might be encountered in situations where the production facility is itself responsible for assigning due dates. A third method examined was the CON mode, in which due dates represented a constant lead time for all jobs, and a fourth method was the RDM mode, in which due dates were assigned randomly. In each case a "tightness" parameter could be set so that all modes resulted in comparably tight due dates on the average. Table 8.7 displays the comparison of FCFS, SPT, EDD, and S/OPN for each of the four modes. The striking result is that S/OPN, which achieved the best performance under the TWK mode, performed worse under the other modes and in fact yielded the worst performance among the four rules under CON and RDM. On the other hand, SPT was the least sensitive to the due-date mode and dominated

Table 8.7

Dispatching Rule	Mode			
	TWK	NOP	CON	RDM
FCFS	44.8	39.9	33.8	41.2
SPT	5.0	6.2	11.0	19.8
EDD	17.8	26.7	43.9	48.8
S/OPN	3.7	21.6	48.1	52.6

Table 8.8

| Dispatching | Utilization | | |
Rule	88.4%	90.4%	91.9%
FCFS	44.8	57.7	67.3
SPT	5.0	6.1	7.3
S/OPN	3.7	30.9	54.8

the other rules when TWK was not employed. This behavior suggests that S/OPN may be relatively ineffective when due dates are set arbitrarily.

A second question involved the effect of shop load on the relative performance of dispatching procedures. Conway generated two additional job files that created greater congestion in the shop, resulting in utilizations of over 90% in both cases. Table 8.8 compares the percentages of jobs tardy in each of these three cases for the rules FCFS, SPT, and S/OPN. As would be expected, the performance of a given rule suffers when utilization is increased. However the performance of S/OPN is quite sensitive to this increase. The numerical results suggest that when shop loads are quite heavy the mean-oriented strategy SPT is preferable, while at moderate loads the variance-oriented strategy S/OPN is preferable. Thus there appears to be a crossover point as utilization increases, beyond which SPT achieves better performance than S/OPN. Under the experimental conditions of Conway's study this crossover point occurred for a utilization near 90%, but it is not difficult to imagine that the location of this point is subject to several factors, including the manner in which due dates are assigned and the tightness of the due dates themselves. This type of behavior makes it quite difficult to select a "best" dispatching rule in practice and may even make the use of a combination rule more inviting.

One of the most comprehensive studies of the mean tardiness performance measure was carried out by Carroll (6). One of the main themes in Carroll's experiments involved a parametric family of priority dispatching rules called COVERT rules. This type of rule is based on two pieces of information about each waiting operation: a projected delay cost (c_j), as measured by anticipated tardiness for the associated job, and the operation processing time (t_j). The priority assigned to a waiting operation is the ratio c over t (c_j/t_j), and the dispatching rule selects the operation with the largest ratio to be sequenced next. Hence the procedure is similar to WSPT sequencing, although it uses an elaborate means of calculating the delay cost c_j. Critical jobs are those without slack: that is, even if the remaining operations were to be completed without any delay, the job still could not be completed early. These jobs are assigned an anticipated delay cost of $c_j = 1$. At the other extreme there may be noncritical jobs for which the length of time until the due date exceeds the amount of waiting time anticipated in addition to the remaining processing time required. These jobs are assigned an anticipated delay cost of $c_j = 0$. For jobs between these two extremes there is positive slack, but it is insufficient to meet the waiting time requirement that is anticipated. Let t denote the time at which the dispatching decision must be made, and for job j let Q_j denote the anticipated waiting time for remaining operations and let R_j denote the remaining processing time required. Then the delay cost is

$$c_j = \frac{Q_j - (d_j - R_j - t)}{Q_j}$$

and for this set of jobs $0 < c_j < 1$. Finally, the ratio c_j/t_j is calculated for each waiting operation and the dispatching rule selects the operation with the largest ratio.

Carroll's experiments compared the COVERT rule with two benchmark rules (FCFS and FASFS) along with SPT, TSPT, and S/OPN. Carroll tested a version of S/OPN in which job slack was calculated only when an operation arrives at a machine queue. The priority was not updated while the operation waited in queue, so that the procedure represents an adaptation of S/OPN that is static with respect to a particular operation. There is no reason to believe, however, that the behavior of dynamic S/OPN is very different. Figure 8.2 exhibits a set of results for a pure job shop containing eight machines operating at a utilization of 80%, and from the data it is clear that the COVERT rule is quite effective. The figure contains sketches of the lateness distributions for each of the rules and explains graphically the good performance of the COVERT rule.

Carroll also examined a parametric generalization of the basic COVERT rule in an attempt to find a variation that attained an even smaller mean tardiness. He examined a family of rules that assigned a delay cost of the form

$$c_j = \frac{kQ_j - (d_j - R_j - t)}{kQ_j}$$

For $k = 0.5$ in the same experiment, he achieved $\overline{T} = 1.4$. This result is analogous to some of Conway's results using combination rules: although the setting of an additional parameter may provide slightly better performance, the difficulty of selecting the proper parametric setting may render its use impractical. Carroll also found that the performance of COVERT rules was somewhat sensitive to the choice of a k value.

In additional simulation runs, Carroll examined the relative performance

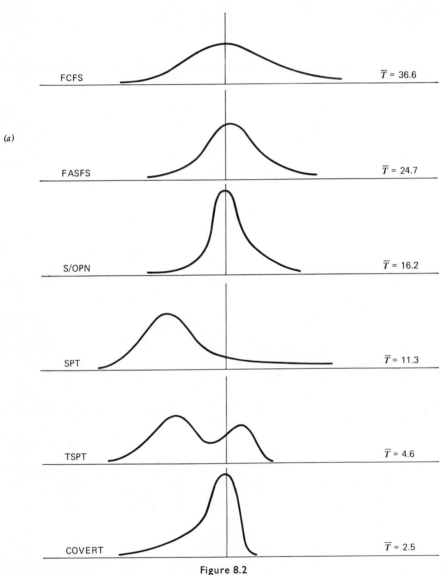

Figure 8.2

A graphical interpretation of Carroll's results for comparative lateness performance.

of the COVERT procedure for different experimental conditions. In particular, COVERT's good performance persisted under different shop loads and with different due-date allowances. Although the COVERT rule is more complex than SPT or S/OPN, and more difficult to implement, Carroll's experiments indicate that the COVERT strategy may well be desirable in a variety of shop environments.

Table 8.9

Dispatching Rule	All Jobs			Revised Jobs	
	Mean Flowtime	Percent Tardy	Mean Tardiness	Percent Tardy	Mean Tardiness
Light load					
SPT	162.1	13	17.0	29	34.1
SPTEX	166.4	22	9.3	15	5.5
FCFSEX	168.2	23	10.6	17	7.2
Heavy load					
SPT	419.4	45	223.4	63	224.1
SPTEX	456.7	89	232.0	74	179.3
FCFSEX	488.2	92	262.0	88	223.1

In shops concerned about meeting job due dates it is an accepted custom to single out certain urgent jobs and give them special priority. The process of flagging rush jobs in this way is called *expediting*, and has been studied in a series of simulation experiments carried out by Hottenstein (*12*). His simulation model involved a six-machine shop normally operating with SPT dispatching and with due dates assigned in the TWK mode. However, a novel feature was added to the assignment of due dates: certain customers would request their jobs to be completed one-fourth sooner than specified at the time the job was released to the shop. These revised requests occurred randomly, but affected an average of 20% of the due dates and were allowed only during the early part of the job's progress in the shop.

In addition to the normal SPT mode of job dispatching, Hottenstein tested two expediting modes. In each of these modes jobs were segmented into normal and high priority classes. Jobs qualified for membership in the high priority class if (1) their due dates had been subjected to customer revision or (2) their slack had diminished to or below zero. In the SPTEX mode high priority jobs are dispatched by SPT, and in the FCFSEX mode high priority jobs are dispatched by FCFS. Hottenstein examined the effects of three factors on the comparative performance of the dispatching rules: shop configuration, shop load, and tightness of due dates. Two configurations were examined—a pure flow shop and a hybrid shop in which the routing matrix was somewhere between that of a pure flow shop and that of a pure job shop. In addition, two shop loads (corresponding to utilizations of roughly 72 and 94%) and three due-date settings (loose, moderate, and tight) were also examined.

The selected results shown in Table 8.9 for the hybrid shop with moderately tight due dates are rather typical of the findings. As might be anticipated, expediting mechanisms sacrifice mean flowtime performance, and the degree of this sacrifice depends largely on the shop load. In all cases SPTEX was the better of the two expediting modes, but the question of whether expediting itself is desirable appeared to be fairly complicated. The expediting device was definitely better suited to the mean tardiness measure than to the proportion of jobs tardy and perhaps slightly better suited to light shop loads than to heavy shop loads. These qualifications aside, the expediting device seemed to be best suited to situations in which performance in meeting the customer-revised due dates is much more important than aggregate performance measures, for expediting frequently led to deterioration of aggregate measures. The SPT rule was distinctly superior in minimizing the proportion of all jobs that were tardy, a result that reinforces the earlier findings in Conway's experiments.

5. SUMMARY

Several important themes emerge from the extensive job shop simulation experiments that have been reported. Perhaps the most noticeable aspect in the job shop studies is the great variety of simple, rational, and effective dispatching procedures that have been developed and tested. The practitioner who is faced with the responsibility of selecting and implementing a priority dispatching scheme can consider a rich variety of priority rules in order to choose a strategy that is appropriate and useful. Moreover, an encouraging theme in job shop work is the efficacy of local rules that utilize only a limited information base. In addition, the implication that SPT in particular does not suffer drastically if input information is unreliable suggests that the simplifications often made in experimental models may not be crucial to the adaptation of simulation results to actual shop control. On the discouraging side, however, is the accumulating evidence that the selection of a "best" priority rule for a tardiness-based measure may depend critically on such factors as the level of shop load, the manner in which due dates are set, and the tightness of the due dates. This means that a certain amount of caution is necessary when attempting to apply the conclusions of a simulation study to a different type of system.

An important consideration in applying simulation results to actual systems is the role of the typical model assumptions delineated in Section 2. When these assumptions do not hold, there may be systematic factors that should be considered. For example, Wayson (21) explored the effects of relaxing the assumption that each operation required a unique machine. In his model, certain operations could be performed by one of several alternate machines, so that an imminent operation could sometimes avoid a congested queue if an alternate machine assignment was technologically feasible. Wayson compared the effect of this structure on the relative behavior of FCFS and SPT dispatching when the performance measure is mean number of jobs in the system. He found, for example, that the behavior of SPT under unique machine assignments was not very different than that of FCFS when alternate selection could be exploited about 20% of the time. In addition, he observed that as the degree of potential alternate selection rose, the differences between the two dispatching rules became less significant.

Wayson's study illustrates that the modification of basic model assumptions may complicate the comparison of priority dispatching rules, yet the systematic effect of this modification on the results may well be predictable, at least qualitatively. The same theme can also be found in other studies, which have relaxed such assumptions as the linear precedence structure (14), sequence-independent setup times (2), or the implicit assumption that the shop can only be machine-limited as opposed to labor-limited (16).

In conclusion, the simulation approach has been reasonably effective in studying the dynamic job shop. As stated at the outset of this chapter, the primary objectives of the simulation work have been to compare specific operating procedures, to test broad conjectures about scheduling rules, and to develop greater insight into the nature of job shop operation. This brief review should indicate that the experimental work has been distinctly successful in these respects. A discussion of the scheduling systems that have been implemented recently in some large job shops can be found in Buffa and Taubert (5).

REFERENCES

1. Baker, C. T., and Dzielinski, B. P. "Simulation of a Simplified Job Shop" *Management Science*, Vol. 6, No. 3 (April, 1960).
2. Baker, K. R. "Priority Dispatching in the Single Channel Queue with Sequence-Dependent Setups," *Journal of Industrial Engineering*, Vol. 19, No. 4 (April, 1968).
3. Baker, K. R. "Control Policies for an Integrated Production-Inventory System," Ph.D. dissertation, Department of Operations Research, Cornell University (September, 1969).
4. Berry, W. L. "Priority Scheduling and Inventory Control in Job Lot Manufacturing Systems," *AIIE Transactions*, Vol. 4, No. 4 (December, 1972).
5. Buffa, E. S., and Taubert, W. H. *Production-Inventory Systems*, Richard D. Irwin, Inc. Homewood, Illinois, 1972.
6. Carroll, D. C. "Heuristic Sequencing of Single and Multiple Component Jobs," Ph.D. dissertation, Sloan School of Management, M.I.T., 1965.
7. Conway, R. W. "Priority Dispatching and Work In Process Inventory in a Job Shop," *Journal of Industrial Engineering*, Vol. 16, No. 2 (March, 1965).
8. Conway, R. W. "Priority Dispatching and Job Lateness in a Job Shop," *Journal of Industrial Engineering*, Vol. 16, No. 4 (July, 1965).
9. Conway, R. W., Maxwell, W. L., and Miller, L. W. *Theory of Scheduling*, Addison-Wesley, Reading, Mass., 1967.
10. Day, J. E., and Hottenstein, M. H. "Review of Sequencing Research," *Naval Research Logistics Quarterly*, Vol. 17, No. 1 (March, 1970).
11. Emery, J. C. "Job Shop Scheduling by means of Simulation and an Optimum-Seeking Search," Proc. Conference on Simulation, Los Angeles (December, 1969).
12. Hottenstein, M. P. "Expediting in Job-Order-Control Systems: A Simulation Study," *AIIE Transactions*, Vol. 2, No. 1 (March, 1970).

13. LeGrande, E. "The Development of a Factory Simulation System Using Actual Operating Data," *Management Technology*, Vol. 3, No. 1 (May, 1963).

14. Maxwell, W. L., and Mehra, M. "Multiple-Factor Rules for Sequencing with Assembly Constraints," *Naval Research Logistics Quarterly*, Vol. 15, No. 2 (June, 1968).

15. Moore, J. M., and Wilson, R. C. "A Review of Simulation Research in Job Shop Scheduling," *Production and Inventory Management*, Vol. 8, No. 1 (January, 1967).

16. Nelson, R. T., "A Simulation Study of Labor Efficiency and Centralized Labor Assignment in a Production System Model," *Management Science*, Vol. 17, No. 2 (October, 1970).

17. Nanot, Y. R. "An Experimental Investigation and Comparative Evaluation of Priority Disciplines in Job Shop-Like Queueing Networks," Ph.D. Dissertation, UCLA, 1963.

18. Pai, A. R., and McRoberts, K. L. "Simulation Research in Interchangeable Part Manufacturing," *Management Science*, Vol. 17, No. 12 (August, 1971).

19. Rowe, A. J. "Sequential Decision Rules in Production Scheduling," Ph.D. Dissertation, UCLA, 1958.

20. Russo, F. J. "A Heuristic Approach to Alternate Routing in a Job Shop," Master's Thesis, MIT, 1965.

21. Wayson, R. D. "The Effect of Alternate Machines on Two Priority Dispatching Disciplines in the General Job Shop," M.S. Thesis Department of Operations Research, Cornell University, 1965.

CHAPTER 9

NETWORK METHODS FOR PROJECT SCHEDULING

1. INTRODUCTION

The techniques of network analysis are valuable tools for scheduling. Network models have been widely used in the formulation of resource allocation problems and sequencing problems; therefore, it is appropriate to think of network models as fundamental in scheduling. The purpose of this introductory treatment of network methods is twofold. The first objective is to describe the elements of network models, since many of the scheduling problems discussed later can be visualized more clearly and analyzed more effectively with the use of network concepts. The second objective is to discuss the basic elements of CPM and PERT, which are well-known techniques for network scheduling.

Traditionally, CPM (Critical Path Method) and PERT (Program Evaluation and Review Technique) have been regarded as tools for planning and scheduling large, nonrepetitive projects, although their potential usefulness has a much broader scope. They have won rapid acceptance as useful, practical techniques, and have been successfully employed in a variety of areas, including research and development, construction, maintenance, marketing, and production.

For the purposes of using network methods in project scheduling, a *project* represents a collection of well-defined tasks called *activities;* when all of these activities are carried out, the project is said to be completed. (In job shop terminology a project is called a job, and an activity is called an operation.) The activities of a project are subject to certain logical constraints, which restrict activity scheduling to certain feasible sequences. Within a feasible sequence, however, activities may be started and stopped independently of each other, as long as the logical constraints are not violated. (This property rules out, for example, conveyor-driven processes in which stopping one activity—by shutting down the conveyor—also stops other activities along the line.) The network model is essentially a means of representing the logical constraints, but it also provides a basis for analyzing the effects of scheduling decisions.

Section 2 deals with the construction of network models to display logical information. Section 3 discusses the fundamentals of analyzing simple, deterministic activity networks. Sections 4 and 5 treat two important extensions of the analysis of simple networks.

2. LOGICAL CONSTRAINTS AND NETWORK CONSTRUCTION

Network representations of logical constraints were introduced in Chapter 4 for describing sets of dependent jobs. In the same way a network model can be used to describe the precedence relations among the dependent activities in a project. The particular network model employed in previous chapters essentially represented activities as nodes in the network and represented direct precedence relations as directed arcs. This type of network is referred to as an activity-on-node (AON) network because of its structure. An alternative model is an activity-on-arc (AOA) network, which is more frequently employed in project scheduling. This section deals with the construction of AOA networks for project models.

Networks are made up of nodes and directed arcs. In an activity-on-arc network, the arcs represent activities and the nodes represent events. The distinction between activities and events in AOA networks is subtle but important. Activities are processes and are associated with intervals of time over which they are performed; events are stages of accomplishment and are associated with points in time. For example, in the development of a prototype of an automobile emissions control device, "testing cold-weather performance" might be an activity, while "test completed" would be an event.

In a network, the direction of arcs indicates precedence relations. Thus if $A < B$, an appropriate network representation would be:

Here, event 1 (node 1) represents the start of activity A and event 3 represents the completion of activity B. Event 2 has two interpretations: it can be considered the completion of activity A or the start of activity B. The network structure indicates that these two events are not logically distinct. In other words, while they may occur *temporally* at different points, they occur *logically* at the same point. If two activities, C and D, are allowed to be concurrent but $C < E$ and $D < E$, the network representation is:

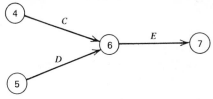

Here the interpretation of node 6 in logical terms is the completion of both activities C and D (or, equivalently, the start of activity E, which requires that both C and D be complete.) Similarly, if $F < G$ and $F < H$, where G and H can be concurrent, then the network representation is:

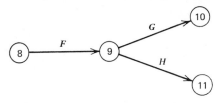

Here the interpretation of node 9 in logical terms is the completion of activity F or, equivalently, the potential start of either activity G or activity H, or both.

Several conventions are usually prescribed for the construction of AOA networks. Here are the principal rules.

1. The network should have a unique starting event (a single origin node).

2. The network should have a unique completion event (a single terminal node).

3. The nodes should be numbered so that the completion event for any activity has a larger number than its starting event. (Such a numbering can always be found unless the network contains logical inconsistencies.)

4. No activity should be represented by more than one arc in the network.

5. No two activities should share both a starting event and a completion event.

Rule 5 may create a problem for the basic AOA network. For example, consider the following simple project (planning and holding a fund-raising concert) and the network representation that follows it.

Activity	ID	Predecessors
Plan concert	A	—
Advertise	B	A
Sell tickets	C	A
Hold concert	D	B, C

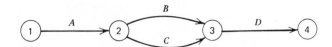

For informal purposes or hand calculations, this network diagram is sufficient. To avoid violating rule 5, however, it is necessary to include a dummy activity (dotted arc), as shown below.

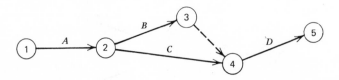

The dummy activity allows the same logical relationships to be accommodated without violating rule 5, or some other rule. Clearly, there is no physical process that corresponds to the dummy activity, but it is often necessary to use dummy activities to exhibit correct logical relationships under the conventions listed above. Also, computer programs for project scheduling techniques often rely on the ability to use dummy activities.

Given these conventions, the task of constructing a suitable network requires two types of input: a detailed list of the individual activities and a specification of their precedence relations. To help provide the latter information, the following questions should be answered for each activity:

Which activities precede it? (What controls its start?)
Which activities follow it? (What are its consequences?)
Which activities may be concurrent with it?

With this information available, the next step is to draw an intelligible network diagram. Often, this will be a trial-and-error process, and many textbooks caution the novice to approach this task armed with a good eraser. Battersby (1) offers the following guidelines for drawing good networks.

Avoid drawing arrows that cross.
Keep all arrows as straight lines.
Avoid too wide a variation in arc lengths.
Keep the angles between arcs as large as possible.
Keep a left-to-right component in each arc.

The use of AON networks leads to a different approach to constructing network diagrams for project scheduling. Recall that in an AON network the nodes represent activities and the arcs represent the logical constraints. Since each arc corresponds to a direct precedence relation between two activities, there is never any need to use dummy activities. For example, here is the AON network for the fund-raising concert.

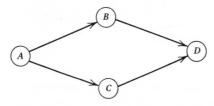

The direct correspondence of arcs with precedence information, and the fact that dummy activities are not necessary for expressing logical constraints, make AON networks somewhat easier to construct than AOA networks. For this reason, when network models are used in formulating scheduling problems that contain logical constraints, the AON type of network is usually employed. Nevertheless, in practical application of CPM and PERT there are good reasons for using AOA networks. First, when computer programs are used to perform the requisite calculations for large projects, the computational task can be carried out more efficiently with AOA formulations. Second, the event orientation of AOA networks can be advantageous from a project management point of view. In particular, events in the network represent milestones—points in time when project status can be conveniently updated, prospects can be reevaluated, and plans can be revised with new decisions. Because of the particular usefulness of event-oriented networks in project scheduling, the discussion of CPM and PERT in the following sections will emphasize AOA networks.

9.2 EXERCISES

2.1 Suppose that the tasks in changing a flat tire are as follows.

ID	Predecessors
A Remove flat tire from wheel	—
B Repair puncture on flat tire	A
C Remove spare tire from trunk	—
D Put spare on wheel	A, C
E Place repaired tire in trunk	B, C

(a) Find an error in the following AOA network diagram for the above project.

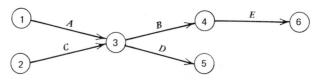

(b) Draw a correct AOA network diagram for the project of changing a flat tire.

2.2 Consider the following set of precedence restrictions among five activities.

$$A < D \qquad B < E$$
$$B < D \qquad C < E$$

(a) Draw an AOA network diagram for these logical constraints.
(b) Draw an AON network diagram for these logical constraints.

2.3 Consider the following set of precedence restrictions among six activities.

$$B < D \quad A < D \quad C < E$$
$$B < F \quad A < E \quad C < F$$
$$A < F$$

(a) Draw an AOA network diagram for these logical constraints.
(b) Draw an AON network diagram for these logical constraints.

2.4 Consider this set of precedence restrictions.

$$A < D \quad C < F \quad B < E$$
$$A < E \qquad\qquad B < F$$

Given these logical constraints, someone in the project control staff proposes the AOA network diagram shown below.

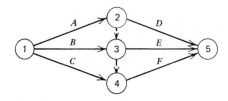

(a) Identify the error in the given network.
(b) Construct a correct AOA network diagram for the project.
(c) Construct a correct AON network diagram for the project.

3. TEMPORAL ANALYSIS OF ACTIVITY NETWORKS

The underlying motivation of temporal analysis involves the question "When will the project be complete?" A closely related question is "Which activities will contribute directly to the duration of the project?" To help answer both questions, the network is analyzed under the simplifying assumption that all activity durations are deterministic.

To begin with, "time" refers to a point in time, and is associated with the occurrence of an event; "duration" refers to an interval in time and is associated with an activity. Associated with each event in the network are two time values: an *early event time* (ET), which is the earliest point in time at which the event could possibly occur, and a *late event time* (LT), which is the latest point in time at which the event could occur without delaying the completion of the project. These are obviously complementary definitions, and suggest complementary ways of calculating their values.

Calculation of early event times

1. The origin event is assigned an ET of zero.
2. Employing the node numbering convention of Rule 3, the events are considered in numerical order. For each event the following calculation is made to find the associated ET.
   (a) To the ET of each directly preceding event add the duration of the connecting activity.
   (b) Select the maximum of the sums found in (a).

Calculation of late event times

1. The terminal event is assigned an LT equal to the project due date.
2. The events are considered in reverse numerical order and the following calculation determines the LT for each event.
   (a) From the LT of each directly succeeding event subtract the duration of the connecting activity.
   (b) Select the minimum of the differences found in (a).

Thus a forward pass calculates ET values and a backward pass calculates LT values. If the project does not have an explicit due date, the backward pass is initialized by using the ET for the terminal event as the due date. Once all ET and LT values are computed, attention shifts to activity information. In particular, four quantities are calculated for each activity.

Early start time (ES).   The earliest time at which the activity could possibly be started (equal to the ET of the activity's starting event).

Early finish time (EF).   The earliest time at which the activity could possibly be completed (equal to the sum of ES and the activity duration).

Late finish time (LF).   The latest time at which the activity could be completed without delaying the project beyond its due date (equal to the LT of the activity's completion event).

Late start time (LS).   The latest time at which the activity could be started without delaying the project beyond its due date (equal to the difference between LF and the activity duration).

To illustrate these calculations, consider the collection of activities shown on pp. 243. The corresponding network diagram is shown in Figure 9.1, where each arc is labeled with both an activity ID and a duration. The forward and backward passes produce the ET and LT values displayed in Figure 9.2. (Since no project due date was given, the late event time for event 6 is taken

Activity ID	Direct Predecessors	Duration
A	—	5
B	—	4
C	—	3
D	A	1
E	C	2
F	C	9
G	C	5
H	B, D, E	4
I	G	2

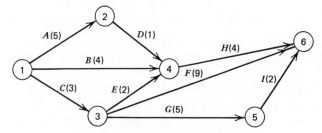

Figure 9.1

Network model for the example project.

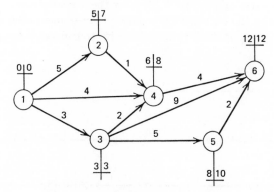

Figure 9.2

Labeled network for the example project. The two numbers associated with each node are the ET and LT of the corresponding event.

to be 12, its early event time.) With this data it is possible to calculate the activity information[1] displayed in Table 9.1.

One of the motivating questions has now been answered. Assuming that activity durations are deterministic, the ET of the terminal event represents the minimum project length. The project can be completed by this time as

[1] An analogous labeling procedure can be used in AON networks (9).

Table 9.1

Activity	Duration	ES	EF	LF	LS
A	5	0	5	7	2
B	4	0	4	8	4
C	3	0	3	3	0
D	1	5	6	8	7
E	2	3	5	8	6
F	9	3	12	12	3
G	5	3	8	10	5
H	4	6	10	12	8
I	2	8	10	12	10

long as sufficient resources are available and no delays occur. To address the second question, it is necessary to understand what accounts for the project length.

Activities that contribute directly to the duration of the project are called *critical*. Hence any delay in a critical activity will ultimately cause a delay in the completion of the project. The chain of arcs formed by the critical activities is called the *critical path:* it is the longest path from the origin event to the terminal event and may not be unique. In the network of Figure 9.1, the critical path is CF. Because the logical constraints require that the activities on the critical path be carried out sequentially, there is no way that event 6 can be realized prior to time 12. In general, if the project is to be

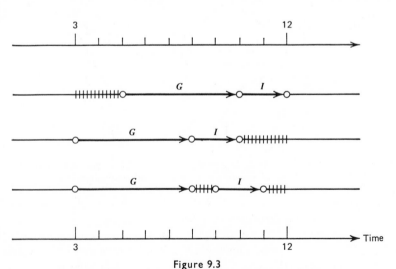

Figure 9.3
Three different ways of scheduling activities *G* and *I*.

completed by the ET of the terminal event, there is no room for any delay along the critical path.

For noncritical activities, however, there is some scheduling flexibility. Consider the scheduling of activities G and I in Figure 9.2. Activity G can start no earlier than time 3 and, to avoid delaying the project, activity I must be completed by time 12. Since seven units of time are required to carry out activities G and I in sequence, and since an interval of length 9 is available, there is some flexibility in scheduling. The two extra units of time can be absorbed before or after either activity, or perhaps in some combination, as shown in Figure 9.3. This kind of flexibility is called *float*. Along the critical path (or critical paths, if there are several) there is by definition no float, while along other paths there is some amount of float. There are a variety of ways to quantify this measure of scheduling flexibility with respect to individual activities in the network.

To describe the various measures of float concisely, consider activity j and let:

$t_j = $ duration of activity j

$i = $ start node of activity j

$k = $ completion node of activity j

$ET_i = $ early event time corresponding to node i, etc.

Then for activity j, with start node i and completion node k, the four measures of float are:

Total float (TF) $= LT_k - ET_i - t_j$

Safety float (SF) $= LT_k - LT_i - t_j$

Free float (FF) $= ET_k - ET_i - t_j$

Independent float (IF) $= \max \{ET_k - LT_i - t_j, 0\}$

Of these four measures, the most frequently used is total float, which—as observed above—actually measures float along a path. The total float represents the delay in start time that could be absorbed by an activity without delaying the project, assuming no other activity on the path is delayed further. The safety float is similar, but assumes that the direct predecessors of an activity have already been delayed as much as possible. Free float measures the delay in start time that could be absorbed by an activity without preventing any other activity from being started at its own early start time. Finally, independent float, which is perhaps the most useful measure of individualized activity float, represents the delay in start time that can be absorbed by an activity unconditionally, that is, independent of any scheduling decisions made elsewhere in the network. The calculation of the four types of float for the example network introduced above is shown in Table 9.2. Note that the critical activities are identified by the condition $TF = 0$.

Returning to the two questions posed at the outset of this section, it is

Table 9.2

Activity	TF	SF	FF	IF
A	2	2	0	0
B	4	4	2	2
C	0	0	0	0
D	2	0	0	0
E	3	3	1	1
F	0	0	0	0
G	2	2	0	0
H	2	0	2	0
I	2	0	2	0

possible to see how the temporal analysis of a network provides answers. If we assume that activity durations are known constants, the duration of a project is equal to the length of the longest path in the network. The critical activities, those which lie along this longest path, are the activities that contribute directly to project length. Any delay in a critical activity will lead to a delay in the project. Furthermore, for noncritical activities, the amount of scheduling flexibility available, and the nature of that flexibility, is represented by the various measures of activity float.

The assumption of constant, deterministic activity durations on which temporal analysis is based certainly has some shortcomings. To address these flaws, and to develop more practical forms of network analysis, the basic project model has been extended in two important ways. The first extension (usually associated with PERT) allows activity durations to be probabilistic, and answers the motivating questions in probabilistic terms. The second extension treats each activity duration as a function of the amount of a certain resource applied, and formulates a resource allocation problem in which resource levels (and therefore activity durations) are decision variables. These extensions are discussed in the next two sections.

9.3 EXERCISES

For each of the projects diagrammed below,
  (a) Determine the critical path and its length.
  (b) Calculate ES, EF, LS, and LF for each activity in the project.
  (c) Calculate TF, SF, FF, and IF for each activity in the project.

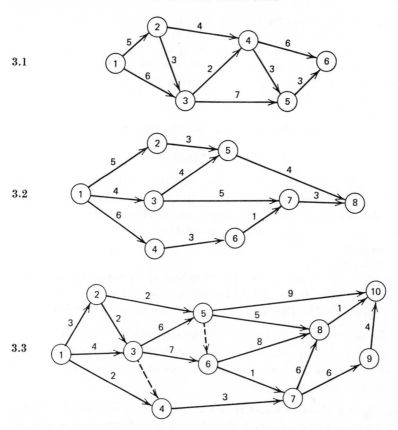

3.1

3.2

3.3

3.4 A precedence matrix P is shown below, where $p_{ij} = 1$, if activity i is a direct predecessor of activity j. From the matrix, construct a network diagram, and then find the critical path of the project using the activity durations shown.

	A	B	C	D	E	F	G	H	I	J	Duration
A	—	0	0	1	1	0	0	0	0	0	5
B		—	0	0	0	0	1	1	0	1	9
C			—	0	0	1	1	1	0	0	8
D				—	0	0	1	1	0	1	6
E					—	0	0	0	1	0	10
F						—	0	0	0	1	7
G							—	0	1	0	3
H								—	0	0	12
I									—	0	8
J										—	10

3.5   Consider the project of Exercise 3.3. Suppose that a special piece of equipment is required to carry out activities (5, 8) and (6, 7).
   (a) Can the entire project still be carried out in the same total length of
       time as if unlimited resources were available?
   (b) Can each activity be started at its early start time?

4.   PROBABILISTIC NETWORK ANALYSIS

4.1   The PERT Method

   Once again the motivating question is "When will the project be complete?" The objective of probabilistic analysis is to answer this question with
explicit recognition that activity durations are uncertain. Let

   T_j = duration of activity j (a random variable)

   μ_j = mean of T_j, or $E[T_j]$

   σ_j^2 = variance of T_j

The analysis therefore recognizes that T_j is indeed a random variable, and
begins with the assumption that μ_j and σ_j^2 are known (or that they can at
least be estimated). The PERT model requires two basic assumptions:

A1.   The activities in the network are probabilistically independent.

A2.   The critical path in the network (as defined below) contains a large
      enough number of activities so that the central limit theorem applies
      when analyzing its length.

The central limit theorem states that the sum of a large number of independent random variables has a distribution that approaches a normal
distribution as the number of components of the sum grows large. Moreover,
the mean of such a sum is equal to the sum of the individual means, and the
variance of the sum is equal to the sum of the individual variances. If L_p
denotes the duration along path p in the network, then

$$L_p = \sum_{j \in p} T_j$$

$$\mu_p = E[L_p] = \sum_{j \in p} E[T_j] = \sum_{j \in p} \mu_j \tag{1}$$

$$\sigma_p^2 = \sum_{j \in p} \sigma_j^2 \tag{2}$$

Furthermore, the central limit theorem states that the distribution of the
random variable L_p can be closely approximated by a normal distribution
with mean μ_p and variance σ_p^2, provided there are a large number of activities on path p.

   The PERT recipe identifies the critical path by taking μ_j to be the duration
of activity j and performing the temporal analysis described in the previous

section on the resulting deterministic network. Let $p = \pi$ denote the critical path in this analysis. Then L_π is the length of this path, and L_π has approximately a normal distribution with parameters μ_π and $\sigma_\pi{}^2$. (Notice that in a particular realization of the network, the path π may not be the actual longest path in the network; it is merely the path with the longest mean length.) The PERT method then substitutes L_π for the length of the project, so that the distribution of L_π is interpreted as the distribution of the project length.

The PERT method thus obtains a distribution that it uses to approximate the actual distribution of project length. The motivating question posed above can then be answered in probabilistic terms. If we use the PERT approximation, the probability that the project will be completed by a deadline d is

$$\Phi\left(\frac{d - \mu_\pi}{\sigma_\pi}\right)$$

where $\Phi(\cdot)$ denotes the cumulative distribution function for a standard normal random variable.

To provide this kind of analysis, the method relies on knowledge of the individual activity parameters μ_j and $\sigma_j{}^2$. Frequently there will be no data from which to estimate these parameters, and it may be difficult even for knowledgeable personnel to provide good estimates. For such situations, PERT provides a mechanism for obtaining μ_j and σ_j from estimates that are easier and perhaps more meaningful to obtain. For a given activity, let

a = an optimistic duration; that is, an estimate of the activity duration under the most favorable conditions.

b = a pessimistic duration; that is, an estimate of the activity duration under the least favorable conditions.

m = a most likely duration; that is, the duration that is most likely to occur.

These three parameters are incorporated in a beta distribution (see Figure 9.4) as a probabilistic model for the duration of the activity. The values a and b are the minimum and maximum values of the distribution, and m is the mode of the distribution. The beta distribution is widely accepted as a reasonable subjective model for the distribution of an activity duration. It has a rather flexible density function, which can be symmetric or else skewed in either direction depending on the values of a, m, and b. With the hypothesis of an underlying beta distribution, the PERT method provides for μ_j and $\sigma_j{}^2$ to be obtained as follows:

$$\mu_j = \tfrac{1}{6}(a + 4m + b) \tag{3}$$

$$\sigma_j{}^2 = \tfrac{1}{36}(b - a)^2 \tag{4}$$

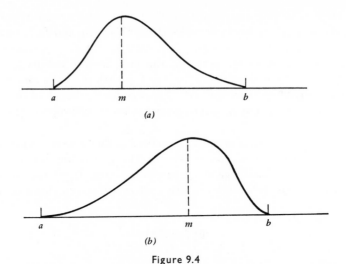

Figure 9.4

The density function of a beta distribution. (*a*) and (*b*) indicate that the distribution can be skewed in either direction, depending on the parameters *a*, *m*, and *b*.

Thus, even when μ_j and σ_j^2 are not known at the outset, PERT offers a technique for calculating the two parameters from the estimates *a*, *m*, and *b*.

As an example, consider the project described in Table 9.3, in which the values of μ_j and σ_j^2 are calculated from equations 3 and 4 by using the given values of *a*, *m*, and *b*. The next step is to construct the network diagram and to label activity *j* with its mean duration, μ_j, as shown in Figure 9.5. Then, by using these mean values we can identify the PERT critical path as *B–F–I*. From these calculations, it can be seen from equations 1 and 2 that the length of the path *B–F–I* has a mean of 16 and a variance of 2.44. If we use

Table 9.3

Activity	Predecessors	*a*	*m*	*b*	μ	σ^2
A	—	2	4	12	5	2.78
B	—	3	6	9	6	1.00
C	A	1	2	9	3	1.78
D	A	3	3	9	4	1.00
E	B	1	2	3	2	0.11
F	B	2	8	8	7	1.00
G	C	1	2	9	3	1.78
H	D, E	4	5	12	6	1.78
I	F	1	3	5	3	0.44

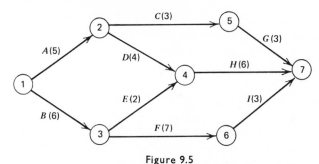

Figure 9.5
Network representation of the project in Table 9.3.

the probabilistic characteristics of this path as a model for project duration, the probability that the project will be completed by time 15 is then

$$\Phi\left(\frac{15 - 16}{\sqrt{2.44}}\right) \simeq 0.26$$

In summary, PERT recognizes that the duration of the project is a random variable and that questions about the completion of the project can be answered only in probabilistic terms. This being true, PERT utilizes mean-value "certainty equivalents" and deterministic analysis to identify the critical path, π. Then assumptions A1 and A2 are invoked to characterize the length of this path, L_π. The properties of the random variable L_π are then substituted for the duration of the project to make statements about project completion. Finally, where information about the duration of individual activities is scarce, PERT uses the beta distribution model for activity durations, based upon estimates of a, m, and b, and the relations 3 and 4. Although many theoretical objections can be raised to the PERT method, its practical value has still been very real. In many cases, the advent of PERT made available a powerful planning tool where no comparable tool had formerly existed. This very substantial contribution to project management is probably PERT's greatest achievement. Also, in the years that have passed since the PERT technique was introduced, several refinements have been developed to compensate for some of its theoretical flaws.

4.2 Theoretical Aspects of PERT

The purpose of this section is to discuss the principal theoretical shortcomings that are present in the PERT method, and to provide references that contain more detailed examinations of such problems. Essentially, the objections that are most often raised about PERT fall into two categories: problems arising at the project level and problems arising at the individual activity level.

Perhaps the most popular indictment of PERT is that its estimate of mean project duration is biased downward. While the true mean project duration is of the form $E[\max_p \{L_p\}]$, PERT substitutes $\max_p \{E[L_p]\}$. Since $\max_p \{L_p\} \geq L_\pi$, it follows that

$$\text{True mean} = E\left[\max_p \{L_p\}\right] \geq E[L_\pi] = \max_p \{E[L_p]\} = \text{PERT mean}$$

That is, the mean project length obtained via PERT will always be less than or equal to the theoretical mean. In this sense, PERT is inherently optimistic—it always underestimates the true mean.

The extent of the error that is involved in this calculation depends on the structure of the network and the array of activity distributions. For example, suppose that the different path lengths in Figure 9.5 are independent and have normal distributions. By using the PERT statistics, the four paths can be described as follows:

p		μ_p	$\sigma_p{}^2$
1	(A–C–G)	11	6.33
2	(A–D–H)	15	5.67
3	(B–E–H)	14	2.89
4	(B–F–I)	16	2.44

According to the PERT method, B–F–I (path 4) is the critical path, yet there is a probability that B–F–I will not be the longest path in a given realization of the project. In particular, under the assumption that L_2 and L_4 are independent random variables, $\Pr \{L_4 < L_2\} = 0.36$. The distributions of the L_p are sketched in Figure 9.6a, and the degree to which other distributions overlap the distribution of L_4 indicates that there is a significant probability that path 4 will not be the longest path. On the other hand, if there is little or no overlap of the distribution of L_π (as sketched for a hypothetical example in Figure 9.6b), then the project duration is essentially identical to the random variable L_π. In that case

$$E\left[\max_p \{L_p\}\right] \doteq \max_p \{E[L_p]\}$$

and the PERT estimate is quite good.

Several authors have studied the general problems of improving the PERT estimate of mean project duration. The basic approach in finding improvements is discussed by Fulkerson (4). Subsequent refinements and extensions can be found in articles by Clingen (2) and Elmaghraby (3).

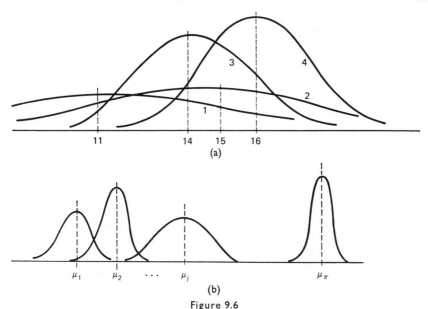

Figure 9.6

Distributions of individual paths in a network for (a) the example project and (b) a hypothetical project.

A second shortcoming in PERT concerns its identification of critical activities. By employing deterministic analysis to identify the critical path, PERT necessarily partitions the activities into two distinct subsets: the critical activities and the noncritical activities. Because the network is probabilistic, it is possible that an activity that lies on the deterministic critical path may not lie on the longest path in a particular realization of the project. Furthermore, the two-way partition of PERT may not reflect the likelihood that the various activities will be critical. For example, in the project of Figure 9.5, the PERT method identifies activities B, F, and I as critical. Nevertheless, an intuitive argument can be made that B is somehow "more critical" than F because B is critical whenever F is and, in addition, B is also critical when $B-E-H$ turns out to be the longest path.

A similar, but more extensive comparison can be based on the network shown in Figure 9.7, which is adapted from (10). Suppose that the distributions of activity duration are discrete and, specifically, that the durations a, m, and b are each realized with probability $\frac{1}{3}$. If all possible realizations of the project are enumerated, the following properties emerge (see Table 9.4).

1. Although the deterministic critical path is $A-C-G$, a theoretical analysis reveals that $A-C-G$ will be the longest path with a probability of 0.27, which is less than the probability that $A-D$ will be the longest path.

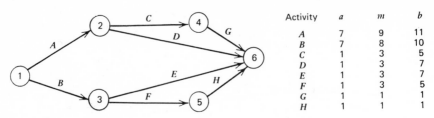

Activity	a	m	b
A	7	9	11
B	7	8	10
C	1	3	5
D	1	3	7
E	1	3	7
F	1	3	5
G	1	1	1
H	1	1	1

Figure 9.7
Network representation for a small project.

2. Although the PERT method identifies activity C as critical, it will be on the actual longest path with a probability of only 0.27.

3. Although the PERT method identifies activity B as noncritical, it will be on the actual longest path with a probability of 0.42.

The broad implication of such an analysis is that the concept of "criticality" tends to be blurred in the presence of random activity durations. Moreover, the activities along a single path may be critical to different degrees, suggesting that criticality is more a trait of individual activities than of entire paths. Unfortunately, the difficulties inherent in general analytic approaches to the problem are substantial. Instead, a more practicable vehicle appears to be the use of Monte Carlo simulation, as described by Van Slyke (15). Van Slyke demonstrated that for medium-sized networks the Monte Carlo technique can provide good information about both the distribution of project length and the criticality of individual activities. Related discussions can be found in Klingel (8), Hartley and Wortham (7), and Garman (6).

A third problem with the PERT calculations involves its assumption A1

Table 9.4

Activity	Probability Activity Lies on Longest Path
A	0.58
B	0.42
C	0.27
D	0.30
E	0.24
F	0.19
G	0.27
H	0.19

that the activity durations are independent. A comprehensive analytical treatment of more general situations requires a model for dependence among activities, and it would seem to be quite difficult to propose (much less analyze) such a model. A start in this direction can be found in the work of Ringer (*13*), and it should be noted that the basic approaches of Fulkerson and Van Slyke (referenced above) can accommodate some dependence.

At the level of individual activities in the network, an entirely different set of PERT assumptions can be challenged.

1. The true form of the distribution of an activity duration may not be a beta distribution.

2. The true distribution may be a beta distribution, but its mean and variance may not be those prescribed in equations 3 and 4.

3. The estimates on which the entire procedure is based (i.e., estimates of *a*, *m*, and *b*) may be inaccurate.

Qualitative and quantitative discussions of these problems can be found in MacCrimmon and Ryavec (*10*), Swanson and Pazer (*14*), Parks and Ramsig (*12*), and Levy and Wiest (*9*).

9.4 EXERCISES

4.1 What is the probability that the following project will be completed in 20 days?

Activity	Predecessors	*a*	*m*	*b*
A	—	1	4	7
B	—	1	5	9
C	A	3	6	9
D	B	1	2	3
E	A	1	2	9
F	C, D	2	4	6
G	C, D, E	2	9	10
H	F	2	2	2 days

4.2   What is the probability that the following project will be completed in 18 days?

Activity	Predecessors	a	m	b
A	—	3	5	7
B	—	4	6	20
C	A	1	2	3
D	A	3	3	3
E	A	1	2	9
F	B, C	0	6	6
G	B, C	2	5	14
H	D	1	8	9
J	E, F	1	3	11
K	G	2	2	2

4.3   In the project shown below, all activities have normal distributions with means μ and standard deviations σ as given. What is the probability that A–C–E–G will be the longest path in the network?

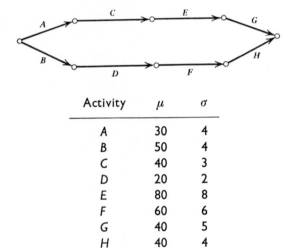

Activity	μ	σ
A	30	4
B	50	4
C	40	3
D	20	2
E	80	8
F	60	6
G	40	5
H	40	4

5. THE TIME/COST TRADE-OFF

The second generalization of the basic deterministic model treats activity durations as decision variables. The premise from which this kind of analysis develops is that activity durations can be shortened by the application of greater amounts of labor, capital, or both. More simply, this means that the expenditure of more money can reduce the duration of an activity. There is therefore a time/cost trade-off for each activity in the project, and an overall trade-off involving project duration and project expense.

To illustrate the structure of a time/cost model, suppose that the relationship between activity duration and cost satisfies the following properties:

1. Each activity duration is a linear function of the costs incurred in carrying out the activity.

2. Each activity has a minimum feasible duration and a maximum feasible duration.

Under these conditions, the time/cost trade-off for a given activity can be represented by the graph shown in Figure 9.8. Here is the notation.

m = minimum feasible duration
M = maximum feasible duration
t = activity duration
c = cost per unit time of expediting the activity
K = total cost incurred in carrying out the activity

Within this type of framework, it is possible to formulate several problems in finding minimum-cost project schedules.

Suppose that in addition to the activity-related costs described in Figure 9.8, there is also a fixed overhead cost, c_f, incurred on a daily basis until the

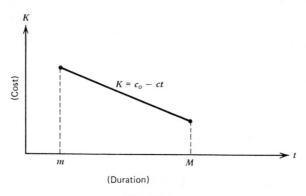

Figure 9.8
Graphical representation of the time/cost function for an individual activity.

project is completed. The following brief example illustrates the decision procedure involved in finding a minimum cost schedule. First, suppose that all activities are scheduled at their maximum durations. The corresponding

Activity (j)	Predecessors	M_j	m_j	c_j	c_{oj}
A	—	3 days	1 day	$40	$140
B	A	7	3	10	110
C	A	4	2	40	180
D	C	5	2	20	130

Fixed cost $c_f = \$45/\text{day}$.

network diagram, displayed on a time scale, is shown in Figure 9.9a. The total cost of this project is broken down as below. In order to reduce costs,

Component	Cost
Activity A	$20
Activity B	40
Activity C	20
Activity D	30
Overhead	540
Total	$650

a reduction must be made in the length of the project. In other words, the length of the critical path (A–C–D) must be reduced in a manner which will reduce costs. Among the critical activities, D is the least expensive to expedite. A two-day reduction in its duration (costing $40) achieves a reduction in overhead costs of $90. At this stage, activity B is also critical (see Figure 9.9b) and the alternatives for reducing the length of the project are:

1. Expedite activity A at $40/day.
2. Expedite activities B and C at $50/day.
3. Expedite activities B and D at $30/day.

Clearly the third alternative is most desirable, but a reduction of only one day is possible, since activity D must be at least two days in length (Figure 9.9c). A further improvement requires alternative 1 in the above list. Activity A can be scheduled at its minimum duration, and the resulting total cost is

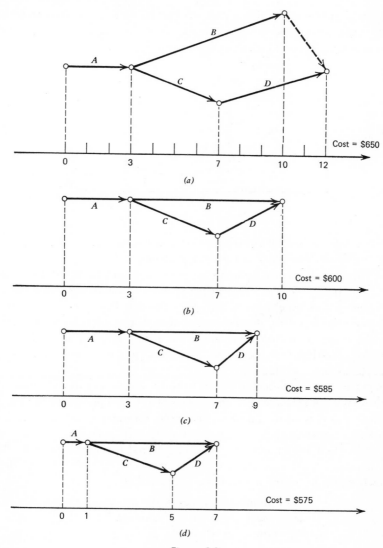

Figure 9.9
A sequence of schedule modifications in the solution of the example problem.

lowered to $575 (Figure 9.9d). At this stage, only alternative 2 on the list is a feasible way of reducing the length of the project, but alternative 2 is not cost-effective. The cost of a one-day reduction in activities B and C more than offsets the savings in overhead cost; therefore the cost of $575 is optimal.

As this simple example illustrates, when variable activity costs and fixed project costs are of concern, it can be expected that total costs will behave (approximately) as the function sketched below:

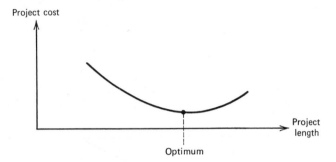

In such a case, finding an optimal project length—and an associated project schedule—is a meaningful optimization problem.

For larger projects, the heuristic solution method illustrated above will seldom be practicable. With a great many more activities present there will be more stages at which several paths are critical. The identification of all alternatives for reducing project length in such cases can be a formidable task, not to mention that there might be a very large number of stages. Therefore, solutions to large-scale time/cost problems rely heavily on computer-oriented techniques.

When the cost functions are linear, as in the situation just described, the power of linear programming as an optimization technique can be harnessed. The basic structure of the linear programming formulation is relatively easy to describe. Let activity j be characterized by start node i and completion node k. In other words, activity j can be referred to as activity (i, k). The basic decision variables are the activity durations or, equivalently, the times at which the nodes in the network are realized. Let

$$N = \text{number of nodes in the network}$$
$$x_i = \text{early event time of node } i(ET_i)$$
$$t_{ik} = \text{duration of activity } (i, k)$$

Then the length of the project is $(x_N - x_1)$ or simply x_N, if x_1 is taken to be zero. The two feasibility constraints on activity durations may be expressed in this way.

$$t_{ik} \leq M_{ik} \quad \text{for each activity } (i, k)$$
$$t_{ik} \geq m_{ik} \quad \text{for each activity } (i, k)$$

And the relationship between early event times and activity durations may be written

$$x_k - t_{ik} - x_i \geq 0 \quad \text{for each activity } (i, k)$$

The criterion is simply the sum of project costs and activity costs, or

$$c_f x_N + \sum_j (c_{oj} - c_j t_j)$$

Since the sum of the c_{oj} values is a constant, the objective is essentially to minimize $c_f x_N - \sum_j c_j t_j$. The full linear program, with activities represented by double subscripts (i, k) is shown below.

$$\text{Minimize} \quad c_f x_N - \sum_{(i,k)} c_{ik} t_{ik}$$

$$\text{Subject to} \quad x_k - t_{ik} - x_i \geq 0$$

$$\left. \begin{array}{c} t_{ik} \leq M_{ik} \\ t_{ik} \geq m_{ik} \end{array} \right\} \quad \text{for all } (i, k)$$

$$x_i, t_{ik} \geq 0$$

The linear programming formulation is significant primarily because it is a direct way of stating the problem and because it can accommodate some important variations of the problem described here (see Exercise 5.1). Special purpose formulations and solution algorithms have been developed for certain variations (5).

Returning to properties 1 and 2 assumed at the outset of the discussion of time/cost problems, an important generalization of the model clearly involves nonlinear time/cost functions. Solution approaches to such a problem can in principle utilize nonlinear programming and integer programming techniques but may not be practical for large projects.

9.5 EXERCISES

5.1 Formulate the following version of the time/cost trade-off problem as a linear program:

Given a linear time/cost relation for each activity, minimize the total cost of completing the entire project within an interval of length y.

5.2 A small maintenance project consists of the jobs in the table on page 262. With each job is listed its normal time and a minimum, or crash, time (in days). The cost in dollars per day of crashing each job is also given.

| Job | | Normal Days | Minimum | Cost of Expediting |
i	j	Duration	Duration	(Dollars/Day)
1	2	9	6	20
1	3	8	5	25
1	4	15	10	30
2	4	5	3	10
3	4	10	6	15
4	5	2	1	40

(a) What is the normal project length and the minimum project length?

(b) Determine the activity-related costs of schedules ranging from normal length down to, and including, the minimum length schedule. That is, if L = length of normal schedule, find the minimum costs of schedules that are L, $L - 1$, $L - 2$, and so on, days long.

(c) Overhead costs total \$60/day. What is the optimum length schedule in terms of both expediting and overhead costs? List the scheduled durations of each job for your solution.

6.　SUMMARY

Network models are building blocks for scheduling, and this introduction to network methods has been aimed at both pedagogical and practical objectives. Since logical constraints often appear as basic elements in scheduling problems, the ability to visualize and describe logical relationships with network structures is a fundamental aspect of scheduling. This presentation introduced the activity-on-arc network as a model for precedence relationships.

As suggested earlier, the significance of CPM and PERT lies primarily in their role as useful tools for project planning and project management. The success of these network-based techniques in finding rapid acceptance among practitioners can be attributed to several factors. First, the basic model provides information in a useful form. It analyzes the project in a way that makes pertinent information explicit and that can be used as a basis for communication throughout the administrative organization. In addition, the model accommodates sufficient detail so that important aspects of the project will not be overlooked, and it provides a framework for testing and evaluating alternate project management strategies.

The basic versions of CPM and PERT address themselves to two central aspects of project planning by supplying information about the length of the project and by identifying the particular activities on which the project duration depends. The simplest approach to these topics is through temporal analysis of deterministic networks with constant activity durations. This type of analysis is enriched by the two extensions introduced in this chapter: the recognition of probabilistic factors and the recognition of the time/cost trade-off. Another important extension involves project scheduling with limited resources, which can also be viewed as a generalization of the job shop problem. Project scheduling under resource constraints is the subject of the next chapter.

REFERENCES

1. Battersby, A. *Network Analysis for Planning and Scheduling*, Macmillan London, 1967.
2. Clingen, C. T. "A Modification of Fulkerson's PERT Algorithm," *Operations Research*, Vol. 12, No. 4 (July, 1964).
3. Elmaghraby, S. E., "On the Expected Duration of PERT Type Networks," *Management Science*, Vol. 13, No. 5 (January, 1967).
4. Fulkerson, D. R., "Expected Critical Path Lengths in PERT Networks," *Operations Research*, Vol. 10, No. 6 (November, 1962).
5. Fulkerson, D. R., "A Network Flow Computation for Project Cost Curves," *Management Science*, Vol. 7, No. 2 (January, 1961).
6. Garman, M. B., "More on Conditional Sampling in the Simulation of Stochastic Networks," *Management Science*, Vol. 19, No. 1 (September, 1972).
7. Hartley, H. O., and Wortham, A. W., "A Statistical Theory for PERT Critical Path Analysis," *Management Science*, Vol. 12, No. 10 (June, 1966).
8. Klingel, A. R., "Bias in PERT Project Completion Time Calculations for a Real Network," *Management Science*, Vol. 13, No. 4 (December, 1966).
9. Levy, F. K., and Wiest, J. D. *A Management Guide to PERT/CPM*, Prentice-Hall, Englewood Cliffs, N.J., 1969.
10. MacCrimmon, K. R., and Ryavec, C. A., "An Analytical Study of the PERT Assumptions," *Operations Research*, Vol. 12, No. 1 (January, 1964).
11. Martin, J. J., "Distribution of the Time Through a Directed Acyclic Network," *Operations Research*, Vol. 13, No. 1 (January, 1965).
12. Parks, W. H., and Ramsig, K. L., "The Use of the Compound Poisson in PERT," *Management Science*, Vol. 15, No. 8 (April, 1969).
13. Ringer, L. J., "A Statistical Theory for PERT in which Completion Times

of Activities are Interdependent," *Management Science*, Vol. 17, No. 11 (July, 1971).

14. Swanson, L. A., and Pazer, H. L., "Implication of the Underlying Assumptions of PERT," *Decision Sciences*, Vol. 2, No. 4 (October, 1971).

15. Van Slyke, R. M. "Monte Carlo Methods and the PERT Problem," *Operations Research*, Vol. 13, No. 1 (January, 1965).

CHAPTER 10

RESOURCE-CONSTRAINED PROJECT SCHEDULING

1. INTRODUCTION

The resource-constrained project scheduling model contains both types of constraints that characterize scheduling decisions. Recall from the discussion in Chapter 1 that scheduling decisions are generally subject to both precedence constraints and resource constraints. The preceding chapters have dealt with a variety of situations in which one or both of these types of constraints are relaxed, or at least simplified. In a sense, the difficulties present in those simpler problems are superimposed in resource-constrained project scheduling.

A general precedence structure accommodates arbitrary precedence relations, such as those found in the network models of the preceding chapter. In that analysis, however, the critical path calculations assumed that resources of the appropriate type and amount were sufficiently available and that resource capacities would never be binding on scheduling decisions. In Chapter 4 some problems involving precedence constraints were treated, but only one resource type was involved. In the treatment of the flow shop and job shop problems, where more general resource models were introduced, the precedence relations were restricted to special structures.

A general resource structure contains multiple units of each of several different resources. Models with resource parallelism were introduced in Chapter 5, but only for one resource type; and the multiple-resource models of the flow shop and the job shop contained only one unit of each resource. The extension to parallel resource structure involves combinatorial problems in a whole new dimension.

The relation of this topic to the material in earlier chapters can therefore be interpreted two ways. First, the resource-constrained project scheduling problem can be formulated by adding explicit resource requirements and resource capacities to the basic network model of CPM and PERT. Alternatively, the problem can also be formulated by allowing general precedence structures in the job shop problem and replacing machines by machine groups, for parallelism. This latter viewpoint will be taken at the outset, to stress that the philosophy of solving job shop problems carries over to the more general context. But the main approach of this chapter is to synthesize much of the previous material in order to deal with the resource-constrained project scheduling problem.

2. EXTENDING THE JOB SHOP MODEL

In the terminology of network models, we can state the problem as scheduling a project consisting of several activities in the presence of limited resources. The purpose of this section is to show how the job shop approach of Chapter 7 can be adapted to the resource-constrained project scheduling problem, where general precedence structures and general resource structures apply.

To begin with, suppose that each activity requires one unit of a unique resource while it is being processed. Let

P_j = the set of all direct predecessors of activity j
Q_j = the set of all direct successors of activity j
p_j = the number of elements in P_j
r_j = the resource type required by activity j

Also, let n now denote the total number of activities to be scheduled and let m denote the number of resource types.

The concepts of schedule classification carry over directly from the job shop discussion. Therefore, where regular measures of performance are concerned, it is sufficient to examine active schedules in the search for an optimum. In this context, an active partial schedule is a feasible schedule for a subset of the activities with the property that no scheduled activity can be started earlier without delaying the start of some other activity in the partial schedule. As in Chapter 7, PS_t refers to a partial schedule containing t activities. Now for a given partial schedule let u_j denote the number of activities in P_j that are contained in the partial schedule. Then the set S_t of schedulable activities corresponding to a given PS_t is defined by

$$S_t = \{j \mid u_j = p_j \text{ for } j \notin PS_t\}$$

Given an active partial schedule PS_t and an activity j in the corresponding set S_t, the conditional early start and early finish times associated with activity j are defined, respectively, by

$$\sigma_j = \max \{\max [C_i \mid i \in P_j], \max [C_i \mid i \in PS_t \text{ and } r_i = r_j]\}$$
$$\phi_j = \sigma_j + t_j$$

Notice that σ_j and ϕ_j are defined only with respect to a given partial schedule. Thus, if activity j appears in several of the schedulable sets S_t that occur successively in the construction of a complete schedule, then the associated σ_j might change dynamically at various stages. By contrast, the analogous CPM times, ES_j and EF_j, are static quantities and are not conditioned upon a given partial schedule.

When arbitrary precedence structures are introduced into the job shop model, the procedure for generating all active schedules is a straightforward extension of Algorithm 7.1 and is given below.

ALGORITHM 10.1
(Active Schedule Generation)

Step 1. Let $t = 0$ and begin with PS_t as the null partial schedule. Initially S_t contains all activities for which $p_j = 0$.

Step 2.   Given PS_t, determine $\phi^* = \min_{j \in S_t} \{\phi_j\}$ and the resource r^* for which ϕ^* could be realized.

Step 3.   For each activity $j \in S_t$ that requires resource r^* and for which $\sigma_j < \phi^*$, create a new partial schedule in which activity j is added to PS_t and started at time σ_j.

Step 4.   For each new PS_{t+1} formed in Step 3, update the data set as follows:
(a) Remove activity j from S_t.
(b) For each activity $i \in Q_j$ increment u_i by one.
(c) Form S_{t+1} by adding to S_t those activities $i \in Q_j$ for which $u_i = p_i$.
(d) Increment t by one.

Step 5.   Return to Step 2 for each PS_{t+1} created in Step 3, and continue in this fashion until all active schedules have been generated.

The next step in extending the job shop model is to incorporate resource parallelism. Such an approach is illustrated in the model used by Johnson (*6*), which contains only one resource type but allows activities to require more than one unit of the resource. (This kind of single-resource model is particularly relevant to certain construction and maintenance problems in which manpower is the critical resource.) The crucial difference in Johnson's method occurs in Step 3, where it is necessary to examine not just single activities, but groups of activities as well. Basically, a new partial schedule can be generated at Step 3 for any subset of schedulable activities that can be accommodated by available resources. The task is then to eliminate the subsets that do not result in active partial schedules and keep all of the rest for Step 4. The partial schedules are denoted PS_{t+k} at Step 4 since several activities might have been added to PS_t. Note that although complete schedules may be generated in far fewer than n stages, the implementation of Step 3 involves a combinatorial generation scheme in itself. Nevertheless, Johnson found that the computational requirements of his algorithm seemed reasonable for $n \le 50$, and the approach could logically be extended to problems containing several resource types. Further generalizations of Algorithm 10.1 could also be pursued for problems in which there is resource substitutability or in which activities require several different resources simultaneously. Finally, once the generation scheme is designed, it is possible to use it as the basis for a branch and bound method for determining an optimum.

Lower bounds in the resource-constrained project scheduling problem can be developed using the concepts introduced in Chapter 7 in connection with the job shop problem. For example, an activity-based bound can be obtained by ignoring all resource constraints, while a resource-based bound can be obtained by ignoring all precedence constraints. To illustrate these ideas, consider a problem containing general precedence structure and unit resource availabilities (so that Algorithm 10.1 applies) and assume that makespan is the criterion. For each activity j let π_j denote the length of the longest path in the project network from the completion of activity j to the end of the project. (In other words, π_j is the critical path length for the subproject containing all of the successors of activity j.) Then, by ignoring the resource constraints, the following lower bound on the makespan can be calculated for a given partial schedule:

$$b_1 = \max_{j \in S_t} \{\sigma_j + t_j + \pi_j\}$$

In this type of calculation σ_j depends on the commitments in the partial schedule, but π_j need be calculated only once at the outset for each activity. To illustrate the derivation of resource-based bound, let U_k denote the set of unscheduled jobs that require resource k. Then, by ignoring the precedence constraints, the following lower bound on the makespan can be calculated:

$$b_2 = \max_k \left[\max \{C_j \,|\, j \in PS_t \quad \text{and} \quad r_j = k\} + \sum_{i \in U_k} t_i \right]$$

It should be easy to see that in the job shop problem these calculations are reduced to the bounds derived in Section 4 of Chapter 7.

These two simple bounds can be strengthened somewhat by accommodating some resource constraints in the activity-based bound and some precedence information in the resource-based bound, as suggested by Schrage (9). A combination activity-based bound explicitly considers the resource availabilities, one at a time. Temporarily, number the activities in set U_k in nondecreasing order of their critical path lengths π_j. (In this way, activities near the end of the project will appear relatively early in the numbered list.) Then, taking the activities in numbered order, calculate

$$\lambda_j = \max \{\lambda_{j-1}, \pi_j\} + t_j$$

where $\lambda_0 = 0$. Let the last of these λ_j be denoted W_k. Then

$$b_3 = \max_k [W_k + \max \{C_j \,|\, j \in PS_t \quad \text{and} \quad r_j = k\}]$$

A combination resource-based bound explicitly considers precedence relations among all activities that require a given resource. This time, number the activities in U_k in nondecreasing order of their early start times σ_j. (In this way, activities near the beginning of the project will appear relatively early in the numbered list.) Then, taking the activities in this numbered order, calculate

$$\mu_j = \max \{\mu_{j-1}, \sigma_j\} + t_j$$

where $\mu_0 = 0$. Let the last of these μ_j be denoted V_k. Then

$$b_4 = \max_k \{V_k\}$$

Obviously the bounds b_3 and b_4 are at least as tight as b_1 and b_2, and generally tighter, although they require some additional calculations. A composite bound is therefore $B = \max \{b_3, b_4\}$.

As an example of these calculations, consider the project described in Table 10.1, containing 10 activities and two resources. At an intermediate

Table 10.1

Activity j	t_j	r_j	P_j	π_j
A	4	1	—	2
B	3	2	—	5
C	2	1	—	5
D	4	2	—	8
E	4	2	D	4
F	2	1	B	3
G	2	2	C	3
H	1	1	E	3
I	2	2	A	0
J	3	1	F, G, H	0

stage in the generation of active schedules, the partial schedule shown in Figure 10.1 might be generated. In this PS_2, activity A occupies resource 1 beginning at time 0 and activity D occupies resource 2 beginning at time 0. With these two activities constituting PS_2, the set of schedulable activities is $S_2 = \{B, C, E, I\}$. First, with respect to PS_2 we have

$$\sigma_B = \sigma_C = \sigma_E = \sigma_I = 4$$

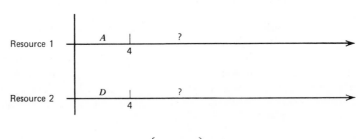

$$S_t = \{B, C, E, I\}$$
$$U_1 = \{C, F, H, J\}$$
$$U_2 = \{B, E, G, I\}$$

Figure 10.1
A partial schedule for the project in Table 10.1.

and

$$b_1 = \max \{4 + 3 + 5, 4 + 2 + 5, 4 + 4 + 4, 4 + 2 + 0\} = 12$$

Next we have

$$\max \{C_j \mid j \in PS_2 \quad \text{and} \quad r_j = 1\} = 4 = \max \{C_j \mid j \in PS_2 \quad \text{and} \quad r_j = 2\}$$

and

$$b_2 = \max \{4 + 8, 4 + 11\} = 15$$

In calculating b_3, the activities requiring resource 1 are considered in the order J–H–F–C and $W_1 = 8$. The activities requiring resource 2 are considered in the order I–G–E–B and $W_2 = 12$. Thus

$$b_3 = \max \{4 + 8, 4 + 12\} = 16$$

Finally $V_1 = 13$ and $V_2 = 15$ so that $b_4 = 15$. Hence b_3 is the tightest bound for this PS_2, indicating that the optimal makespan must be at least 16.

Although there has been little research involving optimizing techniques for resource-constrained project scheduling problems with criteria other than makespan, the basic approach is similar. First of all, a tree-structured schedule generation scheme, such as Algorithm 10.1, is the basis for constructing schedules. An activity-based bound is obtained by ignoring resource constraints and dealing with the resulting CPM network. A resource-based bound is obtained by ignoring precedence constraints and dealing with the single-machine sequencing problem that results. The success of such an approach depends on the utility of the solutions to these subproblems and on the difficulty of obtaining those solutions.

10.2 EXERCISES

2.1 Describe how Algorithm 10.1 can be modified to generate all active schedules in the following cases:
   (a) Each activity requires two or more different resources simultaneously.
   (b) Each activity requires one of several alternative resources (i.e., substitutable resource types).

2.2 Show how the bound b_2' in Section 4 of Chapter 7 can be generalized to the resource-constrained scheduling problem.

2.3 Show how the bounds b_1 and b_2 are affected when resources are available in multiple amounts.

3. EXTENDING THE PROJECT MODEL

To illustrate how the temporal analysis of CPM can be useful in resource-constrained problems, consider the project model in which all activities require just one resource type. Let

a_j = resource units required to perform activity j

A = total resource units available

An *early start schedule* is constructed by starting each activity in the project at its own early start time, as calculated by CPM. If the resources required in this schedule never exceed availabilities, then this schedule achieves the minimum possible duration. Similarly, a *late start schedule* is constructed by starting each activity at its late start time and, if this schedule is resource-feasible, then it achieves the minimum possible duration. If neither schedule is feasible, it is still possible to extract some information for the calculation of a lower bound on project duration.

Let G_t denote the set of activities in process at time t in some given schedule with duration D. In addition let

$$r_E(t) = \sum_{j \in G_t} a_j \qquad \text{for the early start schedule}$$

$$r_L(t) = \sum_{j \in G_t} a_j \qquad \text{for the late start schedule}$$

$$r_S(t) = \sum_{j \in G_t} a_j \qquad \text{for some arbitrary schedule } S$$

In other words, $r_E(t)$ represents the resource consumption at time t under the early start schedule, and so on. If we examine cumulative resource consumptions, we will find that

$$\sum_{u=1}^{t} r_E(u) \geq \sum_{u=1}^{t} r_S(u) \geq \sum_{u=1}^{t} r_L(u) \qquad \text{for all } t \tag{1}$$

where we are treating time as discrete only for convenience. The following properties address the question of whether a feasible project schedule can be found to achieve the given duration D.

Theorem 10.1

If $\sum_{u=1}^{t} r_L(u) > tA$ for any t, $1 \leq t \leq D$, then no feasible schedule of length D exists.

Theorem 10.2

If $\sum_{u=D-t}^{D} r_E(u) > tA$ for any t, $1 \leq t \leq D$, then no feasible schedule of length D exists.

Proof

Under the hypothesis of Theorem 10.1, it follows from (1) that $\sum_{u=1}^{t} r_S(u) >$ tA. In other words there are insufficient resources available to carry out the activities in an arbitrary schedule of length D. An analogous argument will establish Theorem 10.2.

As an example, consider the single-resource project described in Table 10.2.

Table 10.2

Activity j	Duration t_j	Predecessors P_j	Resources a_j	Early Start Time ES_j	Total Float TF_j
12	4	—	1	0	6
13	3	—	4	0	4
14	2	—	3	0	5
15	4	—	4	0	0
56	4	4	3	4	0
37	2	2	2	3	4
47	2	3	6	2	5
67	1	5	4	8	0
28	2	1	5	4	6
78	3	6, 7, 8	3	9	0

Suppose that $A = 7$, and consider the question of whether it is possible to complete the project by time 12 (the length of the critical path). First construct the resource profile of the late start schedule, shown in Table 10.3.

Table 10.3

Time, t	1	2	3	4	5	6	7	8	9	10	11	12
Resources, $r_L(t)$	4	4	4	4	7	10	11	12	13	4	8	8
Cumulative resources	4	8	12	16	23	33	44	56	69	73	81	89

Verify that the hypothesis of Theorem 10.1 holds for $t = 9$, so that the critical path length cannot possibly be achieved. (A similar conclusion can be reached by applying Theorem 10.2 to the early start schedule.) Suppose instead that $A = 8$. Then neither theorem will apply; yet it is not possible to conclude that a schedule of length 12 can be found when eight resource units are available.

It is also possible to develop a resource-based bound using the information in the early and late start schedules. Let the total resource requirement in the project be

$$R = \sum_{u=1}^{D} r_E(u)$$

Then clearly a feasible schedule of length D cannot exist unless

$$R \leq DA \tag{2}$$

In effect, (2) yields a lower bound on project duration, but this can be strengthened somewhat by examining the first part of the early start schedule and the last part of the late start schedule, as suggested in (11). Let α represent the first time t at which $r_E(t) > A$. Then the resources that are not used in the beginning of the early start schedule sum to

$$\sum_{u=1}^{\alpha-1} [A - r_E(u)]$$

These resources cannot be utilized by any feasible schedule. Analogously, let β represent the latest time t at which $r_L(t) > A$. Then, an expression for additional resources that cannot be utilized by any feasible schedule of duration D is

$$\sum_{u=\beta+1}^{D} [A - r_L(u)]$$

Therefore the inequality 2 can be amended to reflect usable resource capacity. Hence a feasible schedule of length D cannot exist unless

$$R \leq DA - \sum_{u=1}^{\alpha-1} [A - r_E(u)] - \sum_{u=\beta+1}^{D} [A - r_L(u)] \tag{3}$$

This bound is sometimes called the *skyline bound* because it makes use of the profile of resource requirements in the schedule.

Theorems 10.1 and 10.2, and the bound in (3) are all based on conditions that can be examined before a schedule generation procedure begins. In order to adapt the bounds for use at intermediate stages of a branch and bound scheme, the inequalities must be generalized to accommodate fluctuating resource availabilities (see Exercise 3.3). In addition, the same type of analysis can be extended to problems in which there are several resource types and problems in which activities require different resources simultaneously.

Researchers have explored several variations on the themes discussed in this section and the last. Unfortunately, all implicit enumeration approaches to the determination of an optimal schedule appear to be susceptible to the combinatorial nature of these problems when they are tested on the large versions typically found in practice. In two recent surveys (1, 4) of the optimum-seeking methods currently available, there is no evidence that such techniques can reliably handle multiple-resource versions of a problem that contains more than 50 activities.

10.3 EXERCISES

3.1 Use Theorems 10.1 and 10.2 to answer the following questions about the project in Table 10.2:
    (a) When $A = 7$, what is a lower bound on the project duration?
    (b) When $A = 6$, what is a lower bound on the project duration?

3.2 Apply Theorems 10.1 and 10.2 to compute a bound on the duration of the project in Table 10.1. (Notice that the theorems can be generalized to multiple-resource problems.)

3.3 Show how to generalize Theorems 10.1 and 10.2, and the inequality of (3), to situations in which resource availabilities vary with time.

4. AN INTEGER PROGRAMMING APPROACH

A fairly general problem formulation has been proposed by Pritsker, Watters, and Wolfe (8), whose integer programming approach is reasonably efficient in its use of decision variables. For purposes of exposition, consider the extended version of the model in which an activity may simultaneously require several units of more than one resource. Let

a_{jk} = amount of resources of type k required by activity j
A_k = total resource units of type k available

A discrete-time formulation is necessary, and the primary decision variable is

$x_{jt} = 1$ if activity j completes in time period t
    $= 0$ otherwise

At the outset a scheduling horizon H is chosen so that x_{jt} may be defined for $1 \leq j \leq n$ and $1 \leq t \leq H$. For activity j the precedence constraints are written

$$\sum_{t=1}^{H} tx_{it} + t_j \leq \sum_{t=1}^{H} tx_{jt} \qquad \text{for all } i \in P_j \tag{4}$$

where $x_{it} = 0$ if activity j has no predecessors. In order to reduce the number of variables in the problem, note that x_{it} need not be defined for $t < EF_i$, where the early finish time of activity i is determined by the usual temporal analysis that ignores resource constraints. Analogously, if there is an absolute project deadline then x_{it} need not be defined for $t > LF_i$.

To develop inequalities for resource constraints, notice that activity j is in process at time t if and only if

$$\sum_{u=t}^{t+t_j-1} x_{ju} = 1 \tag{5}$$

Therefore the summation in (5) is a means of indicating whether activity j is consuming resources in period t. Hence the resource constraints become

$$\sum_{j=1}^{n} a_{jk} \sum_{u=t}^{t+t_j-1} x_{ju} \leq A_k \qquad 1 \leq k \leq m \qquad 1 \leq t \leq H \tag{6}$$

Finally, the requirement that all activities be processed is simply

$$\sum_{t=1}^{H} x_{jt} = 1 \qquad 1 \leq j \leq n \tag{7}$$

To minimize project duration the problem is

$$\text{Minimize} \quad \sum_{t=1}^{H} t x_{nt}$$

Subject to (4), (6), and (7), with x_{jt} equal to 0 or 1

where activity n is the terminal activity. The formulation can easily be adapted to other criteria when performance measures are functions of activity completion times. In general, let the value f_{jt} denote the component of the objective function associated with the completion of activity j in time period t. Then the objective function can always be written in the form $\sum\sum f_{jt}x_{jt}$. In their original presentation, Pritsker, Watters, and Wolfe also discuss the extension of the integer programming formulation to projects with substitutable resources, concurrency requirements, and preemptable activities.

As with other mathematical programming approaches, the crucial question is whether the formulation is practical. Although the size of the problem formulated this way is generally difficult to characterize, it may have as many as $n + mH + N$ constraints (where N is the number of direct precedence relations) and nH integer variables. The role of the scheduling horizon makes this formulation quite different from the formulations of Chapters 6 and 7, and there has been little computational experience with this type of problem. An example presented in the original paper with $m = 3$, $n = 8$, and $H = 10$ turned out to be 37 by 33 and required only a few seconds to solve. However, since the performance of integer programming codes is often unpredictable on moderate-sized problems, it is difficult to evaluate the practical usefulness of this approach.

4. EXERCISES

4.1 Use the integer programming model of this section to formulate the job shop scheduling problem in Exercise 6.2 of Chapter 7.

4.2 In the above problem, what objective function would be employed if the objective were to minimize mean job flowtime?

4.3 Use the integer programming model to formulate the problem of minimizing makespan for the project in Table 10.1.

5. HEURISTIC METHODS

In resource-constrained scheduling for large projects or for several projects the size of the problem may render optimal methods computationally impracticable. In such cases, the problem is most amenable to heuristic problem solving, using fairly simple scheduling rules capable of producing reasonably good suboptimal schedules.

Kelley (7) outlined two single-pass strategies that require modest computational effort and can provide useful results. (The strategies are called "single-pass" strategies because once they schedule a particular activity, it is never rescheduled.) The common convention in AOA networks is to number the nodes in the network so that for each arrow the head node has a larger number than the tail node. This node-numbering scheme is generally not unique for a given project, but has the convenient property that if the activities are sorted by head-node number, then no activity will appear in the sorted list before any of its predecessors. A feasible schedule can be constructed by considering the activities in order of their appearance on such a list and scheduling them one at a time as early as precedence constraints and resource availabilities permit. Kelley called such a strategy a *serial* method.

For a given set of node numbers, the sorting procedure discussed above is not uniquely defined, since several activities can share the same head-node. One way to resolve the sorting question is to order activities according to tail-node number when they share the same head-node. However, other mechanisms for determining an order are intuitively appealing, since a scheduling criterion is involved. For example, critical activities (i.e., activities that lie on the critical path as defined in CPM) should be given preference over noncritical activities if the scheduling objective involves meeting project deadlines. Depending on the nature of the objective function, preferences could be determined on the basis of such factors as resource requirements, activity duration, total float, weighting factor, or some combination. Since the construction of a schedule by serial methods is computationally rapid, it would be possible to try several combinations of sorting factors and to select the best schedule among those that are constructed. Moreover, as Kelley also observed, since the node-numbering itself is usually not unique, this process could be repeated for several numberings, after which the best schedule could again be selected among those generated.

Kelley used the term *parallel* method to refer to a strategy by which several activities are scheduled at once. At any point in time during the construction of a schedule, there exists a set of schedulable activities whose predecessors are complete. From this schedulable set, a preferred subset can be scheduled up to the resource capacities and into the future. At some future point in time, a new set of schedulable activities is encountered and the preferred subset can be reconstructed. By this method, a schedule can be created by proceeding chronologically forward.

The effectiveness of the parallel method depends on the mechanism for constructing the preferred subset of schedulable activities. Once again, such factors as total float, resource requirement, activity duration, or weighting factor can be employed in a decision rule that generates the subset and ultimately determines the schedule. And, again, the best schedule can be selected from among several developed from a variety of scheduling rules.

In general terms, the serial and parallel strategies represent the basic heuristic approaches to the solution of large-scale problems.

Again, consider the 10-job problem of Table 10.2. (The network representation of this project is displayed in Figure 10.2.) If the single resource were available in unlimited amounts, it would be possible to start each job at its associated early start time and the entire project could then be completed in 12 time units, as depicted in Figure 10.3. As shown in the accompanying resource profile, as many as 15 units of the resource would be required during at least one time period in order to meet this schedule. Now suppose that eight resource units are available in each time period, and consider the problem of minimizing project duration.

To illustrate a serial method for solving this problem, suppose the head-node, tail-node ordering is used to sort the activities. (This is the order in

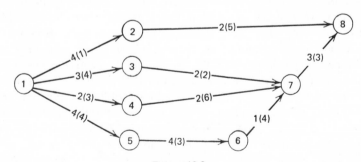

Figure 10.2
Network representation of the project in Table 10.2.

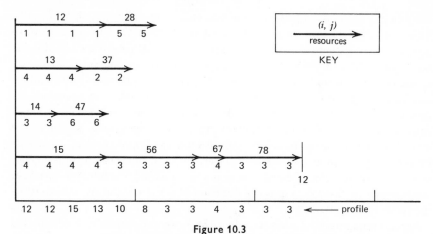

Figure 10.3
An early start schedule for the example project.

which the activities are listed in Table 10.2.) Activities 12, 13, and 14 are taken from the list and scheduled to start as early as possible, which is at time 0 in each case. This occupies seven resource units through the first two time periods and five resource units in the third. Activity 15, which is next on the list and which requires four resource units, cannot be started until the completion of activity 13. With activity 15 scheduled the method proceeds to the next one on the list (activity 56) and schedules it as early as possible. The serial method continues in this fashion and eventually constructs a complete schedule with a duration of 17, as shown in Figure 10.4.

To illustrate the parallel method, suppose that at every time period the schedulable activities are sorted in nondecreasing order of the total float in

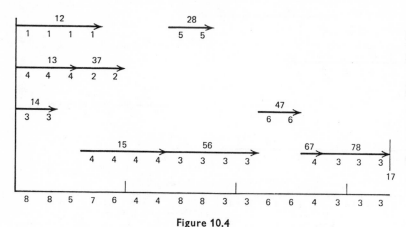

Figure 10.4
A schedule constructed with the use of a serial method.

the original table. At time 0 the schedulable set, in order, is {15, 13, 14, 12}. Thus activities 15 and 13 are scheduled to start at time 0, occupying all eight resource units for the first three time periods. At time 3 the schedulable set becomes {37, 14, 12}. After activities 15 and 37 are scheduled for period 4, activity 14 cannot be started in time period 4, but activity 12 can be started (because of its smaller resource requirement). At time 4, activity 56 becomes schedulable, and the schedulable set is {56, 37, 14}. (A potential issue at this point is whether the activities are preemptable, for there are now sufficient resources to accommodate activities 56, 37, and 14 if activity 12 can be preempted and resumed later. For the purposes of illustration, however, suppose that preemption is not permitted.) Pursuing the parallel method in this fashion, a project duration of 15 is ultimately achieved, as shown in Figure 10.5.

Several computerized heuristic algorithms are commercially available for scheduling large projects, and in most cases, the actual solution procedure is proprietary information. Perhaps the most widely exposed heuristic program is SPAR-1, developed by Wiest (*10*). SPAR-1 is based on a parallel strategy, but is not limited to a one-pass procedure. At the heart of the parallel strategy is a priority scheme based on total float. At any stage in the construction of a schedule, the activities whose predecessors have been completed are considered for scheduling in order of their float. As the algorithm moves forward in time, the total float of each schedulable activity is revised, so that a dynamic priority scheme results.

To suggest how such a heuristic might work, again consider the example in Table 10.2. At time 0, the priority-ordered set of schedulable activities, along with their total floats is {15(0), 13(4), 14(5), 12(6)}. Just as in the

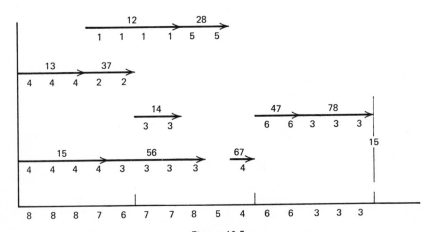

Figure 10.5
A schedule constructed with the use of a parallel method.

parallel algorithm described earlier, activities 15 and 13 are scheduled to start at time 0. After one period of time, the schedulable set becomes {15(0), 13(4), 14(4), 12(5)}, where the total float of activities not scheduled is revised. After two time periods, the set becomes {15(0), 13(4), 14(3), 12(4)}. At this stage a SPAR-type algorithm would, in principle, have the flexibility to preempt activity 13 in favor of activity 14, because the latter has become more critical. However, suppose as before that no preemption is allowed. The next opportunity to schedule an activity arises at time 3, when the schedulable set is {14(2), 12(3), 37(4)}. Activities 15, 14, and 12 are scheduled, consuming all available resources. Then at time 4 the set becomes {56(0), 37(3)}. With no preemption allowed, activities 14, 12, and 56 are scheduled, and the total float associated with job 37 continues to decrease. As should be clear, this mechanism of revising total floats creates a structure in which some activities may appear for the first time in the schedulable set with a priority different than their original total float. Figure 10.6 represents a complete schedule constructed this way.

SPAR-1 has several other features. It accommodates flexible resource requirements, so that an activity duration might be a function of the amount of resources allocated to it. Therefore, in attempting to schedule a critical activity, it may be possible to borrow resources from a previously scheduled activity. The program explores the possibility of borrowing this way and then considers the possibility of rescheduling noncritical activities already assigned in order to locate sufficient resources to perform the critical activity. Subsequently, if excess resources remain in the schedule, the procedure applies them to scheduled activities in order to reduce their durations.

In implementing the parallel strategy, SPAR-1 also uses a randomized selection procedure in the spirit of biased random sampling. Thus a sampling

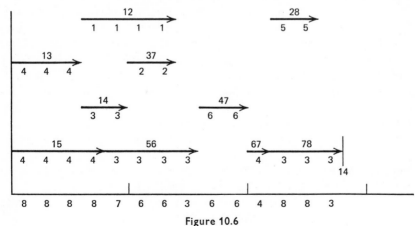

Figure 10.6
A schedule constructed with the use of a dynamic priority mechanism.

device is used for selecting activities from the preferred set to be scheduled. The whole scheduling program can be repeated several times with this random device, generating a sample of full schedules from which the best can be chosen.

One of the most important characteristics of SPAR-1 is its flexibility. The basic approach can be adapted to situations characterized, for example, by multiple-resource requirements, time/cost tradeoffs, preemptive scheduling, comprehensive objective functions, and specialized constraints. As Wiest observed, one of the more essential traits of a heuristic procedure is its practical usefulness, and SPAR-1 was certainly developed with usefulness in mind.

Scheduling rules for the simultaneous processing of several independent projects have generally been proposed as generalizations of the rules that performed well in extensive job shop studies (Chapter 8). Following the emphasis of the job shop scheduling work, most of the emphasis in project scheduling experiments has been on dispatching rules—that is, procedures in which the choice of the activity (or activities) to be processed next by an available resource is made from among the jobs waiting for that resource at the time it becomes available.

Fendley (5) studied the scheduling of multiple PERT projects with probabilistic activity times. He tested several basic dispatching strategies under a variety of performance measures. His simulation experiments indicated that for makespan and tardiness performance measures, the dynamic minimum total float priority assignment was particularly effective. Fendley also observed that this priority yielded high utilization of resources and also led to relatively uniform behavior among the different projects.

Calica (2) proposed, but did not test, a dispatching priority mechanism based on parametric combinations of four kinds of information in multi-project problems. To compute the priority of a given task, he combined activity duration, total float, project slack, and "node density" (a measure of the interdependence associated with an individual activity). Activities with smaller processing times tend to get preference in priority assignment, to take advantage of some of the desirable properties of shortest-first sequencing. Those activities with small total float or belonging to projects with little slack get preference in an attempt to avoid undue tardiness. These two characteristics change over time and must be recomputed dynamically in determining priorities. Activities with high node densities tend to be predecessors of substantial parallel processing and, therefore, merit some importance in priority decisions. Calica's priority number was determined by weighting these four measures of importance to provide a priority assignment for dispatching purposes. In analogy to the approaches of Kelley and Wiest, several schedules could be generated by varying the weighting parameters in computing priorities and eventually choosing the best schedule from among those generated.

Any number of heuristics can be devised along these lines; unfortunately there exists little accessible, documented comparative work examining the advantages and limitations of various methods, and some of the results that do exist are conflicting. One exception is a recent experimental investigation reported by Davis and Patterson (3), involving single-project problems containing activities with multiple-resource requirements. The comparative study examined parallel strategies utilizing eight different priority rules aimed at minimizing project length. Davis and Patterson found that, on the whole, three of the priority rules tended to be most effective, but observed that even the effective rules were sometimes unreliable. The three rules were

1. Select activity j according to min LS_j (dynamic).
2. Select activity j according to min LF_j.
3. Select activity j according to min δ_{jk}, where

$$\delta_{jk} = \max_{k \neq j} [\max \{0, EF_j - LS_k\}]$$

Rule 1, the dynamic late start time rule, is analogous to MST, and rule 2, the late finish time rule, is analogous to EDD. Rule 3 minimizes the potential incremental delay in the whole project caused by scheduling activity j before activity k. The authors noted, however, that rules 2 and 3 had not performed as well in separate studies of multiproject scheduling, and they suggested that different priority rules might be effective in scheduling multiple projects.

10.5 EXERCISES

5.1 Describe how to incorporate random sampling techniques and biased random sampling techniques in Kelley's serial strategy.

5.2 Construct a schedule for the example project in Figure 10.2 by employing a parallel strategy and the dynamic late start time rule.

6. SUMMARY

The scheduling of a project in the presence of limited resources is a challenging decision-making problem. It is a full-blown scheduling problem in the sense that solutions must cope with both technological constraints and resource availability constraints. In its general forms, it is a combinatorial problem of such magnitude that virtually all existing methods for finding optimal schedules are impractical for problems of realistic dimensions. As Bennington and McGinnis (1) observe, the problem has also been a frustrating one in the discipline of scheduling. First, the problem is fairly easy to state and to visualize. Second, the problem involves extension of the CPM and PERT models, which themselves have been readily and widely adapted to practical network scheduling problems. Third, the substantial literature on the subject contains any number of sophisticated and clever optimum-seeking schemes, yet the barrier of computational practicality still exists.

For relatively small problems, two viable methodologies for determining optimal schedules are integer programming and branch and bound. An integer programming approach can harness the power of classical constrained optimization techniques and accommodate fairly general criteria. A branch and bound approach, based on the implicit enumeration of all active schedules, is more flexible in its structure and may provide better insights into the nature of the solution. In addition, the tree structure imbedded in the branching procedure may provide a basis for the implementation of heuristic techniques in larger problems. Just as in the job shop problem, the use of priority dispatching procedures and biased sampling schemes appear to be effective heuristic devices. Such suboptimal approaches are quite rapid and are the most flexible in their ability to accommodate realistic criteria and decision constraints. On the other hand, they achieve their speed and flexibility at the expense of not being able to guarantee optimality. As mentioned earlier, many heuristic programs are commercially available, although their details have often been withheld on proprietary grounds. As up-to-date guide to the features of these algorithms, together with a survey of their applications can be found in the review paper by Davis (4).

REFERENCES

1. Bennington, G. E., and McGinnis, L. F. "A Critique of Project Planning with Constrained Resources," in *Symposium on the Theory of Scheduling and its Applications*, S. E. Elmaghraby, Ed., Springer-Verlag, New York, 1973.
2. Calica, A. "Fabrication and Assembly Operations," *IBM Systems Journal*, Vol. 4, No. 3 (1965).
3. Davis, E. W., and Patterson, J. H. "A Comparison of Heuristic and Optimal Solutions in Resource-Constrained Project Scheduling," Working Paper 73-15, Harvard Business School (March, 1973).
4. Davis, E. W. "Project Scheduling under Resource Constraints—Historical Review and Categorization of Procedures," *AIIE Transactions*, Vol. 5, No. 4 (December 1973).
5. Fendley, L. "Toward the Development of a Complete Multi-Project Scheduling System," *Journal of Industrial Engineering*, Vol. 19, No. 10 (October, 1968).
6. Johnson, T. J. R. "An Algorithm for the Resource Constrained Project Scheduling Problem," Ph.D. thesis, MIT, 1967.
7. Kelley, J. E. "The Critical Path Method: Resources Planning and Scheduling," Chapter 21 in J. Muth and G. Thompson, Eds., *Industrial Scheduling*, Prentice-Hall, Englewood Cliffs, N.J., 1963.
8. Pritsker, A. A. B., Watters, L. J., and Wolfe, P. M. "Multiproject Scheduling with Limited Resources: a Zero-One Programming Approach," *Management Science*, Vol. 16, No. 1 (September, 1969).

9. Schrage, L. E. "Obtaining Optimal Solutions to Resource Constrained Network Scheduling Problems," *Proc. Systems Engineering Conference,* Phoenix, February, 1971.

10. West, J. D. "A Heuristic Model for Scheduling Large Projects with Limited Resources," *Management Science,* Vol. 13, No. 6 (February, 1967).

11. Zaloom, V. "On the Resource Constrained Project Scheduling Problem," *AIIE Transactions,* Vol. 3, No. 4 (December, 1971).

APPENDIX A
SIXTEEN TEST PROBLEMS FOR THE $\bar{T}$ PROBLEM

Problem	Job Number j:	1	2	3	4	5	6	7	8	Optimum[a]
1	t_j	121	147	102	79	130	83	96	88	755
	d_j	260	269	400	266	337	336	683	719	
2	t_j	101	87	79	92	103	133	110	67	668
	d_j	471	476	340	387	357	400	329	324	
3	t_j	84	123	102	91	122	114	98	50	378
	d_j	122	587	645	474	341	321	129	598	
4	t_j	99	68	70	108	102	26	120	108	675
	d_j	336	369	324	382	379	363	321	324	
5	t_j	124	110	105	125	135	96	136	86	364
	d_j	415	361	547	443	739	673	598	476	
6	t_j	89	64	105	124	64	100	107	78	478
	d_j	408	359	362	467	394	479	328	442	
7	t_j	97	93	117	89	129	113	67	79	820
	d_j	311	372	127	393	318	458	481	282	
8	t_j	129	84	116	125	97	111	128	108	1292
	d_j	382	343	366	437	338	362	333	420	
9	t_j	42	115	111	96	117	93	95	98	63
	d_j	260	283	616	622	452	624	447	749	
10	t_j	138	132	153	89	141	131	107	103	1300
	d_j	466	459	402	422	478	392	368	385	
11	t_j	111	84	78	121	78	59	82	97	662
	d_j	160	540	518	447	251	124	319	46	
12	t_j	69	71	82	106	84	104	88	69	531
	d_j	352	396	353	393	328	388	387	337	
13	t_j	118	92	133	81	65	116	96	132	271
	d_j	380	303	691	334	180	433	724	514	
14	t_j	115	125	101	109	104	120	98	72	936
	d_j	437	327	467	386	401	450	370	395	
15	t_j	116	94	80	103	57	91	115	104	708
	d_j	548	31	67	510	427	42	322	622	
16	t_j	129	99	114	151	106	105	114	115	1285
	d_j	477	344	321	438	363	369	394	367	

[a] Total tardiness.

APPENDIX B
A DYNAMIC PROGRAMMING CODE FOR SEQUENCING PROBLEMS

In developing a computerized version of the dynamic programming algorithm described in Chapter 3, the central problem is to accommodate the recursion relation

$$G(J) = \min_{j \in J} [g_j(q_J + t_j) + G(J - \{j\})] \qquad \text{(B1)}$$

The values of the function $G(J)$ can be treated as elements of a G-vector once a device is adopted for representing each subset J by a unique integer. An efficient device for this purpose is to associate with J an integer whose binary equivalent identifies the members of J. For example, suppose $n = 4$. Then there are 15 distinct subsets, and the integers between 1 and 15 can be used to identify subset membership as shown in the table below.

Integer	Binary Equivalent	Subset Members	Integer	Binary Equivalent	Subset Members
1	0001	1	6	0110	3, 2
2	0010	2	7	0111	3, 2, 1
3	0011	2, 1	8	1000	4
4	0100	3	9	1001	4, 1
5	0101	3, 1	10	1010	4, 2

Integer	Binary Equivalent	Subset Membership
11	1011	4, 2, 1
12	1100	4, 3
13	1101	4, 3, 1
14	1110	4, 3, 2
15	1111	4, 3, 2, 1

Thus, to find the particular subset associated with a given integer, the first step is to express the integer as a binary number. It is then possible to read off the location of 1's in this expression, and these positions identify the members of the subset. In the computer code given below, this conversion is carried out by the subroutine MEMBS.

Conversely, to find the integer corresponding to a given subset, simply let $\delta_j = 1$ if job j is in the subset and let $\delta_j = 0$ otherwise. Then the desired integer is

$$\sum_{j=1}^{n} \delta_j (2^{j-1})$$

The elementary vectors in this construction are the powers of 2, and in the computer code the vector $E(I)$ represents the power 2^{i-1}. The subset containing all the jobs is represented by the integer $2^n - 1$, and this number is denoted MAX in the code.

The computer code calculates $G(J)$ for $J = 1, 2, \ldots, $ MAX; but in order to reconstruct the optimal sequence, the program must save the minimizing value of j in the expression B1 each time a $G(J)$ is calculated. This minimizing value represents the lead job for a given subset and is coded as LEAD(J), for $J = 1, 2, \ldots, $ MAX.

The subroutine MEMBS has three arguments: J, M, and JSIZE. The input to the subroutine is the integer J. The subroutine determines the members of the subset corresponding to J, and stores these elements in the vector M. The subroutine also determines the size of the subset and returns this value in the variable JSIZE.

A glossary for the code, and the Fortran code itself are shown below. The code will handle job sets of size $n \leq 12$. (Notice that the vectors are dimensioned either at 12 or at $2^{12} - 1$, as appropriate.) Also, generic READ and PRINT statements are listed.

GLOSSARY

Vectors

T, **D**, and **W** denote processing time, due date, and weight, as usual.

SLACK denotes **T** − **D** for each job, for convenience in the calculations.

E(I) holds the constant 2^{i-1}.

M is the vector containing the members of the current subset. Also, in the last phase of the algorithm, it contains the optimal sequence.

LEAD and **G** are described in the text above.

Variables

N denotes the number of jobs, n.

MAX becomes the constant $2^n - 1$.

TSUM becomes the sum of the processing times.

J denotes the integer representing the subset currently being treated.

JSIZE denotes the number of elements in subset J.

Q becomes the sum of the processing times in J.

TARD is the weighted tardiness, first for the lead job, and subsequently for all jobs, in J.

J1 is the subset J with its lead element removed.

FORTRAN CODE

```
      IMPLICIT INTEGER (A – W)
      DIMENSION T(12), D(12), W(12), SLACK(12), E(12), M(12)
      DIMENSION LEAD (4095), G(4095)
      READ N
      READ (T(I), D(I), W(I), I = 1, N)
      MAX = 1
      E(1) = 1
      DO 10 I = 2, N
      E(I) = 2* E(I – 1)
   10 MAX = MAX + E(I)
      TSUM = 0
      DO 20 JB = 1, N
      SLACK(JB) = T(JB) – D(JB)
   20 TSUM = TSUM + T(JB)
      J = 1
      IF(TSUM – D(1)) 40, 40, 30
   30 G(1) = W(1) * (TSUM – D(1))
      GO TO 100
   40 G(1) = 0
  100 J = J + 1
      CALL MEMBS (J, M, JSIZE)
      Q = TSUM
      DO 120 I = 1, JSIZE
  120 Q = Q – T(M(I))
      G(J) = 1000000
      DO 150 I = 1, JSIZE
      TARD = W(M(I)) * (Q + SLACK(M(I)))
```

```
      IF(TARD .LT. 0) TARD = 0
      J1 = J − E(M(I))
      IF(J1 .EQ. 0) GO TO 130
      TARD = TARD + G(J1)
130   IF(TARD .GT. G(J)) GO TO 150
      LEAD(J) = M(I)
      G(J) = TARD
150   CONTINUE
      IF(J − MAX) 100, 200, 200
200   M(1) = LEAD(J)
      DO 220 I = 2, N
      J = J − E(M(I − 1))
220   M(I) = LEAD(J)
      PRINT TARD, (M(I), I = 1, N)
      STOP
      END
      SUBROUTINE MEMBS(J, M, JSIZE)
      DIMENSION M(12)
      I = J
      JSIZE = 0
      K = 1
15    IA = I/2
      IREM = I − 2 ∗ IA
      I = IA
      IF(IREM .EQ. 0) GO TO 20
      JSIZE = JSIZE + 1
      M(JSIZE) = K
20    IF(I .EQ. 0) GO TO 30
      K = K + 1
      GO TO 15
30    RETURN
      END
```

A DESIGN STRATEGY FOR A
BRANCH AND BOUND CODE

Many reports and technical papers deal with the results of implementing a branch and bound code, but few authors take the time to discuss how they designed the code. There are some good reasons why this topic is somewhat neglected: (1) computer programming is an individualistic activity and one programmer is seldom comfortable with another's organization and logic; (2) the most convenient way to implement a given strategy may depend on the programming language being used; (3) a given strategy may be obviated by the peculiarities of the computer on which the implementation is carried out; and, (4) there may be unique ways of exploiting special problem structure that do not carry over to other branch and bound approaches. In addition, it has been said that no matter how many branch and bound algorithms a programmer has developed, he can always learn new insights by tackling one more.

These comments notwithstanding, the purpose of this appendix is to describe a branch and bound scheme suitable for permutation problems, such as those in Chapters 3, 4, and 6. The scheme is based on a backtracking strategy rather than the jumptracking strategy introduced in Section 5 of Chapter 3. This choice should make things a little bit easier for the novice because the storage demands of a backtracking code are not severe. Therefore the programmer need not be overly concerned about organizing his data in sophisticated ways in situations where core memory is a scarce resource. Backtracking also avoids the need to deal with a large ranked list (of active nodes), which can often be a source of computing inefficiencies.

Backtracking is described in Chapter 3 as the strategy of always branching from the node corresponding to the most nearly solved subproblem. (This is

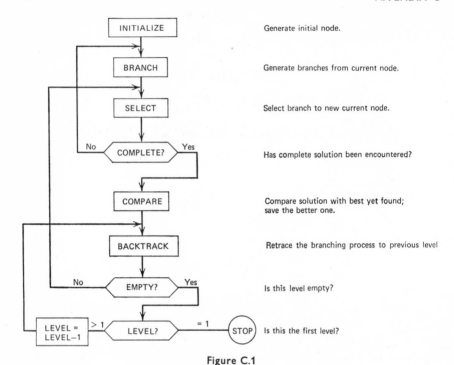

Figure C.1

called the *current node* each time.) Stated more explicitly, this means that backtracking attempts to find a complete solution in the most direct way, and then to retrace its steps only so far as necessary to find the next closest solution in the tree. The elementary logic of this approach is represented by the flow chart in Figure C.1, and the following description of its significant steps.

INITIALIZE: At the outset, all counters, pointers, and constants must be initialized; and it is at least necessary to generate the initial node (corresponding to a null partial sequence) and place it on the list of active partial schedules. It is also a good idea at this point to construct a complete solution, by means of a quick heuristic procedure, since an on-hand solution can be of value early in the algorithm.

BRANCH: Remove the current node from the tree and replace it with the nodes formed by assigning the next open position in sequence. It is at this step that dominance properties should be checked, so that dominated nodes are discarded instead of being placed on the tree. Also at this step, lower bounds are calculated in an attempt to fathom nodes rather than to place them on the tree.

SELECT: Among the nodes most recently added to the tree, select the one with minimum lower bound to be the new current node. Update the cumulative information that must be stored to maintain a sufficient description of the current node.

COMPLETE: Determine whether the current node is a complete solution. If not, return to BRANCH; otherwise, proceed.

COMPARE: Calculate the objective function value associated with the newly encountered trial solution and compare it to the on-hand best solution yet found. Keep track of the better of these two.

BACKTRACK: Retrace the branching process by returning to the node from which the current node was created. Update the information stored regarding this node by "peeling off" the job in the last assigned position in sequence. This node then becomes the current node.

EMPTY: Determine whether there are any nodes remaining that were previously generated from the current node. If so, return to SELECT; otherwise, proceed.

LEVEL: Test whether the empty level just encountered was actually the first level. If so, this means that all solutions have been implicitly enumerated and the on-hand trial solution is optimal. If the empty level is not the first, then return to BACKTRACK.

In utilizing this algorithm for the single-machine tardiness problem, for example, we see that the cumulative information stored for the current node σ includes q_σ, v_σ, b_σ, and perhaps an indicator vector to show which jobs remain unscheduled. Then the process of peeling off job j during backtracking entails the addition of t_j to q_σ and the subtraction of T_j from v_σ.

Finally, we consider an efficient means of representing the tree internally. Define TREE(I, J) to be an $n \times n$ matrix. Row i of this matrix corresponds to level i of the branching tree and contains the indices of the jobs that correspond to newly generated nodes each time the BRANCH step is executed. To illustrate how this matrix is manipulated, consider the following four-job problem, in which the objective is to minimize total tardiness.

Job j	t_j	d_j
1	6	9
2	4	10
3	7	8
4	5	6

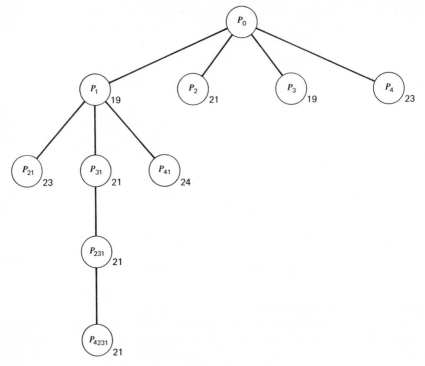

Figure C.2

At level 1 the nodes corresponding to $\sigma = 1$ and $\sigma = 3$ both have lower bounds of 19 when b_σ is employed as a lower bound. Selecting $\sigma = 1$ arbitrarily, and pursuing the tree to level 4, leads to the tree shown in Figure C.2. The corresponding TREE matrix takes the following form:

$$
\begin{array}{cccc}
1 & 3 & 2 & 4 \\
3 & 2 & 4 & \\
2 & & & \\
4 & & &
\end{array}
$$

The indices in row 1 of this matrix correspond to the nodes at level 1 of the tree, ranked by lower bound. (The values of b_σ are displayed next to each node in Figure C.2.) Similarly the indices in row 2 correspond to the nodes at level 2, ranked by their lower bounds. In row 3 there is only one entry because Dominance Property 3.1 was invoked during the BRANCH step. In row 4 there is one entry simply because no alternatives remain after three sequence positions have been filled. The complete sequence thus constructed is $\sigma = 4\text{-}2\text{-}3\text{-}1$, which can be read from the first column of the TREE matrix. In order to peel off a job from the current partial sequence, simply delete the first element in the appropriate row of TREE. Upon backtracking, the active nodes remaining at level 2 are fathomed since the complete solution has a total tardiness of 21. When the algorithm next encounters a complete sequence, the TREE matrix takes the form:

$$
\begin{array}{ccc}
3 & 2 & 4 \\
1 & 2 & 3 \\
2 & & \\
4 & &
\end{array}
$$

Thereafter all remaining active nodes can be fathomed.

This implementation strategy requires core storage of the TREE matrix and a corresponding matrix containing lower bounds. No other large commitment of storage space is required, and relative little additional information is necessary to carry out the algorithm.

With a few modifications, the same approach can be adapted to finding optimal traveling salesman tours (Chapter 4), optimal permutation schedules in flow shop problems (Chapter 6), and solutions to a variety of similar combinatorial problems.

INDEX